Ethical Exploration in a Multifaith Society

Catherine Shelley

Ethical Exploration in a Multifaith Society

palgrave
macmillan

Catherine Shelley
Independent Scholar
Croydon, United Kingdom

ISBN 978-3-319-46710-8   ISBN 978-3-319-46711-5 (eBook)
DOI 10.1007/978-3-319-46711-5

Library of Congress Control Number: 2017932110

Cover illustration: Jan Wlodarczyk / Alamy Stock Photo

Printed on acid-free paper

This Palgrave Macmillan imprint is published by Springer Nature
The registered company is Springer International Publishing AG
The registered company address is: Gewerbestrasse 11, 6330 Cham, Switzerland

Acknowledgements

No acknowledgements can ever do justice to all those whose support and inspiration help to bring a book into being. However, there are some milestones and people that stand out and these I want to name for particular reasons, as follows:

To Birmingham University School of Philosophy, Theology and Religion for inviting me to teach Theological Ethics and in particular to Stephen Pattison for the course I inherited, Isobel Wollaston and Karen Wennell for their support and to several students whose questions and feedback also encouraged me to write.

To Manchester University and in particular Elaine Graham, Caroline Bridge and Peter Scott for their respective encouragement and challenges in my PhD research and to Martin Seeley and others at Westcott House for their support at important points.

To friends, fellow curates, colleagues at Lee Bolton Monier-Williams and in particular to Alison Joyce for giving me some belief in my writing and to Anne and Martin Shelley, Andrew McCall and Andrew Manson Brailsford.

And finally to the team at Palgrave Macmillan, who supported me in the commissioning and production of the book.

Contents

List of Tables

1

Introduction to Philosophical and Theological Ethics

'He has a really Scriptural approach to his Sermons, so we are learning much more about the Bible and less about contemporary living!' This recent feedback from a parishioner in a church with a new priest highlights one of the problems with religion and ethics. There can be a perception and tendency in some parts of the Christian community – and consequently wider society – to assume that focusing on the Bible necessitates ignoring how it applies to contemporary life. Alternatively it can mean interpretations that are radically at odds with contemporary life. Some argue that is as it should be, as Christianity should be counter-cultural; others blame such interpretations for making Christianity irrelevant. Similar tensions apply to most religious traditions and faith communities grappling with the challenges of how or whether a faith and tradition with roots going back several millennia has any application in secularized modern or post-modern societies. For what are seen as minority faiths or those of 'foreign' origin, which includes Christianity with its Middle Eastern origins, the tensions include transitions of culture as well as time.

Simultaneously the impact of Enlightenment scepticism about the perceived divisiveness and lack of empirical proof of religious belief not

© The Author(s) 2017
C. Shelley, *Ethical Exploration in a Multifaith Society*,
DOI 10.1007/978-3-319-46711-5_1

only relegated religion to the private sphere but actively sought to exclude it from the public square. Yet despite this privatization, decline in church attendance, the downgrading of Sunday observance and other secularizations of society, religious practice and belief remain alive and well. The Church of England remains established, whatever that means and a diversity of Christian communities continues to flourish alongside higher levels of belief than practice in Christian heritage communities. Faith also remains strong and key to identity amongst many of non-Christian traditions, who often do not understand or recognize the Western[1] Enlightenment's public/private divisions. The protection of religion and conscience in the European Convention on Human Rights[2] has also brought religious practice into public legal fora. All of which means that religious belief and practice remain important in the ethics and decisions of many of the UK's citizens and therefore need to be taken into account in public life. This exploration seeks to show not only that religious belief and ethical traditions have a place in public as well as private life but also that faith has positive things to offer to public life and decision-making, at both local and global levels.

Theological Ethics

Any exploration of theological ethics has to address dilemmas posed by arguments around relevance, distinctiveness, counter-cultural trends and interpretations and whether religion really is divisive or irrational. The exploration that follows throughout this book seeks to address these issues by examining premises, authority, use of reason and various methodologies for ethical analysis that are based on or include theological assumptions.

Teaching and writing about theological ethics in the UK has tended for the most part to be Christian ethics, often with consideration of how

---

[1] 'Western' is used to distinguish the European philosophical revolution that rejected religion from public life & ethics from enlightenment in other e.g. *dharmic* traditions. Space precludes use of the term each time.

[2] Imported into English law via the Human Rights Act 1998.

theological ethics relates to what are described as secular ethics. Biblical sources and the natural law tradition are considered alongside but often in distinction from post-Enlightenment modes of ethical reasoning found in utilitarianism and Kantian deontology. This approach to theological ethics now seems limited for at least two reasons.

The first and more obvious is that in a society now acknowledged to be multifaith other sets of religious beliefs have a claim to be considered as part of theological ethics. Whilst the majority belief remains Christian, at over 59% according to the 2011 census, higher percentages of those smaller faith communities are often more actively involved in their faith and express it more publicly. Across the world religious beliefs as a factor in peoples' lives, whether for good or ill, remain stronger than in the UK.[3] The greater diversity of faith-based ethics poses fresh challenges to the ethical framework set by a Christian establishment and necessitates greater engagement with religious beliefs and religious literacy, for an understanding of society and many areas of professional practice. For example, social workers, medics, teachers and educational establishments at all levels, as well as workplaces need to be able to consider the impact of peoples' religious beliefs on their client or student populations. Professionals need awareness of how clients' beliefs and ethical perceptions may affect decision-making as well as reflecting on how their own beliefs might affect perceptions of clients and their decisions.

The second is whether theological and secular ethics are as divorced from each other as often portrayed. In some cases the roots of theological ethical methodology are found in non-theological, or at least non-monotheistic, traditions. Natural law theology is a good example; Greek and particularly Aristotelian philosophical tradition forms a basis for ethical exploration and reflection in Christianity, Judaism and Islam. Correspondingly there are concepts, now seen as secular that can be shown to have their origins in religious traditions and beliefs. One example is human rights, which tend to be portrayed as eminently liberal and secular, yet which are considered by at least some from both Christian and Muslim traditions to have roots in their respective religions.

---

[3] Davie G. *The Sociology of Religion*. Sage Publishing, 2007, pp. 135–180 (Davie 2007).

Reasons for Excluding Religion

Religious belief has all too often been viewed as alien, irrational and divisive leading in the UK to calls for its exclusion from the public square since Bentham and Mills; a call repeated by contemporary commentators from atheist biologist Richard Dawkins[4] to retired Bishop Richard Holloway.[5] Elsewhere this is reflected by similar calls from Rawls[6] and Jurgen Habermas,[7] although their initial calls for total exclusion have moderated to inclusion on condition of rationality.[8] In some states, notably the US, France and Turkey, legislation and policy aims to keep religion out of the public sphere in terms of debate, practice and dress. In considering the dominant narrative about religion and human rights Banchoff and Wuthnow note that whilst a narrow individual freedom to 'have, practice and change' religion is protected, 'the freedom of religious groups to engage in politics . . . is frowned upon.'[9]

From those who would exclude or at least limit religion in the public square there is a dominant but misleading narrative that opposes religion against science, reason, progress, the empirical and experience, pleasure and what is perceived as humane as well as against rights, autonomy and the secular. Above all religion is rejected as superstitious, bound to unthinking deontology and inherently conflictual. Yet despite accusations that religious belief leads to conflict it is also often presented as homogenous, suggesting that all believers share the same critically benighted views of for example life issues or women's rights. This exploration seeks to address these false oppositions, acknowledging

---

[4] e.g. Dawkins R. *The God Delusion*. Black Swan, 2007 (Dawkins 2007).

[5] Holloway R. *Godless Morality*. Canongate Publishing, 2004 (Holloway 2004).

[6] Rawls J. Public Reason Re-visited. *University of Chicago Law Review* 64 (Summer 1997), pp. 765–807 (Rawls 1997). Bailey T & Gentile V. *Rawls and Religion*. Columbia University Press, 2015 (Bailey and Gentile 2015).

[7] Habermas J. *Between Naturalism and Religion*. Cambridge Polity Press, 2008. pp. 114–147 (Habermas 2008) re-evaluation of total exclusion of religion from the public square.

[8] Holloway R. *Godless Morality: Keeping Religion Out of Ethics*. Edinburgh University Press, 1999 (Holloway 1999).

[9] Banchoff T & Wuthnow R. *Religion and the Global Politics of Human Rights*. Oxford University Press, 2011, p. 4 (Banchoff and Wuthnow 2011).

those places where there are disagreements but setting out the reasons for them and the wide diversity of factors and methodologies that are found within theological ethics.

Religion and the Secular Narrative

Although seen as a fundamental division religion is not necessarily opposed to the secular. As Dechant and Fasching observe *secular* meant 'of the world' contrasted with the heavens or transcendent; it did not mean an exclusion of God.[10] Whilst the sacred was set apart as a reminder of the things of God, the holy saw God in all aspects of creation, including issues of ethics and justice. Part of the genius and challenge of religion and theological ethics is to bridge the gap between aspirations to heaven and the wisdom of the transcendent whilst living solidly in the world. The two are intertwined.

As noted above the history of theological ethics includes significant overlap of common cultural and philosophical roots for ideas and practices, such as natural law and more recently secular ethical methods like Critical Social Theory. This is not to take a syncretistic approach or pretend that all traditions really have the same beliefs or ethical frameworks; it is clear that there are differences. However, the differences are not necessarily as major as some would like to assert. Theological ethics is open to ideas and experience from non-religious sources to illustrate, interpret, analyse and apply religious understandings of the world.

Contrary to the myth spread most persistently by Richard Dawkins religion is not opposed to science either. As will be seen in Chapter Three natural law theologians, particularly in the Muslim tradition, were often scientists and medics as well as theologians. Theological ethics is primarily applied and its material is therefore empirical experience. Discerning how meta-ethical principles apply to that experience requires processes of analysis and reasoning, particularly in changed social

---

[10] Fasching DJ, Dechant D & Lantigua DM. *Comparative Religious Ethics: A Narrative Approach to Global Ethics*. Wiley Blackwell, 2011, pp. 9–20 (Fasching et al. 2011).

conditions such as diaspora, which many traditions experience. Arguments for the irrationality of religion vary. Whilst secular humanists who adopt the line taken by Dawkins argue that religion can never be reasonable because it is based on the idea of God, which in Dawkin's opinion is a lie. Holloway, effectively following Kant, would exclude religion from ethics because it lacks empirical proof, meaning that it falls back on unprovable deontological command.

Contrary to this perception significant contributions to theological ethics are premised on reason as a God-given faculty common to all humanity, religious or not; exploring the role of reason in theological ethics illustrates this amply. Theological ethics uses both deductive and inductive analysis to assess the empirical world. What might differ from purely philosophical ethics are the premises used, concepts from scripture or other religious sources and authorities. However, even these differences may not be so significant. For example, ethical principles founded in scriptural sources, like the Golden Rule to love neighbour as oneself, can make sense to those without a religious belief or who reject the Bible as divinely revealed truth.

Yet whilst both early and contemporary theologians embrace natural science as part of exploring God's creation they also recognize the limits of science in the face of the transcendent and eternal. This recognition of transcendence, eternity and the non-material as part of human experience tends to be excluded by post-Enlightenment narratives but is intrinsic to the theological quest and understanding of ethics. Whether it is the earth and heavens of Hebrew scripture, paradise of the Qu'ran or *pavritti* and *nvritti* in *dharmic* traditions both dimensions of experience are embraced, through pleasure and joy in creation or abstinence in pursuit of the holy.

Besides recognizing the limits of reason in the face of transcendence, theology also recognizes the limits of reason as the sole arbiter of human experience and decision-making. It is important but theology recognizes humanity as more than just reason. Despite the criticism of religion as irrational increasingly debate in British and western society, driven by traditional and social media, is based on human story, appealing to emotion and intuition. David Hume recognized that intuition and emotion also have a place in human decision-making and ethics and it is notable that the purported reason of the utilitarian hedonic calculus relies on subjectively evaluated criteria. Theological ethics recognizes these different aspects of humanity and theological methodologies include all human faculties in making good ethical decisions and discerning appropriate ethical responses.

Autonomy versus Heteronomy

Religion and theological ethics are also often criticized as opposed to progress, autonomy and human rights. Charges that theology has a communal approach at odds with vindicating individual rights may be well-founded in some instances but the numbers of cases defending religious rights under the Human Rights Act suggests faith communities' acceptance of rights in practice. Religion is sometimes portrayed as a forum where believers suspend their own conscience to assent to their leaders' teachings; heteronomy replaces autonomous responsibility. Whilst there are elements of heteronomous authority, religious traditions retain a strong sense of personal responsibility for actions, emphasized by theologies of final judgment or *karma* and reincarnation. Theological ethics also assumes free will by contrast with some contemporary philosophies[11] that are sceptical about the extent to which human beings can make genuinely free decisions. The role of conscience, free will and dynamics of autonomy and heteronomy are further areas of exploration, raising important questions about human nature. At the heart of all religion are the prayer and worship that provide distinctively theological ways to process ethical decisions drawing on reason, emotion, intuition and openness to the larger, transcendent perspective of eternity, afterlife and community beyond the self. All of these human capacities provide a richer context and perspective for ethics than pure deductive reasoning highlight the role of conscience in ethics.

Conscience, discernment and personal judgment mean that all religious communities are prone to differences of opinion and that religion and theological ethics are not homogenous either across the spectrum of

---

[11] e.g. Pierre Bordieu's theory of the *habitus,* Bourdieu Pierre. *The Logic of Practice.* Polity Press, 1990 (Bourdieu 1990).

traditions or within them. To this extent criticism of religion as conflictual may have a point. However, religion is hardly unique in its scope for differences of opinion and suggestions of being uniquely absolutist seem unfounded in the face of secular absolutes about nationalism or the supremacy of science, technology or capital. Religious belief is not and never has been the only source of division and difference of belief, nor of war. Difference arises from culture as much as religion, just as in all societies. Differences of opinion of various sorts lie at the core of most ethical approaches, religious or secular. As an essential principle Utilitarianism assumes that 'harm' is a universal concept and to be avoided. Yet 'harm' is contested; for example, some believe that corporal punishment harms children, whilst others argue that its absence is harmful. There are those with religious views and those without on both sides of the argument. This exploration recognizes the essentially democratic nature of theological ethical disagreement and seeks to show how and why approaches to faith, both within and across traditions, reach different ethical conclusions and stances in relation to dominant ethical trends in society. Differences arise over initial premises, sources of revelation and their interpretation, approaches to authority and both processes and methods of theological analysis. This also enables an examination of charges that theological ethics either makes no difference or makes such an alarming difference that it needs to be discounted from the public square.

Methodology

The lack of homogeneity in faith communities means that approaches to ethics that seek to compare what different faiths believe about particular ethical issues,[12] whilst providing useful insights, can risk portraying a homogeneity that is illusory. To the extent that insights from different faiths will be considered by way of analysis and illustration a comparative

---

[12] e.g. Morgan P & Lawton C. *Ethical Issues in Six Religious Traditions,* 2nd edition. Edinburgh University Press, 2007 (Lawton 2007).

approach will be adopted to explore the role and diversity of theological and faith-based ethics in wider society. However, the difficulty of making definitive assertions about any religion's ethical views on particular issues means that illustrations will be given rather than strict or systematic comparisons of faith with another. The illustrations and examples used are drawn insofar as possible from sources within the faith in question rather than external commentators.

There are various rationales for selecting the particular traditions chosen. Christianity and Judaism enable an engagement with religions that to a degree share religious scriptures yet are shaped by very different histories and self-concept. For example, Christianity as missionary people versus Judaism as a self-contained chosen people; Christianity as an empire, Judaism repeatedly at the mercy of exile and empire. Whilst not sharing quite the same scriptures Christianity and Islam do share some similarities as missionary faiths with imperial histories. This has implications for theologies of war, politics and governance as well as contemporary challenges of adjusting to minority status in secular worlds. Christianity is also the tradition with which the writer is most familiar which explains any disproportionate focus on that tradition and the Abrahamic faiths more generally.

Distinctive insights, premises and wisdom from particular traditions will be shared along with the particular theological methodologies and how they vary. Reference has already been made to revelation and natural law theology, both of which will be considered in greater detail, along with other areas of ethics to which they give rise, such as human rights and virtue ethics. Liberation theology and various approaches to theological deontology are also considered for their own methodology as well as the specific developments and trajectories that have grown from them. Methodological and conceptual parallels with ethics derived from non-theological sources are also considered.

Theological sources that underlie theological ethics are explored as distinct areas of difference. Differential interpretations of scripture, exercise of religious authority and development of tradition are analysed for their impact on both the ethical conclusions reached and the stance of faith communities affected. It is worth noting that talk of methodology, system, paradigms and other forms of intellectual or academic ordering is alien to some religious understandings. This in itself is another feature of religious ethics that is worth considering for the insights it can furnish about ethical praxis in charismatic and mystical traditions. The comparative place of religious leaders, scholars, jurists, the faith community and the operation of autonomy versus heteronomy also lead to significant diversity. Diversity operates both in terms of premises and ideals about where the authoritative voice of the community lies which in turn has an impact on ethics, particularly in traditions with a predominantly male leadership. Dynamics within religious communities are another perceived area of religious distinctiveness when compared with the personal autonomy and equality of wider secular society. The reality or otherwise of this distinction is another issue for examination.

Bridging the Gap of the Centuries

One of the major issues for theological ethics to address is the significant differences between the societies in which the major religious worldviews began and scriptures written down and our contemporary global village. Despite their age there is much wisdom still to be distilled from such scriptures and traditions but to do so requires an awareness of interpretive context. Theological ethics requires an exercise in translation to glean and read religious scriptures in ways that are relevant to our times yet authentic to the spirituality and wisdom of their original vision.

There are several methodologies for reading scripture and religious tradition in ways that enable a genuine appreciation and living of the tradition. Tradition in its original meaning is not about preserving something in aspic or a pure historical state but is rather, from the Latin verb *trader*, about handing things on from age to age. An examination of these methodologies and the ways that tradition is lived and grows throughout time is a key part of ethical exploration. The same approach applies to Greek and other philosophies and not just to religious views. Even the 'modern' utilitarianism dates from two centuries ago.

Yet religion suffers from the charge, both from some within faith communities and disenchanted sceptics outside the traditions, that failure to live precisely as scripture says is to be unfaithful. Some argue that such failure is to 'play' at the religion, to seek cheap grace (to use a Christian term) or to betray it. In practice at no stage and in no faith has a pure religion ever existed. Whilst pointing to the transcendent religion is also irretrievably human; it is the means by which countless human beings over the ages have sought meaning and direction in life, in terms of ethics and vocation, the personal and communal. All these circumstances are embedded in particular cultural, social, material and historical contexts, which overlap to greater or lesser degrees with other contexts. It is therefore impossible in any worldview to find a faith or religion that is free from cultural limitations and expressions or more pejoratively baggage. The same applies to non-theological ethics. It is hoped that by outlining varied methodologies for interpreting scripture, ethics and living faith from generation to generation those accusations will be answered or at least muted.

As the exploration of themes, stories, methodologies and issues illustrates, such overlapping contexts and narratives may or may not lead to common ethical conclusions. To the extent that consensus can be achieved there is a convergence with Rawls' theory of ethics as overlapping consensus. Yet, whilst religion is not the only cause of division and difference, no religion is homogenous. Therefore the reasons for divergent interpretations of scripture, theology, tradition and ethical presumptions are also part of the exploration.

Ordering the Arguments

The way in which the various questions, inter-relationships and distinctions are ordered and the arguments developed seeks to demonstrate the interweaving of religious and secular thought, challenging assumptions on both sides of that divide. The second chapter traces ways in which reason has been employed in both philosophical and theological ethics over time, in different traditions. Overlapping influences, like the impact of Greek ethical thought on the Abrahamic faiths, are explored and arguments from history evaluated. The different trajectories of *dharmic* thought are also considered. Processes of ethical reasoning in religious paradigms are compared with post-Enlightenment ethics that seek to exclude religious sources.

The history challenges perceptions that religion lacks reason, is incapable of tolerance or that the current multicultural settlement is uniquely the product of Englightenment.

Chapter Three continues the exploration of religious reasoning via theologies of natural law and virtue ethics, their derivation from Aristotelian ethics and the ways in which they mirror or depart from secular versions of the same ethical theory. The role of nature in the *dharmic* faiths is also considered and compared with western and Abrahamic approaches. The complex interaction of nature and perceived role or class that underlay understandings of virtue in the Athenian *polis* and Hindu caste is also assessed. Historical understandings of nature and virtue are compared with contemporary perspectives both religious and otherwise. Natural law and virtue ethics also provide a framework for considering arguments about relative versus universal or absolute ethics and norms. These paradigms are also considered via the modern development of human rights from natural law, which is considered by reference to both theological and secular engagement with human rights instruments. This exploration considers whether human rights can provide a universal code of ethics, transcending differences of worldview.

Chapter Four assesses utilitarianism and Kantian deontology as two modern approaches to ethical theory and decision-making, in reaction against theological ethics. Their application is considered in relation to contemporary arguments over abortion and euthanasia, just war, poverty and distribution of resources. The use of utilitarian and deontological arguments within religious reasoning is explored, illustrating that theological ethics also resorts to such paradigms in some instances. Thus, what is now seen as secular ethical theory is shown to be implicit in much religious debate, both contemporary and historical, alongside religious sources of authority.

Having considered the interplay of secular with theological reasoning and vice versa, Chapter Five considers various forms of authority that influence both secular and theological ethics. It is arguable that it is sources of authority and approaches to them that cause the greatest divergence between theological and philosophical ethics. Personal autonomy is explored as informed by personal and social experience, the nature of conscience, intuition, care and relationships. The role of law as ethical authority is evaluated as applied to both secular and religious paradigms, recognizing the varying attitudes to law and written authority within different theological traditions. The relationship between secular or state law and the religious laws and legal fora of specific communities are also examined by assessing their accommodation in English law.

A significant authority for theological ethics is religious scripture, which includes not only written texts but the oral traditions that preceded the writing and continue to be used in exposition and interpretation. The sixth chapter considers ways in which scripture is a source of ethical authority for religious traditions and the challenges posed by historical and contemporary context, language and interpretation. The varied role and force of scripture within and between different traditions is another challenge of scriptural authority. For example, Scriptural sources of revelation are foundational to Judaism, Christianity, Islam and Sikhism yet within each tradition there is a range of interpretive principles, with significant implications for the construction and application of ethical norms.

Interpreting and using texts in the *dharmic* faiths is possibly even more complex thanks to the variable adoption of particular scriptures, lack of unifying authority and the comparative lack of a clear canon. The chapter analyses scripture with particular reference to modes of interpretation, religious reasoning and the relationships of scripture to other sources of ethical authority. The challenges of differential contexts and societal developments for scripture, and theological ethics generally, are illustrated by reference to contemporary debates over gender and sexuality. The extent to which religious texts may have relevance, or parallels in secular thought, for those outside the faith are also explored.

Having considered how religious authority and scripture inform theological ethics Chapter Seven outlines the varied ethical stances that can result vis-à-vis dominant ethical paradigms. The analysis is based on RH Niebuhr's thesis in *Christ and Culture*,[13] originally developed in relation to Christian communities but more recently applied by Keith Ward,[14] amongst others, to other religious traditions.

---

[13] Niebuhr RH. *Christ and Culture*. Bravo Limited Press, 2002 (Niebuhr 2002).
[14] Ward K. *Religion and Community*. Oxford: Clarendon Press, 2000 (Ward 2000).

The paradigm explores the dilemmas for religious ethics and communities of living 'in but not of the world'. This can vary from maintaining religious authenticity through isolation from the wider community to losing religious identity by assimilation to broader social *mores*. Ethical dilemmas for wider society are also raised by the degree to which religious communities want to maintain a counter-cultural stance or public engagement, with or without assimilation. Counter-cultural epistemological authority as well as ethical authority is also assessed. Finally, the impact of communal authority and communal decision-making processes are considered. To illustrate the communal impact of theological difference this chapter addresses ethical issues in relation to power, gender and minorities with some analysis of how far these issues are acknowledged or addressed in various ethical paradigms and worldviews. The concepts of idealized ethical stances and community identity[15] are also relevant here.

Chapter Eight reviews and compares several recognized methods by which theological ethics brings together the factors addressed in earlier chapters so as to reflect on experience, scripture and authority. These include liberation theology, middle axioms, narrative theologies alongside theologies considered earlier such as natural law. As a further consideration of the inter-twining of theological and secular reasoning this chapter considers theological ethics that draw explicitly on secular philosophy, socio-political theory and knowledge for example feminist, black and political theologies. Chapter Nine continues this exploration focusing on the impact of globalization, and consequently global ethics, within religious and theological paradigms. The international profile, membership and reach of religious communities raise further ethical dilemmas, for example perceived tensions between national citizenship and religious loyalties. Theologies of welcoming the stranger, responses to poverty and war and environmental ethics are also raised by global ethics. These areas of ethics emphasize that religious ethics are not limited to personal morality.

---

[15] Roald AS. Research on Muslims, pp. 5–22. In *Women in Islam: The Western Experience*. London: Routledge, 2001 (Roald 2001).

The concluding chapter reviews and summarizes overlapping areas, paradigms and dilemmas for ethical argument in both theological and philosophical reasoning and identifies areas in which differences remain. Consideration is given to how far diversity can be accommodated by agreements to disagree and those areas in which bridging of the gaps is needed. By way of conclusion options are explored for bridging the gaps through conversation, theological language, common epistemology and frameworks like human rights. This chapter, like the book, aims to provide a platform for further conversation and ethical exploration by others with an interest and stake in developing and applying common ethical norms.

Terminology

Clarity over terminology is important as overlapping and confused use of terms can cause problems. The following terms are defined so as to assist clarity.

Religion or Theology? Strictly speaking theology is 'theo' 'logos', God-word, human talk about God though not 'the word of God,' because that is scripture. Some argue that faiths like Buddhism cannot be theological for the lack of a monotheistic deity, unlike the Abrahamic faiths and Sikhism. However, Buddhism, Hinduism and other *dharmic* faiths have a sense both of a transcendent order to the universe and practices of transcendence in meditation, prayer and worship. On that basis they are theological as well as religious. Even the Christian theologian Thomas Aquinas concedes that we cannot say with any certainty what this transcendent God looks like. Theology as 'Talk-of-God' is a discipline engaged in by members of a tradition but can equally be enjoyed and participated in by those outside, as an academic discipline. By contrast, whilst religion can be commented on and observed by academics it can only be fully engaged in by those who participate at some level in the worship and practices of the tradition. Both have insights for ethics; theology from the perspective of meta-ethical principles and norms, whilst religion tends to be more relevant for descriptive ethics and the norms as they are actually lived.

Ethics or morals? One of the challenges of ethics is the variety of uses of the word and the multiple concepts that can be evoked. The same goes for morality. The English word 'ethics' comes from the Greek *ethike* meaning 'custom' or 'habit'. The equivalent Roman word, *mores,* gave rise to the English 'morals'. Despite the common linguistic origin, in modern use ethics and morals have assumed different connotations. 'Ethics' is the philosophical discipline reflecting on concepts of good and evil, right and wrong, virtue and vice, happiness, empathy, intuition and related facets of human existence, from the personal to the global. It also features questions of justice and law, fairness and equality, human dignity of the person and why people are different from animals – or are they?

Outside the philosophical sphere 'ethical issues' have become, in common usage, what is described as private or personal morality, the privatized aspect of the Enlightenment settlement. They are limited to what people do in the privacy of the home, sex, family, issues of life and death and religion. In the public square, particularly governmental settings like Parliament, these have become issues of conscience, for which party voting mandates are suspended. The divorce of private and public has added a pejorative sense to morality, which now denotes judgmental attitudes exemplified by references to 'the moral majority', for conservative ethical attitudes; by extension that judgment may be extended to religious views.

This legacy has left aspects of life like finance, the operation of capital markets and much public policy, including war, as matters of practical political necessity and discipline, not ethics or conscience. Yet for most of history, many of the population and for faith communities, questions about war, use of public funds, whistle blowing, governing society, integrity at work, crime and punishment, violence and security are matters of ethics just as much as 'private' morality. For the Roman Catholic Church theological ethics remains 'moral theology' rejecting any distinction between ethics and morality. For other faith traditions, particularly Judaism and Islam, the framework for life and scriptural application is far more likely to be called 'law' rather than either morality or ethics. For such traditions, whilst in countries where a faith is in the minority there may be a distinction between the law of the land and religious laws, there is no distinction of religious law from religious ethics. Nor, as indicated above, is there a distinction between public and private morality, public and private life or a sacred versus secular sphere. All life and therefore all morality, ethics and law are under God and subject to the divine rules of the universe, however deity is conceived. The implications of this understanding are considered and illustrated in more depth throughout later chapters. The broad consequence is that being God and faith-focused often provides different ethical motivations for tasks and ethics as compared with secular premises. As will be seen, religious or theological methodology may be no less rational than secular reasoning; the differences lie in the premises, narratives and experience on which it is based.

Ethics also refers to a complex phenomenon that operates in distinct ways, an analytical framework for which includes:

(i) 'Descriptive ethics' discerned from what people actually do, including, in the context of theological ethics the ideas, ethical ideals and practices of faith communities and individuals.

(ii) 'Virtue ethics', considers behaviour and character formation, for example characteristics like 'honour' and dignity, much-encountered in faiths of the Indian-subcontinent or loving-kindness found in Judaism (*hesed*) and Hinduism (*bakhti*).

(iii) 'Normative ethics', is how people ought to behave, laid out in rules, commandments, laws or other guidance that are enforceable and include the distinctive commandments, principles and codes of faith Communities.

(iv) 'Meta-ethics' refers to the broader ethical principles underlying normative ethics and particular decisions; for faith communities these include the theological sources and methodologies used to discern what is faithful and ethical in particular situations.

Each of these distinctive ethical roles is found within the diversity of theological ethics. However different traditions feature or emphasize particular approaches more than others. The terms are not a significant part of the analysis as the main focus is bridging the gap from meta-ethical to normative application. However, the following brief overview illustrates the distinctions by reference to particular traditions.

Descriptive ethics details the particulars of practice in the *vedic* rites and other ritual worship, the full living of Jewish *mitzvot* and daily, weekly and seasonal rites in all traditions. All traditions also celebrate the virtues implicit and developed in the observance of faith, prayer and other regular practices, for example modesty in dress codes, fidelity in prayer, loving kindness or generosity in care of neighbour.

Islam and Judaism approach ethics as law leading to normative and rule-based ethics. The importance of *mitzvot* and *fiqh* is recognized in all branches of Judaism and Islam respectively.[16] For Orthodox, Reformed and Progressive or Liberal Jews the Law is the bedrock of faith and identity; differences lie in modes of interpretation rather than the applicability of the Law. Similarly in Islam, across Sunni and Shia branches and the four different schools of *fiqh* there is no dispute that Shari'a, derived from the Qu'ran is essential to faith and practice. By contrast Christianity has an ambivalent relationship with law, rules and prescriptive norms. Jesus was not keen on lawyers and criticized scribes' and Pharisees' hypocritically restrictive legal interpretations. Yet He was Jewish and called to fulfil not abolish the law, according to the spirit of a loving God, rather than a means to exclude and condemn.[17] Paul was equally ambivalent as he sought to remove law as the key to salvation[18] and navigate the shift from a predominantly Jewish break-away sect to a community of Gentiles. This has left a tension in Christian ethics between ordered norms based on natural reason as opposed to volun-tarist anti-nomian tendencies, appealing to the meta-ethics of revelation or scriptural detail. *Dharmic* faiths are yet more difficult to characterize; laws such as the *manusmriti*, drawn from the *vedic* texts based in the cosmic order, provide guidance for living in harmony with creation rather than codes for personal salvation. Yet the absence of communal rule-making authority within Hinduism or contemporary Buddhism makes for less normative prescription than some traditions.

---

[16] See e.g. Esposito J & Mogaded D. *Who Speaks for Islam*. Gallup Press, 2007 (Esposito and Mogaded 2007); Freud Kandell M & De Lange N. *Modern Judaism an Oxford Guide*. Oxford University Press, 2005 (Freud Kandell and De Lange 2005).

[17] Matthew 5: 17 NRSV.

[18] e.g. Ephesians 2: 15 NRSV; Sanders EP. *Paul, the Law and the Jewish People*. Augsburg Fortress Press, 1983 (Sanders 1983).

Who Is Theological Ethics For?

One challenge for theological ethics is how far it is applicable to wider society, both those of other religious traditions and those outside faith communities altogether. Some traditions, notably Judaism, are profoundly self-contained. A history of persecution has led to a focus that aims simply to live according to their own lights, with little aspiration to share the tradition with or convert others. This, combined with a Jewish narrative of being 'the chosen people' gives rise to a separatist identity that involves being held to a higher ethical standard than other nations. Having said which the seven Noahide commandments, contrasted with the ten given on Mount Sinai, are seen as the basic humane standards for all communities.

Amongst the *dharmic* faiths Hindus and Sikhs operate more like Judaism to the extent that membership is determined to a degree by ethnicity so there is no sense of seeking to convert others to their belief or ethical practices. However, to the extent that Hindu understanding of ethics has a fairly strong natural law premise as the governing force of the universe and Sikhs draw from *dharmic* and Muslim traditions, there is an implicit universalism. Buddhism shares a similar universalist assumption about *dharma,* 'the way,' as the basis for ethics and seeks to encourage others to follow this way to a greater extent than Hinduism.

By contrast with Judaism and Hinduism, Christianity and Islam have historically adopted a greater missionary stance. This has carried with it, for good and ill, a sense of wanting to share a vision of the common good as a valuable contribution for the whole of humanity. The basis for this worldwide vision varies depending upon concepts of salvation. For natural law theologians ethical principles are universally accessible according to God-given reason; ethics are therefore deduced from a shared framework of reason rather than imposing a particular vision or understanding. For liberation theology the basis of shared ethical vision is that all humanity is created by God and deserving of the fullness of life and the justice to make that possible. There are movements in both Islam and Christianity that operate from these ethical and theological premises, assuming a universalism that does not depend on specific belief or membership of the faith community but shares a common vision of ethical goods capable of developing common cause with those outside the faith.[19] However, both Islam and Christianity also include groups whose theological premise is that their understanding of revelation carries a distinctive truth. This truth and the ethics that accompany it are seen as universally accessible but require conversion to that particular revelation and consequent lifestyle as necessary to salvation. This understanding of ethics also posits a chosen people as those who choose conversion and are shaped into ethical patterns by their community. It is the witness of the community that is seen as offering a theological example to the world. The ethics of Karl Barth and Stanley Hauerwas can be seen as examples of this approach.

Overall most understandings of theological ethics are open to universal ethical approaches and application. There are also texts in religious scriptures that can be understood and applied by all regardless of particular belief in a faith tradition. The classic example of such an ethical principle is the Golden Rule, do as you would be done by or 'love your neighbour as yourself'[20] which is found in many traditions and in non-theistic Kantian philosophy. The complexity of theological ethics is that it recognizes and aspires to universalism, yet the diversity of premises for religious beliefs provide many different rationales for ethics at any detailed level. A further contribution that theology can make to ethics is the conscious embracing of the complexity, difference and often paradox of human existence. Amongst these complexities are the challenges of the particular application of universal or general principles and the relationship of personal and communal subjectivities to wider objective truths and reasoning. This also encompasses grappling with issues of absolute and relative norms and the implications of variable understandings of reason, concepts of good and the human person. Additionally theological ethics assumes a relationship with all or any of God, faith, religious authority, sources and values. How people relate to each other, to God and to creation through these various concepts is also explored.

---

[19] Reason and natural law are explored further in Chapters 2 and 3 respectively.

[20] http://www.religioustolerance.org/reciproc2.htm.

Some Preliminary Conclusions

Religious scriptures capture millennia of human wisdom, reflection and human experience. Whilst it is true that many aspects of society have changed since the major religious scriptures were written, there is a good deal about human nature and life that has not. The question of why 'bad things happen to good people', explored in the book of Job amongst others, remains pertinent in this day and age. Questions of how to reconcile the broad principle with the particulars of human experience and difference are also still fully relevant and possibly more so in a global village. Sadly, questions of how to manage conflict, tribalism, violence and distribution of resources remain ever-present, as do increasingly urgent questions of how to live lightly upon the earth in environmental terms. An important corrective of a theological exploration of ethics is the avoidance of reductionism. The diversity of approaches to ethics and wisdom within religious traditions, from commandments to parables, psalms to prophecy, sagas and myths engages with the full complexity of the human situation and the dilemmas that can arise in life. This is captured amongst other approaches by narrative ethics seen in ethical teaching, principles and ideas developed through myth, parable and story. For some, the fact that religious tradition operates at some levels through myth disqualifies it from serious ethical consideration. Yet the prevalence of story, myth and parable throughout human history,[21] in all cultures, is an indication of its ethical power and significance. It is a reminder that linear, deductive rationality is not the only way of representing or seeking ethical insights or truths. Life is too complex and often paradoxical to resolve dilemmas with simplistic or reductionist formulae.

The thesis of this exploration is not that religion has all the answers but rather that there is significant ethical wisdom to be gleaned from religious perspectives on life. That wisdom is not limited in its use or inspiration only to those committed to particular faith perspectives; a

---

[21] Fasching Darrell & Dechant Dell. *Comparative Religious Ethics.* Oxford: Blackwell, 2000.

variety of traditions have relevant insights for wider society. Some of this wisdom is already contained within or shared with secular philosophy, either through drawing, wittingly or unwittingly, on assumptions from the faith context in which they were forged or because faith has adopted methods from other philosophies. Other aspects of religious wisdom, from what are often perceived as 'eastern traditions',[22] may also provide correctives to some of the more mechanistic, rationalistic or materialistic aspects of western philosophy. The sense of cosmic rather than personal consequence found in the theology of the *dharmic* traditions is distinct from the majority of western ethical assumptions, which are predominantly anthropocentric. The development of environmental and global ethics as distinct areas of philosophical enquiry may be correcting the human-centric focus of western ethics but for the *dharmic* traditions the cosmic consequences for the environment have been the starting point.

A further specifically theological source of inspiration is meditation, prayer, ritual and worship. These practices with particular meanings for believers may be seen as exclusively religious but can carry meaning or benefit for those outside the faith. The power of meditative reflection through mindfulness as a context for ethical discernment is an example that has found support in non-religious contexts, including business and the health service. Others find ethical patterns and inspiration through the symbolism and collective reinforcement of corporate worship, an area of ethical enquiry that has formed the basis of *Blackwell's Companion to Christian Ethics*.[23]

Above all, far from being irrational or mindless, theological ethics at its highest requires reflective reasoning, self-knowledge and discernment. Whilst respecting and seeking to understand religious beliefs and ethics in their own confessional terms theological ethics is not itself confessional. Theological ethics questions unthinking or

---

[22] The fact that Christianity is perceived as a 'western religion' is ironic given that its genesis was in the Middle East and some of its early spread was in Africa; Augustine was a Bishop of Hippo, north Africa.

[23] Hauerwas Stanley & Wells Samuel (Eds.). *The Blackwell Companion to Christian Ethics*. Oxford: Blackwell Publishing, 2006 (Hauerwas and Wells 2006).

instinctive assumptions and habits as well as the roles of communal and personal identity in religious ethical approaches to life. Many deeply prayerful members of religious communities grow into this wisdom and discernment without academic training but through the maturing of faithful practice. Yet theological ethics is also an academic discipline.

Theology is about meaning-making in life and is therefore inherently questioning. Thus theological ethics challenges simplistic assertions about ethics based solely on a particular identity or worldview. This applies to secular or humanist assumptions just as much as to religious or theological ones. As with all ethics, theological ethics also clarifies meanings and usage of words and concepts in an area of life where concepts can be easily misunderstood, confused or misapplied. The reality is that, even if ours is an increasingly secular age,[24] a significant majority of the population, even in the UK and especially worldwide, has a religious faith of some sort or another. Some comprehension of religious ethics and theological understandings of the world is therefore necessary simply for sharing the planet. For those whose work brings them into positions of authority, treatment or service of others understanding the diversity of one's client or patient base is important. Equally, for those with a religious faith, a reflective awareness of how that faith relates to, differs from or affects their view of others is necessary. Ethics affects all areas of life; there is no aspect of life that does not have some ethical implication. For the majority of those with a religious faith the same is true, that no aspect of life is unaffected by their faith. Theological ethics therefore deals with the everyday in the light of the transcendent and eternal. It is practical and not given to theoretical speculation or extreme test cases and that is at the heart of this exploration.

---

[24] A contentious point, challenged by some sociologists as summarized by Grace Davie in *A Sociology of Religion: A Critical Agenda.* Sage Publishing, 2013 (Davie 2013), yet a view still promoted for example by Bruce e.g. in Bruce S. The demise of Christianity in Britain. In *Predicting Religion: Christian, Secular and Alternative Futures,* Eds. Davie G, Heelas P & Woodhead L. *Religion & theology in interdisciplinary perspective,* Ashgate, Aldershot, United Kingdom, 2003, pp. 53–63 (Bruce 2003). See too Sharpe M & Nickelson D. *Secularisations and Their Debates: Perspectives on the Return of Religion in the Contemporary West.* Springer Press, 2013 (Sharpe and Nickelson 2013).

2

Reason and Its History in Ethics and Theology

This chapter traces the ways in which concepts and processes of reasoning in ethical thought guided by both philosophy and theology have developed within particular traditions over time. A brief, non-exhaustive timeline traces overlapping influences such as the employment of Greek ethical thought within the Abrahamic faiths. One of the best-known histories of western ethics and Greek thought is that developed by Alistair McIntyre in *After Virtue*[1] and his later *Short History of Ethics*.[2] McIntyre's thesis is considered alongside historical perspectives on ethics from writers in other traditions, particularly Tariq Ramadan from an Islamic viewpoint and David Novak from the Jewish tradition.

The history of ethical thought and understandings of reason and knowledge in the different trajectories of *dharmic* thought are also considered. This exploration highlights very different perceptions of significant ethical and organizational concepts, such as reason, knowledge, the purpose of life and above all the separation of reason

---

[1] McIntyre Alasdair. *After Virtue*. London: Duckworths, 1985 (McIntyre 1985).
[2] MacIntyre Alasdair. *A Short History of Ethics*. London: Routledge, 1993 (McIntyre 1993).

© The Author(s) 2017
C. Shelley, *Ethical Exploration in a Multifaith Society*,
DOI 10.1007/978-3-319-46711-5_2

and faith, sacred and secular. The point of such an overview is to provide a background context for later exploration of particular ethical theories and paradigms.

Enlightenment

One of the most significant events in the history of western ethics and ethical thought is considered to be the Enlightenment, marked as the dividing point of modern from early history and the point at which religion became separated from public life in western society. It is the event, which was more of an historical process than a watershed, that is seen as enabling the development of both the liberal nation state and personal ethical autonomy, belief and conscience. The Enlightenment is both lauded and blamed from different perspectives as the triumph of human reason, the individual, materialism, empirical science and secular organization over religion. The version of religion rejected by those who praise the Enlightenment is an unprovable faith, with autocratic traditions and an ethics of deontological command.

The latter understanding of religious ethics is challenged along with the portrayal of the western understanding of Enlightenment as a triumph of secular, empirical knowledge and reason as the foundation of all that is modern. 'Science' as a touchstone of reality has come to mean technical, material, provable and rationalist knowledge. Its reach is no longer objects and non-human phenomena but also the more variable sphere of human and social sciences. It is a tendency in western thinking that has tended to leave faith and reason, religion and science at odds with each other, which has had an impact on religious communities and their self-understanding, theology and ethics as well as on wider society.

That impact however, is variable. Some religious communities, particularly in western Christianity, see the Enlightenment as simply a development of Christian thought and theological rationalism. They seek to incorporate or integrate science and theology in various different ways within their understanding of faith and the development of ethics.[3] Similarly branches of the Muslim community point to significant historical development of medical science and engineering to show that science and reason are part of their religious history not opposed to it.[4] Such traditions challenge the idea that science, reason and faith are necessarily at odds with each other.

By contrast other trajectories of religious thought set themselves against the rationalist project, being suspicious of human reason and its limitations and fallibility. In some respects Karl Barth[5] provides an example of this theological stance to the extent that whilst he does interrogate science quite extensively he also places revelation first. This is particularly notable in his adherence to a male-female hierarchy based on Genesis 2 but rejection of science that purports to show that men are naturally superior to women. Other theological and religious perspectives reject the apparent Enlightenment reduction of human experience, capacity and political and ethical compass to the secular and material. Contemporary Christian theologians who take this view include Stanley Hauerwas[6] and John Millbank[7] and others in the Radical Orthodoxy camp, blaming the Enlightenment for taking God and religion – in their context Christianity – out of ethics. As Charles Taylor puts it, 'in our secular societies you can engage fully in politics without ever encountering God . . .' yet historically in European society and 'in human history. . . . the whole set of distinctions that we make

---

[3] Bergstrom JC. *Principles of a Christian Environmental Ethic: With Applications to Agriculture, Natural Resources, and the Environment* http://www.leaderu.com/science/bergstrom-enviroethics. html. Accessed 14 May 2016; Dennin Michael. *Divine Science: Finding Reason at the Heart of Faith.* Franciscan Media, 2015 (Dennin 2015); Ward K. *The Big Questions in Science and Religion.* Templeton Press, 2004 (Ward 2004).

[4] For a humorous account of scientific development in Islam see Ziauddin Saddar. *Desperately Seeking Paradise: Journeys of a Sceptical Muslim.* London: Granta, 2004 particularly, pp. 85–121 (Saddar 2004); Ramadan T. *Western Muslims and the Future of Islam.* Oxford: OUP, 2004, pp. 55–61 (Ramadan 2004).

[5] Barth K. *Church Dogmatics. Vol III.4 The Doctrine of Creation.* Eds. Torrance F & Bromily GW. *T&T Clark.* 2010 particularly *Man and woman*, pp. 109–231 (Barth 2010b).

[6] Hauerwas S. *A Community of Character.* University of Notre Dame Press, 1991 (Hauerwas 1991); Hauerwas S. & Wells S. *The Blackwell Companion to Christian Ethics.* Oxford Blackwell Publishing, 2008, pp. 3–50 (Hauerwas and Wells 2006).

[7] Millbank J, Ward G & Pickstock C. *Radical Orthodoxy.* Routledge, 1998; Ed. Millbank J. *The Radical Orthodoxy Reader.* Routledge, 2009 (Millbank et al. 1998b).

between the religious, the political, the economic and the social . . . aspects of our society ceases to make sense . . .'[8]

By contrast with the western understanding of the term 'Enlightenment,' the idea of enlightenment in traditions such as Hinduism and Buddhism could not be more different, both in ethical and broader terms. The Hindu concept of *moksa*, which can variously be translated as 'liberation' or 'release',[9] is an enlightenment that is entirely about transcendence of this-worldly attachment and materialist dualism. Similarly, the Buddhist *nirvana*[10] is a release from desire or attachment to the material and knowledge is the wisdom of acquiring this detachment. Thus 'enlightenment' in the *dharmic* faiths, and the reasoning and ethics that seeking 'enlightenment' fosters, tends in a completely different direction from predominant empirical, material and rationalist western paradigms. This is not to say that *dharmic* faiths ignore material science and reason but their ethical and philosophical premises adopt a wholly different understanding of reality and wisdom.

Theology, Philosophy and History

This brief ethical history traces ages and cultures where non-theological and theological philosophy adopted similar ethical frameworks and the points at which they part company. Above all the overview demonstrates that Western society's division of secular from theological ethics is neither inevitable, nor evidenced in history nor universally accepted across the contemporary world. All human societies regardless of time, culture or religious tradition, have had some form of authoritative ethical norms, rules or laws. The question of why and by what authority people consider particular things ethical is an important consideration. It is in relation to this question of authority – as well as sources for

---

[8] Charles Taylor. *A Secular Age.* Harvard University Press, 2007 (Taylor 2007).

[9] Lipner J. *Hindus Their Religious Beliefs and Practices,* 2nd edition. London: Routledge, 2010, pp. 54–55 (Lipner 2010).

[10] Easwaran, Eknath. *Essence of the Dhammapada: The Buddhist Call to Nirvana.* Nilgiri Press, 2013 (Easwaran 2013).

Table 2.1 Early written ethical and legal codes

King/ City	Ur Nammi	Eshunna	Lipit Ishna	Hammurabi	Hittites	Mosaic/ Jewish
Gods	Utu	Tishpak		Marduk	A'as, Alalus, Arinna, Arinniti Arma	Yahweh
Date BCE	2050	1930	1870	1754	1650–1100	~ 500

Dates drawn from: Sharpes, Donald K. *The Lord of the Scrolls: Literary Traditions in the Bible and Gospels.* New York: Peter Lang Publishing, 2005–2007, pp. 159–163.

ethical ideas and patterns of life – that religion has played a large role and for many people and societies continues to do so.

The brief and non-exhaustive historical overview that follows provides a background for the ethical differences, contrasts and disjunctures examined in later chapters (Table 2.1).

The oldest written code discovered is *the Code of Ur-Nammu*, the King of Sumeria and is dedicated to the Sumerian god Utu. It is dated from 2050 BCE and is considered enlightened to the extent that it includes fines rather than the *lex talionis* or an 'eye for an eye' as punishments.

The *Hammurabi Code*, dated at 1754 BCE was named after King Hammurabi of Babylon who claimed to be a good servant of Marduk the patron god of Babylon. This code does include the *lex talionis*.

Similarly, the laws of the city of Eshunna (1930 BCE), the Hittite empire (1650–1100 BCE), the Code of Lipit Ishtar under the rule of Isin (1870–1860 BCE) and Assyrian codes of a similar period, were all promulgated by kings, with the sanctioning force of their respective local gods.

The beginning of the *Jewish Mosaic Code or Law of Moses* cannot be precisely dated as it was largely passed on orally and was not written and codified until after the destruction of the Temple in 70CE. However, it is thought to have pre-dated the exile to Babylon in 586 BCE. Judaism is believed to have been the first religion with a theology

Table 2.2 Classical Greek philosophy

Philosopher	Socrates	Plato	Aristotle
Key ideas	Practical Reason	The Good	Practical Reason
		Forms as perfect	Nichomachean Ethics
		Transmigration	Natural Law
		of soul; *The*	Virtue Ethics
		Republic	
		Dualistic	
Worldview	Reason over gods of	Athenian gods,	Reason over
	the city	transcendence	Athenian gods
		& afterlife	Integrity of truth
Dates	469/70–399BCE	424–347BCE	384–322BCE

O Sullivan, Maureen. *The Four Seasons of Greek Philosophy*. Efstatiadish Group, S.A.1982/1987.

of one universal monotheistic God.[11] The Mosaic Code's similarities with the laws of neighbouring nations can be cited as an example of universal natural law and reason (Table 2.2).

Socrates – 469/70–399BCE – Socrates gave up the labouring trade of his early life to become a philosopher, much to the annoyance of his wife Xanthippe who was left to care for their three children! Socrates' philosophy based on practical and empirical reason led him to deny the Athenian gods and the emperor. His suicide to preserve his integrity is sometimes compared to Jesus' acceptance of death by crucifixion.[12]

Plato of Athens – 427–347 BCE – Plato was taught by Socrates and in turn taught Aristotle. His concepts of 'the good', perfect Forms of things, immortality and transmigration of the soul, (about which he wrote in *The Phaedo*, a reflection on Socrates' death) and his political philosophy in *The Republic* gave rise to much philosophical and theological thought in later traditions. Plato believed in 'gods' and the

---

[11] Assman J. *Of God and gods: Egypt, Israel and the Rise of Monotheism*. University of Wisconsin Press, 2008 (Assman 2008).

[12] e.g. Bostick William F. Jesus and Socrates. *The Biblical World* 47, 4 (April, 1916), pp. 248–252. University of Chicago Press. http://www.jstor.org/stable/3143019 (Bostick 1916); Ladikos A. The Trials of Socrates and Jesus Christ: A Comparison. *Phronimon* 8, 2(2007), pp. 73–83 (Ladikos 2007).

transcendent but not a monotheistic Abrahamic understanding of God. His thought was dualist, i.e. mind/soul distinct from the body, which has significantly influenced western thought about body and soul, sex and gender.[13]

Aristotle of Stagirus, nr Thrace – 384–322 BCE – Aristotle was taught by Plato but rejected Plato's theory of Forms for more practical reasoning. In particular he developed a system of ethics based on natural law, which includes what human nature shares with animals but also analysis of natural reason as distinctively human. He saw body and soul as a unity, with the 'nature' of things defined by *telos* (or purpose). He also developed a theory of the virtues as ways of considering human ethics and what it means to be a good person. Although he had a monotheistic sense, endorsed by later theological writers such as Al Gazali, his ethics unlike Plato's was not dependent on a sense of transcendence or gods.[14]

The Hellenization of Monotheistic Religion: Jews & Early Christians

Much philosophical development within the Greek empire affected communities that were subject to Greek rule and thought. An example is the Christian St Paul, Apostle to the Gentiles, who was a Jew by birth but also Greek in his education and a Roman Citizen.

Key thinkers within the Jewish tradition, a diaspora community by the time of the Greek Empire,[15] and in the early Christian church sought to make sense of Greek philosophy alongside their religious faith. All defended the Judaeo-Christian scriptures and their beliefs arguing that, as accounts of the all-creating God and His engagement with a humanity made in His image, they pre-dated Greek Philosophy. The argument continued that had they known

---

[13] Plato. *The Complete Works*. Kindle Edition, 2015 (Plato 2015); Plato. *The Laws*. Penguin Classics, 1970 (Plato 1970).

[14] Aristotle Ed. Hugh Tredennick *Nichomachean Ethics*. Penguin Classics, 2004 (Aristotle 2004).

[15] As evidenced by Paul's journeys in the New Testament Book of Acts.

about them the Greek philosophers would have accepted the Judaeo-Christian scriptures and ethics.

Those writing from the perspective of theological belief effectively used non-theist ideas to develop their understanding of creation and of God but also sought to synthesize religious with philosophical ideas in a quest for unity. In the longer-term they used their understanding of philosophy to speak to non-believers about the truths of their faith and sought to justify non-monotheist Greek thought in religious terms. Two examples of such thinkers are the Jewish Philo and the early Christian, Origen, both of Alexandria.

Philo of Alexandria[16] – Philo was a 'hellenized (i.e. Greek educated) Jew' – 20 BCE to 40 CE. A fan of Plato, he used Greek philosophy to justify or explain Judaism, arguing that had Plato known about the Torah he would have been a Jewish believer.

Philo had a significant influence on the development of Christian philosophy, theology and ethics via Clement of Alexandria[17] (150–215 BCE), Justin Martyr[18] (100–165 CE), Tertullian[19] (155–240 CE) and Origen (185–254 CE). He may also have influenced St Paul and the authors of John's Gospel.[20] It is clear that the opening passages of St John's Gospel use Platonic philosophy about the Word in a sustained metaphor for the creation of the world and Jesus incarnation.[21]

Origen of Alexandria – 185–254 CE – Origen was one of the first systematic apologists for Christianity. Yet in support of his arguments and defence of Christianity he used neo-Platonist philosophy. Thus he not only sought to convince Greek philosophers by using their own frames of reference to justify Christianity in his work

---

[16] Philo Scholer David M (Foreword), Yong CD (trans). *The Works of Philo: Complete and Unabridged.* Publishers Hendricklson, 1993 (Philo Scholer David 1993).

[17] Oborn E. *Clement of Alexandria.* Cambridge University Press, 2009 (Oborn 2009).

[18] Justin Martyr Eds. Donaldson J & Roberts A. *The Writings of Justin Martyr.* Apocryphile Press, 2007 (Martyr 2007).

[19] Dunn GD. *Tertullian (Early Church Fathers).* Routledge, 2004 (Dunn 2004).

[20] Dodd CH. *The Interpretation of the Fourth Gospel.* Cambridge University Press, 1968 (Dodd 1968).

[21] Bigg Charles. *The Christian Platonists of Alexandria.* Hardpress Publishing, 2012 (Bigg 2012).

Against Celsus[22] but also used the same philosophy against the Gnostic heresy which privileged a dualist spiritualism over the material in *On first principles.*[23]

After Constantine – Christianity as the Religion of Empire[24]

The adoption of Christianity as the religion of the empire, following the conversion of the Emperor Constantine in 313CE, changed its profile and the nature of its ethical challenges. From being a minority, counter-cultural community, living together in small groups and still to some degree persecuted by the Roman authorities, Christianity became an establishment tradition. From an ethic of soldiers giving up their profession in order to embrace Christian pacifism, the Christian empire started to grapple with theories of Just War and maintaining political order. Already influenced by the predominant cultural traditions of Greek philosophy Christian theologians and leaders now found within it further resources with which to address these new ethical dilemmas.

St Augustine, Bishop of Hippo,[25] a Roman citizen, lived from 354 to 430CE, becoming Bishop of Hippo, part of Africa that is now Algeria. Augustine's works (*Confessions, City of God, sermons*) cover personal moral theology, just war theory, political ethics and theology. His range of ethical interests reflects Plato's output. Augustine is respected by those on both Protestant and Catholic sides of the Reformation schism and (though to a lesser degree) by the Orthodox Church, as one of the foremost Christian apologists. As a theologian in the early Christian Empire, free from the persecution of earlier Christian theologians, he was well-placed to reflect on government and the good society, informed by his own experience of secular and episcopal governance.

---

[22] Origen Ed. Chadwick Henry. *Contra Celsum.* Cambridge University Press, 2008 (Origen 2008).

[23] Origen. *On First Principles.* Ave Maria Press, 2013 (Origen 2013).

[24] Potter D. *Constantine the Emperor.* Oxford University Press, 2015 (Potter 2015).

[25] Chadwick H. *Augustine of Hippo: A Life.* Oxford University Press, 2010; Augustine Trans Mary T Clark. *Augustine of Hippo: Selected Writings.* SPCK, 1984 (Chadwick 2010).

Greek philosophical concepts were his education and everyday language; his journey to adoption of the Christian faith led him through a variety of philosophical movements. Although ultimately he found them wanting, Augustine's grappling with various philosophies and their interplay with personal experience, gives his Christian theology an in-depth understanding. However, his exploration led Augustine to mistrust the limitations of human reason; he rejected any philosophy that put an exclusive emphasis on human action as against God. His intellectual sparring partners were Manichean and Gnostic heretics who believed that mind or spirit is superior to the material and bodily and the Pelagian belief that ethical perfection is possible entirely through human effort.

The Rediscovery of Greek Ethics; A Judao-Muslim Golden Age

Some of the greatest developments of philosophical thinking and theological apologetics flourished across Spain, North Africa and the Middle East with an extraordinary cross-fertilizing of ideas and arguments between polymaths from the Jewish and Muslim traditions. It was customary for a well-educated scholar to reflect on philosophy and theology, alongside medical practice and/or the law. Some of these Golden Age thinkers were also respected poets. This flourishing occurred whilst much of northern Europe was languishing in the 'dark ages.'

Saadia Ben Gaon – was born in Egypt in 882/892CE and died in Baghdad in 942. He was a Jewish philosopher and exegete of Jewish scripture and wrote in Arabic as well as in Hebrew. He developed the 'Jewish Kalam' responses to Greek philosophy and explored the relationship of that philosophy to Judaism and to Islamic scholars of the 'Muslim Kalam' school. His book of Jewish apologetics *Emunoth ve-Deoth* or 'Beliefs and Opinions'[26] is a defence of rational Jewish theology, written in reaction against what Ben Gaon saw as confused and superstitious belief

---

[26] Originally written in Arabic as *Kitāb ul-'amānāt wal-i'tiqādāt* the book was translated into Hebrew by Judah ibn Tibbon. English translation: Samuel Rosenblatt in 1948. *Book of beliefs and opinions.* Yale University Press, 1989 (Rosenblatt 1989).

amongst the Jewish population and unbelief in wider society. Ben Gaon views the three main sources of knowledge as natural reason, experience and the revelation of God in scripture. In its exploration of natural reason the book shows evidence of a reading of Aristotle. The form of argument used also follows the rationalist defences of his contemporary Muslim apologists.

Avicenna, also known as **Ibn Sina** who lived from 980 to about 1036 CE was a Persian Muslim philosopher and medic. He came from Bukhara (Uzbekhistan) and travelled as far as Afghanistan. He was inspired by Aristotle through reading a translation of his work by Al-Farabi but he also read other Greek philosophers. In addition, he was influenced by Indian works on maths and astronomy. He wrote 'The book of healing' as well as over one hundred books on philosophy. It is thought that his works on Greek philosophy and his exploration of Muslim theology had an influence on Aquinas' natural law theology.[27]

Al Ghazali, a Persian from Tus in Iran, lived from 1058–1111 CE and came from the Sunni Muslim tradition. He also sought to rationalize the insights of both theology in the Muslim *kalam* school and of Greek philosophy, particularly Aristotle. He did not adopt Greek philosophy uncritically, writing trenchantly against *The incoherence of the Philosophers*. However, his work examined Greek philosophical concepts, particularly approving much of Aristotle, reconciling philosophical science with theology where logically possible whilst retaining theological authenticity. His analysis and methods were followed by later Muslim, Jewish and medieval Christian thinkers.[28] Gazali's exploration also included reflection on scientific and natural phenomena as well as pure philosophy. Al Gazali's work remains significant and much-quoted in contemporary Islam for example as the most-cited of the 11th CE Muslim philosophers by Tariq

---

[27] McGinnis, Jon. *Avicenna*. Oxford: Oxford University Press, 2010, p. 227 (McGinnis 2010); Toulmin S & Goodfield J. *The Ancestry of Science: The Discovery of Time*. University of Chicago Press, 1967. p. 64 (Toulmin and Goodfield 1967); McGinnis, Jon. Scientific Methodologies in Medieval Islam. *Journal of the History of Philosophy* 41, 3 (July 2003): 307–327 (McGinnis 2003).

[28] Sabra AI. The Appropriation and Subsequent Naturalization of Greek Sciences in Medieval Islam: A Preliminary Statement. *History of Science* 25 (1987): 223–243 (Sabra 1987).

Ramadan in both *Western Muslims and the Future of Islam*[29] and *Radical Reform: Islamic ethics and liberation.*

Judah Ha-Levi was born in 1075 (or possibly 1086) and lived to 1141. He was a Jewish philosopher, medic and poet, born in Toledo, Spain but who seems to have spent time in Granada, the part of Spain governed for many centuries by Muslim rulers until ousted by the Christian monarchs Ferdinand and Isabella. He died in Palestine, at that stage an area under attack from the crusades. Like Ibn Sina and others he had a broad knowledge of theology, philosophy and medicine, from Greek and Arabic sources. His philosophical work, like that of Al Ghazali, sought to engage critically with Greek philosophy, using some of their insights where helpful to theology but maintaining the theological revelation as paramount. It seems that he was influenced by Ghazali's work.[30] His major philosophical and apologetic work is *Kitab al Khazari* otherwise known as '*The book of refutation and proof on behalf of the most despised religion*'.[31]

Averroes who lived from 1126 to 1198 CE was also known as **Ibn Rushd.** He was a Muslim Aristotelian scholar; born in Cordoba and who died in Marrakech he was therefore from the Andalucian school. At the request of the Caliph he produced summaries of Aristotle and Plato's works, including the *Decisive Treatise on the Agreement Between Religious Law and Philosophy (Faṣl al-Makāl)* and an *Examination of the Methods of Proof Concerning the Doctrines of Religion (Kashf al-Manāhij)*. His strict rational approach and critique of Al Ghazali led to conflicts with al-Mansur a more Orthodox contemporary who got him banned from a judicial post in Seville and from Marakech. However, his rationalist thinking still holds a place in Muslim theology.[32]

---

[29] Ramada T. *Western Muslims and the Future of Islam.* Oxford University Press, 2004, pp. 39–44, 236–237 (Ramada 2004); *Radical Reform: Islamic Ethics and liberation.* pp. 61–64, 88, 169–170, 191, 298–302, 356 (Ramada 2009).

[30] For further details see Brody H. *Studien zu den Dichtungen Jehuda ha-Levi's.* Berlin, 1895 (Brody 1895).

[31] http://www.sacred-texts.com/jud/khz/index.htm. Accessed 15 May 2016; Stanford Encyclopaedia of Philosophy http://plato.stanford.edu/entries/halevi/. Accessed 15 May 2016.

[32] Averroes Ed. Majid Fakhri Trans. Ibrahim Naijar. *Faith and reason in Islam: Averroes' exposition of religious arguments.* One world publishing, July 2001 (Averroes 2001).

Maimonides otherwise known as **Moshe Ben Maimon or Musa Ibn Maimon** popularly finds his name shortened to **'the RaMBaM'.** He lived from 1135 (or 8) to 1204 and was a Sephardic Jewish Philosopher, who was born in Cordoba, Spain and died in Egypt. He codified the Talmud in the 14 volumes of Jewish law and ethics known as the *Mishneh Torah.*[33] He was also influenced by the Greek classical tradition and Muslim scholars like Avicenna and his contemporary, Averroes. His work is still cited widely in contemporary Judaism including by modern Jewish natural law scholars such as David Novak who has also explored the overlapping natural law theological traditions.[34]

Christian Development of Philosophy

Aquinas who was born in 1225 and lived to 1274 CE was known as the Angelic Doctor. He synthesized Aristotelian philosophy and natural law ethics with Christianity, often referred to as 'baptising' Aristotle's ethics. Both his philosophy, based on Aristotle and his theology, gave rise to the Scholastic movement, which dominated Catholic theology and ethics until the twentieth century.[35]

Aquinas' philosophy is familiar enough in the west to be included in histories of western philosophy.[36] Ironically, although originating in Greek philosophy, particularly Aristotle's *Nichomachean Ethics*, in many ways Aquinas inspiration came from Jewish and Muslim scholars who had explored the theological interface with philosophy in the centuries before Aquinas' birth. Aquinas' systematic approach[37] developed Aristotle's ethical concepts. One example is striving for 'the mean'

---

[33] http://www.mishnehtorah.com/index.html; Avraham Yaakov Finkel. *The Essential Maimonides: Translations of the RamBam.* Yeshivat Moshe Press, 1993/4 (Finkel 1993/4).

[34] Rashkover R. *Tradition in the Public Square: A Novak Reader.* Eerdmans Publishing, 2008. pp. 113–162; 213–252 (Rashkover and Kavka 2008).

[35] Aquinas. *Selected Writings.* Penguin Classics, 1999 (Aquinas 1999).

[36] Bertrand Russell. *History of Western Philosophy.* Routledge Classics, 2004 (Russell 2004); Anthony Kenny. *A New History of Western Philosophy.* OUP, 2012 (Kenny 2012);

[37] His greatest work is not known as the *Summa Theologica* for nothing!.

between extremes of human behaviour i.e. courage between rashness and cowardice, modesty between shame and shyness. He also developed ideas of justice, analysing legal, distributive and corrective justice. His major move however was his 'Christianising' of Aristotle's work.

The Renaissance and Reformation

The development of critical thinking and classical Greek exploration that began with Aquinas in western and northern Europe developed into the Renaissance which has the reputation of a European intellectual Golden Age. Like the 'Judaeo-Muslim golden age' the Renaissance produced intellectual and humanist all-rounders who were men (virtually always) of faith and philosophy as well as statesmanship, literature, arts and sciences, whether astronomy, biology or medicine. Examples of such Renaissance men include the astronomer Nicolaus Copernicus who was also a philosopher, linguist, canon lawyer, physician, governor, diplomat and economist. Leonardo da Vinci, best known as a painter, also revealed a detailed grasp of human anatomy in his art and a turn for engineering in his scientific inventions.

Compared to such polymaths the priest Desiderius Erasmus[38] was comparatively limited to theology, philosophy and languages, with priestly and teaching duties. He lived from 1466 to 1536 and learnt Latin, Greek and Hebrew so as to read the Bible in its original languages. He also studied the Church fathers, amongst them Augustine, Origen and Tertullian and so learnt afresh their understandings of both Biblical and classical thought. His humanist philosophy and theology sought to bring reason, based in natural law theology, to bear upon reform of the western (as opposed to Eastern Orthodox) Church and society, in what was still the Holy Roman Empire. He challenged what he saw as corrupted power but remained a Catholic, even after the Reformation, which formally began towards the end of his life. He was committed to the idea of human reason and

---

[38] Jardine L. *Erasmus Man of Letters: The Construction of Charisma in Print.* Princeton University Press, 2015 (Jardine 2015).

free will following the natural law tradition developed by Aquinas and rejected Luther's complete reliance on revelation.

Martin Luther and the Reformation: Luther was born in 1483 and lived to 1546. He was a pious and gifted Dominican friar but suffered serious psychological scruples in his observance of the religious rule and perfection of religious life. He challenged laxity and corruption in the Church's life, for example condemning the corruptions of simony and nepotism in filling church posts, the raising of money by selling indulgences and usury. Disillusioned by the church and the self-serving fallibility of human reason Luther rejected natural law, reason and human effort for revelation, God's grace, faith and scripture alone.

Although Luther's intention was primarily reform of the Church his stand, when the Church condemned his arguments as heresy, led to the Reformation. The western church was split, eventually giving rise to the schism between Catholic and Protestant. However, this was not only a religious Reformation; it both grew from and brought socio-political changes including the growth of power for secular leaders.

As the maxim *cuius regio, eius religio*[39] took hold, the church's authority declined. Translation of the Bible into the vernacular (people's own languages) also meant the church no longer had a monopoly on interpreting Scripture. The former development led to greater autonomy for the secular state and the idea of nationhood, whilst the latter increased the scope for personal autonomy, at least amongst the wealthier classes of men.

Both of these developments in relation to national and personal autonomy laid significant conceptual foundations for the philosophical thinking of the Enlightenment. The division of the church and then Europe into Catholic and Protestant camps with inevitably divisive political consequences led to the impetus for removing reference to religion from ethical, political and social decisions.[40]

---

[39] Loosely translated – *His the rule, his the religion or the one who rules chooses the state's religion.*
[40] Henrix Scott H. *Martin Luther Visionary Reformer.* Yale University Press, 2015 (Henrix 2015).

Catholic Exploration and Discovery of the 'New World'

Yet the Protestant Reformation was not the only strand of change to lead to modern intellectual and ethical developments. As the Renaissance and Reformation changed the intellectual, social and political framework of Europe from within, the adventures of Columbus and those who followed him to the 'New World' changed European perceptions of the known world. The travels not only of explorers but also of traders and religious missionaries brought Europeans into contact with the cultures, customs and ethics of very different races and nations. The major continents concerned were the Americas, India, China and Southern Africa; it must be remembered that Northern Africa had already been known via the Greek and Roman Empires.

A number of developments arose from this encounter with other continents. One strand of Catholic missionary thought, via the Dominicans and the Jesuits, found the image of God and respect for human dignity and conscience amongst the indigenous tribes of South America. They sought to defend such peoples against forced conversion or forced slavery at the hands of traders. It could be argued that this was the first example of respect for human rights for all peoples, regardless of property, wealth, religion or nation leading eventually to the sorts of twentieth century human rights developed after the Holocaust.[41] The ethical basis of this development seems to have been both Biblical and based on natural law theology, even though the forms of reason found amongst the indigenous Indians were very different from European thought and belief.

On other continents, notably India and China, Jesuit missionaries took the message of Christianity only to be faced with very different, highly sophisticated cultures. This led in some instances to theologies of acculturation, such as practised by Matteo Ricci in China[42] or Francis

---

[41] Roger Rushton. *Human Rights and the Image of God*. SCM Press, 2004 (Rushton 2004); Wolterstorff N. *Justice: Rights and Wrongs*. Princeton University Press, 2010 (Wolterstorff 2010).

[42] Trigault Nicolas SJ. 'China in the Sixteenth Century: The Journals of Mathew Ricci: 1583–1610'. English translation Gallagher SJ, Louis J. New York: Random House, Inc. 1953 (Trigault 1953); Lowney C. *Heroic Leadership*. Loyola Press, 2003. pp. 63–82 (Lowney 2003); Modras R. *Ignatian Humanism*. Loyola Press, 2004 (Modras 2004).

Xavier and Roberto de Nobili in India,[43] in which the ethics and beliefs of Catholic Christianity were explored by reference to the new faiths and worldviews encountered rather than as a field for conversion. Such methods laid the foundations for exploration of ethical and theological pluralism and later movements for interfaith dialogue. This was in stark contrast to the Catholic revival in Spain by which Jews and Muslims who refused to convert to Christianity were expelled or killed thanks to the Inquisition.

Jesuit and Dominican exploration was also a contrast with the polarizing trends of the Reformation, separating Catholic from Protestant across most of Europe. The Golden Age of humanist intellectual exploration, seems to have seen vigorous apologetics. However, mutual respect for those engaging in debate and development of the faith in dialogue with those of similar intellectual traditions, was overtaken by more tribal and politicized approaches to religious identity. The Reformation tenet of salvation by faith alone within Christianity made the importance of belief in the Bible and Christ's saving power more important than a common search for the kingdom of God. Similarly, in the light of schism, the importance of belonging to the Catholic rather than the Protestant Church as the means of salvation moved to the foreground.

Although the adoption of Christianity by Constantine had already created a situation in which religion was politicized, this became more apparent and more conflictual in the post-Reformation era. The breaking down of the Holy Roman Empire into smaller units, in which state leaders chose the religion of the area they governed, led to increased potential for conflict as compared with the comparatively homogenous former empire. In Europe these conflicts led in due course to the Thirty years war from 1618 to 1648.[44] It began as a Catholic versus Protestant war but soon covered the whole of Europe, largely but not exclusively along denominational lines. This acute example of the politicizing of

---

[43] Broderick J. *Saint Francis Xavier (1506–1552)*. London: Burns, Oates & Washbourne Ltd., 1952 (Broderick 1952); Lowney C. *Heroic Leadership*. Loyola Press, 2003, pp. 127–161.

[44] Wilson P. (Professor). *The Thirty Years War: A Sourcebook*. Palgrave MacMillan, 2010 (Wilson 2010).

religion became a major motivating factor behind Enlightenment attempts to get away from religion and seek alternative bases for the protection of human and civic rights, both domestically and internationally.

The Enlightenment

The tensions and wars generated by the post-Reformation settlements, both as between states and to a degree within states, led to thinking that sought to remove religious belief from ethical and legal norms for states. Whilst within Europe the Thirty Years war was a pivotal moment in the move towards the Enlightenment the development of thinking that would take God out of the public sphere had begun before the war broke out.

Hugo Grotius,[45] a Dutch Protestant, jurisprudential lawyer and Attorney General, who was born in 1583 was 35 years of age when the Thirty Years War began. One of his first works, *Mare Liberum*[46] considered the possibility of an international law more systematically than the sixteenth century *ius gentium*[47] (law of the nations) developed by Francisco de la Vittoria.[48] Grotius had already been writing prior to the outbreak of the war about the need for religious toleration and the divorce of particular views about religious doctrine from the governance of the state. On the basis of these views Grotius was asked to formulate an edict for religious tolerance, which became the *Decretum pro pace ecclesiarum*, published in 1613–1614.

Until his death in 1645, shortly before the end of the thirty years war, Grotius continued to develop the application of natural law ideals to international law and political ethics. *De Imperio Summarum Potestatum circa Sacra*[49] considered the relationship of

---

[45] Neff Stephen C. *Hugo Grotius: On the Law of Ear and Peace: Student Edition.* Cambridge University Press, 2012 (Neff Stephen 2012).
[46] On the freedom of the seas 1609.
[47] Law of the nations.
[48] Francisco de la Vitoria Ed. Pagden AG/Ed & trans: Lawrance J. *Vitoria: Political Writings.* Cambridge University Press, 1991 (de la Vitoria 1991).
[49] Of the power of the secular around the sacred.

secular to religious authorities. The three-volume *On the Law of War and Peace (1625)* developed his theories of international law, based on natural law, rights to protect property, rules of war and the regulation of the comity of nations. His ideas upset a few people in the Netherlands forcing him to escape (reputedly in an oak chest) to Paris, where his work was better received. Whilst Grotius himself was a Christian apologist, who also wrote about theology, like Kant he developed codes of ethics and natural law independent of God.

Unlike Grotius **Thomas Hobbes**[50] was not a theologian, had no religious faith and was one of the first atheists amongst the Enlightenment philosophers. Born in 1588 he was a contemporary of Grotius but responded very differently to the world around him. Whereas Grotius envisaged an international law and political ethics based on the natural law tradition and a positive view of human nature and reason, Hobbes' view of humanity was pessimistic. He viewed human nature as inherently competitive and self-interested; law was required as a restraining force for 'base' humanity, his vision grounded not in a positive view of good but in mutually self-interested co-operation. His writings included *De Cive* in 1642, *Elements of law, natural and political* in 1650, *Leviathan* in 1651 and *Behemoth* about the civil wars in England.

The Diversification of Philosophy and Emphasis on Empiricism

Alongside Grotius and Hobbes' quests to find unifying and non-religious ethical and legal norms in the spheres of politics, international law and rights, many other philosophers sought to remove religion from ethics and ethical authority, focusing largely on the human and empirical. Although religion may have disappeared from the ethical scene disagreement over premises and theories did not. The following

---

[50] Thomas Hobbes Ed. MacPherson CB. *Leviathon*. Penguin Classics, 1968 (Hobbes 1968).

non-exhaustive overview illustrates the diversity amongst some of the key Enlightenment philosophies.

René Descartes (1596–1650) a near contemporary of Grotius and Hobbes was more concerned with metaphysical philosophical enquiry than politics and war, although he did see some armed service. His attempt to create or discover an entirely new approach to philosophy, starting with the premise 'I think, therefore I am', earned him the nickname 'father of modern philosophy'. Like many of his Renaissance predecessors he was a polymath, versed in medicine, law, maths, theology and the 'scientific arts' like music as well as philosophy. He rejected the philosophy of his early Jesuit education in favour of empirical reason and worldly experience. However, he retained some concept of God arguing that there must be a thinking cause to have created humanity as thinking beings.[51] He also conceived of a voluntarist God, creating in complete freedom rather than constrained by human (natural law) ideas of creation's ends.

Despite seeking to start with a blank slate Descartes nonetheless drew on aspects of his philosophical heritage including an Aristotelian investigation of nature. He consistently sought to apply observation and deduction from first principles to philosophical enquiry. His moral philosophy assumed happiness or pleasure in a stoical, rationalist sense as the supreme good. However, contrary to Aristotle he argued that happiness lay in rational mental control rather good fortune. These views were set out in the *Discourse on the Method of Rightly Conducting the Reason and Seeking Truth in the Sciences* (1637) and *Meditations on First Philosophy* and *Principles of Philosophy*, published in 1644.

John Locke's[52] birth (in 1632) post-dated the Thirty Years war by a decade but his philosophy was nonetheless affected by its memory. His theory of mind considered the link between the self and the continuity of consciousness, with significant consequences for continuity of conscience and moral accountability. Locke's theory of the social contract

---

[51] Descartes R. Ed. Williams Bernard. *Meditations on First Philosophy 1641.* Cambridge University Press, 1996 (Descartes 1996).

[52] Woolhouse A. *Locke: A Biography.* Cambridge University Press, 2007 (Woolhouse 2007).

sought to justify mutual co-operation in society and the agreement and acceptance of ethical norms and laws without recourse to secular or religious power. Like Kant he believed that it was possible to find common ethical ground through empirical knowledge and reason rather than metaphysics or faith. Yet the lack of an underlying external authority or objective criteria for legal or moral norms means that social contract theory risks complete relativism or the value-less rule of the mob. Locke died in 1704, a reminder that his theory was also developed in the context of a limited democracy, in which voters were members of an elite class far from a universal franchise for men let alone women.

Baruch Spinoza[53] also born in 1632 (died in 1677) was a complex philosopher of Jewish heritage who disowned his faith but developed a pantheistic faith in nature as an expression of God. His conception of nature as God's creation, programmed to do what God wills, undermines ideas of human free will. His theory did however retain the natural law idea that all creation seeks to preserve itself in being i.e. the principle of life.

David Hume's[54] (1711–1776) empiricism led him also to reject the idea of God, seeking material proof as the basis for ethics. He developed the compatibilist theory of free will arguing that humanity has the freedom to exercise agency or will as a social construct, not a God-given faculty. Hume wanted humanity to take greater ownership of its values, agency and motives for action, without reference to external authority, whether divine or human. Hume recognized also that emotions are a part of human decision-making and personhood yet he argued that there is no independent self, just human bundles of emotions and perceptions.

Immanuel Kant's[55] (1724–1804) deontological ethics posit a rational moral law in which things are good if they result from good will in accordance with moral duty i.e. objectively right rather than right

---

[53] Nadler S. *Spinoza: A life*. Cambridge University Press, 2001 (Nadler 2001).
[54] Harris James A. *Hume: An Intellectual Biography*. Cambridge University Press, 2015 (Harris 2015).
[55] Rogers A. *Immanuel Kant: A Biography*. Kindle Edition.

because they are good. He sought to discover and demonstrate that the moral law is the categorical imperative, an objective rationalist reality that all must follow to be good. He explores these themes in *Groundwork of the Metaphysic of Morals* (1785), *Critique of Practical Reason* (1788) and *Metaphysics of Morals* (1797). Whilst Kant grew up as the son of a Christian Protestant pastor and still had respect for faith he argued, following Enlightenment principles, that universal ethical law could be rationally deduced without reference to God.

Moses Mendelssohn[56] a near contemporary of Kant (1729–1786) was a German Jewish philosopher who developed the 'Jewish enlightenment' or *Haskalah*, although his take on Greek philosophy differed from that of his co-religionist Philo seventeen centuries earlier. Following Plato he wrote about the soul in a modern *Phaedo* and *Metaphysics*, arguing for reason as the foundation of ethics. In contrast with Philo's attempt to read Greek philosophy back into religious scripture, Mendelssohn saw reason as the arbiter of ethics and scripture. He promoted freedom of religious conscience, from both state and religious authorities, although he conceded that Jewish law was binding on the conscience of Jews, including converts to Christianity. He translated the Talmud into modern German to make it more accessible to Jewish followers. Mendelsohn's work was entirely consistent with a rationalist Enlightenment approach to faith and ethics, whilst remaining clearly within a religious and theological framework.

Jeremy Bentham's (1748–1832) 'principle of utility' rejected natural law and Kant's Categorical Imperative. He sought an ethical principle that could be widely and practically applied to ethical and legal issues, including social reforms and prisons. The 'Principle of Utility' employs a quasi-scientific calculus to achieve the greatest good, defined as pleasure and minimize the pain or harm in the world. Yet from the beginning what constitutes or counts as pleasure or pain was not defined. However, the quantum of pleasure or pain was evaluated according to the intensity, duration and degrees of certainty and proximity, as well as the extent of

---

[56] Dahlstrom Daniel O. *Moses Mendelssohn: Philosophical Writings.* Cambridge University Press, 1997 (Dahlstrom 1997).

pleasure. Bentham viewed ethics as entirely an applied science, as indicated by his *Introduction to the Principles of Morals and Legislation*. His Panoptican as a means of keeping prisoners under surveillance was a practical application of his theories, which are examined in more detail later.

John Stuart Mill (1806–1873) was Bentham's disciple, literally as he was educated by him as a boy. He also adopted the theory of utilitarianism – and wrote the book of that name[57]– but refined it to reflect different types of pleasure, including what he considered as the higher pleasures of intellectual and cultural pursuits. Unlike Bentham who saw animals as within the principle of utility, as they could suffer pain, Mill famously coined the phrase 'Better a dissatisfied human being than a contented pig'. Accordingly he distinguished 'higher' i.e. more cerebral from 'lower', more material, pleasures and aimed for the 'The Greatest Happiness Principle.' In more formal language his reasoning was:

> *'those who are equally acquainted with and equally capable of appreciating and enjoying both do give a most marked preference to the manner of existence which employs their higher faculties. Few human creatures would consent to be changed into any of the lower animals for a promise of the fullest allowance of a beast's pleasures; no intelligent human being would consent to be a fool, no instructed person would be an ignoramus, no person of feeling and conscience would be selfish and base, even though they should be persuaded that the fool, the dunce, or the rascal is better satisfied with his lot than they are with theirs.'*

It is an argument for quality of pleasure rather than quantity.

In Summary

All these thinkers, philosophers, theologians and ethicists in their different traditions and times saw ethics as a process of reason. For those who believed in God reason was God-given, with law and ethical codes

---

[57] Utilitarianism 1861 Published more recently as John Stuart Mill & Jeremy Bentham *Utilitarianism and Other Essays*. Penguin Books, 1987 (Mill and Bentham 1987).

accorded the reason and order given in nature. For those without religious belief, reason was innately human and gave authority to human action and decision-making. For the majority of such philosophers reason was universal but essentially dictated by western assumptions.

Challenging Received Thought on the History of Ethics

In both *After Virtue*,[58] his best-known discussion of ethics and his later *Short History of Ethics*[59] Alistair McIntyre sets out a theory of the development of western ethics. Picking up the baton from Elizabeth Anscombe's critique of ethics since the Enlightenment,[60] MacIntyre argued that post-Enlightenment ethical theory, particularly utilitarianism and Kantian deontology, uprooted ethics from its historical and cultural moorings. The argument is that ethics depends on common understandings within a society of what is good and just. Without that common societal vision of morality there is simply a bureaucratic process for determining what is most expedient. This leaves a 'thin morality' with boundaries around what is prohibited but no agreement about what constitutes the good nor any goals or criteria for creating a good society.

McIntyre's history posits comparatively self-contained, homogenous communities with a common historical and ethical narrative, capable not only of determining agreed goods but also shaping members according to the values and virtues of the community. There may be an argument for saying that this view of society had some validity in Greek City States, with a limited *polis* in terms of its citizenry and an elite electorate. There might also be an argument for this sort of analysis of ethics within self-contained diaspora communities such as Haredi Jews or the Amish. This is particularly the case where minority

---

[58] McIntyre A. *After Virtue*. London: Duckworths, 1985.

[59] MacIntyre Alasdair. *A Short History of Ethics*. London: Routledge, 1993.

[60] Anscombe E. *Modern Moral Philosophy* first published in *Philosophy* 33 (1958): 1–19; reprinted in *Ethics, Religion and Politics* (*The Collected Philosophical Papers of G. E. M. Anscombe*, Volume 3), Minneapolis, MN: University of Minnesota Press, 1981, pp. 26–42 (Anscombe 1981).

status, sometimes accompanied by discrimination, leads such communities to develop stricter definitive norms as a means of preserving identity and existence. However, even the brief, potted history outlined above indicates a fair degree of philosophical and ethical mixing and cross-fertilization in Europe, the Middle East and beyond, since at least the Greek empire.

This history of overlapping strands of ethical enquiry, traced through Jewish, Muslim and Christian traditions, as well as later secular societies, suggests that the homogenous society, with a single ethical narrative and vision of the good never really existed. Even considering Greek thought alone indicates various different theories about how to live the good life. Perfectionist and dualist Platonic theories of the forms were at odds with Aristotle's more practical, holistic Nichomachean ethics. Epicurean pleasure-seekers, evaluating life by means of experience and sense had a different worldview from the logic-driven and duty bound Stoics. Different groups also claimed the particularity of their philosophical 'camp'; Epicureans debated Stoics, Stoics argued with Cynics and so on. Each group had different conceptions of the good life and narratives about the gods.

Into this mixture of competing Greek ethics and philosophical schools came religious worldviews from the monotheistic religions. Although pre-dating the Greek empire Judaism engaged with Greek thought and culture, at least by the last century BCE. Evidence from both Philo's writing and the New Testament demonstrates this interface. Philo's engagement sought to justify Greek philosophy as compatible with Judaism; he embraced it arguing that Aristotle would have accepted Judaism had he heard of it. Christian writers, like the author of John's Gospel which begins with arguments from Stoic thought, used it as a missionary tool, to convince gentile neighbours of the truth of Christianity. Even St Paul who rejected paganism nonetheless used Greek concepts, for example the Athenian 'unknown God', to illustrate his exposition of Christianity. Augustine, struggling with the good life in classical Greek mode, continued that selective engagement, working out what in his Greek formation was compatible with Christianity.

This Augustinian engagement with Greek philosophy in search of truth, good and justice whilst maintaining an over-arching religious allegiance, mirrors later Muslim philosophers' engagement with Greek philosophy. Like the Christian Fathers Muslim philosophers drew different conclusions about the extent of Greek heritage that was compatible with faith. In assessing the appropriate relationship of Islamic belief to 'the various philosophical sciences', Al Ghazali writes of philosophy as falling into three categories, 'unbelief', 'heresy' and thirdly, 'what is not to be denied at all'. He criticizes those who reject Islam because they limit their enquiry to philosophy or a faith that is provable; he is equally critical of those who limit their understanding of God and faith by rejecting what science has to teach.[61]

Thus neither Greek philosophy nor those faiths that engaged with it were homogenous, a reflection of the diversity of the empire or civilization in which such philosophical development was taking place. What is notable about these monotheistic engagements with Greek philosophy is that they employ styles of argument and rational deduction influenced by Greek philosophical methodology and analysis. The heritage of Greek thought, particularly in the natural law and virtue ethics derived from Aristotle, continues to be acknowledged in contemporary writing. Virtue ethics experienced a twentieth century recovery or rediscovery by Anscombe and McIntyre from Christian backgrounds and Phillipa Foot from a secular perspective.

Natural law philosophy has been embraced and developed by Germaine Grisez, John Finnis and Jean Porter from a Catholic standpoint, by Gustafson from a Protestant perspective and writers from Thomas Hobbes, Hugo Grotius, Kant, Rawls and Onora O Neill amongst others, from various perspectives in secular philosophy. Tariq Ramadan and other Muslim theologians still draw heavily, in their ethics and wider theology, on natural law insights from the writings of Al Ghazali and in turn their Greek philosophical engagement. David Novak and other Jewish theologians, for example former Chief Rabbi Jonathan Sacks, acknowledge the rationalist and natural law development of broader Jewish ethics and its use as a means of engagement with the wider, non-Jewish world.

---

[61] *The faith and practice of Al Ghazali.* Trans. Montgomery Watt W. One world publications; Oxford, 1953 & 1994 p. 32 and p. 34 (Gazali 1953 & 1994).

The history and citations above illustrate the fact that there is no pure development of any particular religious or ethical tradition because ideas are exchanged and develop both within and across different societies and communities. Whilst some religious communities have sought to define particular ideals of ethical purity and construct narratives of exclusive revelation, truth and ethical authority, that self-definition cannot exclude the interpretation of history that suggests and even demonstrates overlapping influences.

The history outlined also suggests that the Enlightenment stigmatizing of religion as uniquely to be avoided because of a propensity to cause conflict seems misplaced. Given that within all communities there are not only differences of philosophical and political opinion but also different camps around which conflicting identities cohere, religion seems to have been made something of a scapegoat. However, insofar as religious communities have sought to define particular ideals of ethical purity and narratives of exclusive revelation, authority, truth or salvation they have perhaps added another dimension to the conflict. This is especially the case where such uniquely revealed forms of ethical purity are imposed on others, whether outside the community or 'deviant' minorities within the community. The issue though is not reason in philosophy but whether religious communities and their theological ethics are sufficiently open to engagement with other philosophies and to a common journey of ethical exploration.

Meanwhile in India

The western world has tended to privilege the role that Greek culture and thought has played in the development of philosophy, along with the privileging of Christianity. A good illustration of this bias is given by Julius Lipner as follows, 'I was asked by a Greek businessman what Hinduism had contributed to the world. "Everyone agrees, of course [he said] that Greek culture exists at the very roots of our civilization. But what contribution has Hindu culture made to civilization?" Lipner's response, having considered 'chess, yoga, meditation and the use of spices in food', was then to realize 'this was perhaps not the best way to answer.' For my Greek interlocutor had assumed that there was a normative perspective . . . He had assumed a Eurocentric stance and expected a Eurocentric response: the dominant criteria of human civilization derived from Europe.'[62]

It is clear, as will be seen in the discussion of Hinduism below and throughout later chapters, that the religious and philosophical traditions that began in the Indian sub-continent, otherwise known as the *dharmic* faiths, feature an immense pluralism. Much of that pluralism and diversity operates within Hinduism itself although there is also development into additional, separately identified faiths such as Buddhism and Jainism. There is an acceptance that Hinduism and *dharma*, although linguistically '*the* way' is actually lived as a variety of paths. Homogeneity is not something that seems to have been sought, perhaps partly because of the conception of the godhead or transcendent as a plurality of deities.

By contrast both Greek philosophy and the monotheistic faiths of the Abrahamic traditions have tended to portray greater homogeneity, focused around single meta-narratives and truths. Yet the reality of Greek philosophy and monotheistic religions is that there is and always has been significant diversity; that seems to be the way that human thought, practice, identities and societies develop and change. The reality of this pluralism in all traditions, as well as overlapping aspects of ethical development, will be explored further as issues of ethical authority are considered throughout later chapters. The supposed cultural superiority of Greek, western and monotheistic thought is also brought into question. Whilst there may be a perception that Greek culture and its development within religious communities has dominated the world of ideas for the past millennia or so, this may simply be a western misperception. As Lipner puts it in relation to the questions of his Greek businessman, 'For historical and political reasons perhaps he was correct. But there is no reason why this must be so in the future . . .'[63]

---

[62] Lipner J. *Hindus: Their Religious Beliefs and Practices,* 2nd edition. Routledge, 2010, p. 2.
[63] op. cit.

The *dharmic* faiths seem to have had far less formal overlap with Greek philosophy than sketched above for Christianity, Judaism and Islam, but there are some parallel lines of thought. Like natural law, *dharma* also has a sense of natural order that is divinely ordained and created, with ethical consequences for actions that contravene *dharma*, 'the way'.[64] There are also strands of the tradition and its narrative epics that promote ethical goods in the form of virtues. However, whilst there may be similar intuitive understandings about a divinely created nature and cosmos in both eastern and western scriptures and traditions, *dharmic* religions follow different premises about how the universe works, along with different processes of reasoning and logic. The *sruti* of Hindu Vedic scriptures sets down a rich diversity of frameworks for Hindu understandings of nature and the good life based on ritual, observation, practice and oral tradition, rather than the more abstract deductive reasoning of Greek thought.

Development of Hinduism

As indicated above Hinduism is invariably described as plural; Julius Lipner refers to it as 'a multi-faceted reality'[65] and goes on to list ten statements about Hinduism that contain diametrically opposed pairings of what it is and particular teachings. In a chapter on Indian ethics Purusottoma Bilimoria queries both whether India or Hinduism as the predominant Indian religion has *an* ethics.[66] The query is based on the fact that Hinduism and Indian ethics are so diverse, arising from the 'complex spiritual and moral aspirations of the people'. However, it is also based on the fact that there is little tradition of 'ahistorical, abstract and formal theorising' equivalent to that seen in western ethics and the systematic approaches to religious ethics that derived from engagement with Greek ethics.

---

[64] Lubin T, Davis DR & Krishnan JK. *Hinduism and Law: An Introduction.* Cambridge University Press, 2010, pp. 17–57; Lipner J., op. cit., pp. 88–125 (Lubin et al. 2010).

[65] op. cit., pp. 3–7.

[66] Bilimoria P. Indian Ethics In *A Companion to Ethics,* Ed. Singer P. Blackwells Publishing, 1991, pp. 43–57 (Bilimoria 1991).

Historically speaking there is written evidence of Hinduism beginning at any time between 2900BCE to 1600BCE, depending on whose theories are believed about migration or indigenous development and dating of the Vedic scriptures. By way of a reference point with the Judaeo – Christian tradition this dates it to a period that included the Biblical patriarch Abraham who is generally placed around 2025 to 1760.[67] It also pre-dates the earliest Greek philosophy of Socrates by at least 1200 years, even on the most conservative estimates. Hinduism in its diversity gave rise to specific alternative *Dharmic* religions, notably Buddhism from around 600BCE and Jainism which developed between 700–500BCE Much later, in the sixteenth century CE Sikhism appeared displaying elements of both the Hindu and Muslim traditions found in India. Whilst Buddhism and Jainism like Hinduism also have a diversity of scriptures the Sikh focus on the Guru Granth Sahib suggests more similarity with Islam at least as regards approaches to definitive scriptural revelation.

Lipner suggests that in terms of its reputation as a founding force in civilization Hinduism suffered from insularity so that the traditions that make up Hindu thought, ritual and practice were not known outside India. Yet through trading exchanges and academic contact there seems to have been some cross-fertilization of ideas about natural, scientific and mathematical enquiry by at least the tenth century CE. It is clear for example that Muslim natural law scholars, like Avicenna (Ibn Sina) studied astronomy, maths and other sciences from Indian as well as Greek sources.

In addition, although less known historically in the west, the *dharmic* traditions did spread East, across India from the Indus Valley and then, particularly through Buddhism, to Tibet, China and Southeast Asia. The way Buddhism spread across the East illustrates a variety of organic development and geographical percolation of ethical and religious ideas, practices and customs. For example, within India Buddhism, like early Christianity, simply spread between communities, in some cases raising suspicion if not hostility from Hindu

---

[67] Generally believed to have been contemporaneous with the Hammurabi kingdom and code.

adherents and leaders.[68] Yet Tibetan Buddhism spread thanks to its adoption by Tibetan rulers who initially simply revered the books of the Pali canon as ritual artefacts before discovering that their contents were even more inspirational.[69]

Some Conclusions

The fact that such a diversity of religions, philosophies and overlapping influences provides evidence that there is no pure religion or philosophical tradition, means that separating one religious viewpoint from another or the secular from the religious is not as neat an exercise as often portrayed in western dialogue. It also illustrates that ethical, theological and philosophical development occurs as the result of social, sometimes political and often reactive growth rather than ordered and systematic planning. The diverse, organic and sometimes overlapping nature of such growth, for which Lipner in relation to Hinduism uses the image of a banyan tree,[70] is a significant challenge to those seeking one normative framework or superior truth.

Yet, a consequence of studying ethical development and theology through a historical and inter-cultural lens is the discovery of some interesting commonalities. An exploration and comparison of religious scripture reveals significant common human traits millennia before the worldwide web gathered the global village into one internet-based electronic community. One strand of ethical similarities is those explored above that arise where different communities consciously use and explore common sources of ethical authority and thinking. Another set of such commonalities can be seen in the development of similar ethical codes in both the Moasic law and the Hammurabi code. These may be considered as the practical outworkings of societies living closely together, warring and trading with each other. This more ancient

---

[68] Experiencing Scripture in World Religions Ed. Harold Coward – Orbis Books, Maryknoll – Interfaith series Ed. Paul Knitter – 2000 (Ward 2000).
[69] Experiencing Scripture in World Religions Ed. Harold Coward – Orbis Books, Maryknoll – Interfaith series Ed. Paul Knitter – 2000.
[70] Lipner J., op. cit., pp. 6–7, 23.

cross-fertilization of ideas, influences and legal codes bears some resemblance to the development of Greek thought by later Abrahamic philosophers. However the development of these ancient ethical codes was possibly more practical and less intentional than the scholarly deliberation of theological philosophers.

What is particularly interesting however, for those seeking evidence of universal ethical realities, is the apparent commonality of stories from quite different traditions where there is less obvious historical encounter. For example, there are stories from the Hindu Mahabarata, thought to have been written around 300-400BCE in India, that seem to demonstrate some similarity of ethical narrative and message with aspects of the Christian Gospels, three or four centuries later. A notable example is the story of the princely leader, Arjuna, who is required to lead his people in a battle to uphold justice and proper order, even against members of his own family who are fighting on the other side. The dilemma of balancing the particular love and bonds of family against the more objective or universal duties of leadership and upholding justice, it seems is not so unique. Arjuna's dilemma, in wrestling with whether or not to fight his relatives to re-establish good order in the kingdom, are not so different from Jesus' claim, shocking and even madness to his disciples, that he comes to set parent against child and brother against brother, also in the interests of truth and the kingdom.

In addition, as will also be seen in later discussion and engagement with particular ethical questions, theories, analyses and ethical dilemmas codified at the Enlightenment were in fact far from new to ethics. Consequentialist calculus is inherent in the consideration of natural law *telos* and the weighing up of costs and benefits seen arguments such as just war theory have clear utilitarian features. Similarly Kant's deontological appeals to duty and the sanctity of life are not constructed *ex nihilo* but developed from his own Protestant background, upbringing and worldview. That sense of duty to leadership, truth and justice is in turn seen, as described above, not only in Gospel stories but also in Hindu narratives.

It is not intended to prove that there is a universal morality nor, in recognizing such commonalities, to argue for any form of religious syncretism. Such commonalities or overlapping ideas are far too tentative to prove convincingly any objective universal reality. Nor do such commonalities make religions the same, as significant differences and pluralism remain alongside the overlapping ideas. It is recognized, as argued by McIntyre and as will be shown in later chapters, that there is wide and significant ethical diversity and many understandings of reason and ethical goods. Yet it is the fact that there are some commonalities that gives rise to theories and possibilities of universal ethical norms. The fact that some of those commonalities and overlapping ideas clearly transcend the divisions between religion and non-religious forms of philosophy, and between philosophy and theology, challenges patterns of thought that have excluded religion from the philosophical table. Conversely the long history of religious engagement with philosophy demonstrates that religions seeking to prove pure faith based on revelation are somewhat in ignorance of their own history. Even if Kant's search to prove an objective set of rational metaphysical norms waiting to be discovered by reason is misguided, this need not be a bar to the discovery or development of norms waiting to be agreed by reasonable peoples.

3

Natural Law, Reason and Religion

The history of overlapping influences and theological approaches to ethical reasoning presented in the previous chapter shows the significant debt of some theological ethics to the natural law ethical tradition originating in Greek philosophy. This chapter continues the exploration of theological reasoning through a more detailed consideration of natural law and virtue ethics. The derivation of natural law theologies from Aristotelian ethics is not without its problems and different theologians engage with the natural law tradition in varying ways. This variety is explored through the work of both historical and contemporary natural law theologians. The ways in which natural law theology and ethics have been reconciled are examined and contrasted with approaches to nature of those who reject natural law, yet still have to engage with the relationship of revelation to the material and natural world of daily experience.

Inevitably consideration of the natural law tradition within theological ethics focuses primarily on Judaism, Islam and Christianity, as the traditions with the most evidenced influence of Greek philosophical engagement. Yet natural law theology following the model of Greek ethics is not the only way that theology and religions engage with the natural world and consider the creation in the light of what it says about

© The Author(s) 2017
C. Shelley, *Ethical Exploration in a Multifaith Society*,
DOI 10.1007/978-3-319-46711-5_3

God and the divine. For the *dharmic* faiths natural order is also a bedrock of ritual, societal order and related ethical frameworks, preserved and reflected in the *vedic* and other scriptures. The ethical world according to *dharmic* understandings of nature and natural law is therefore compared with assumptions about natural law in western and Abrahamic approaches. The comparison covers ways in which theological engagement with nature and experience of the material, human and created world is mediated through scripture, prayer and in some cases ritual worship.

Tensions between natural law, reason, experience, scripture and other forms of religious revelation are explored in several traditions. In some ways these tensions have been exacerbated by the supposed divorce of material science from other branches of knowledge, begun at the Enlightenment and continued in much contemporary science. Yet a proper consideration of natural law theology demonstrates that theology has always engaged with science in its material and empirical sense and that the two are not necessarily in opposition. There is a common search for explanations and meaning in the natural and phenomenological world which is shared by those of faith with humanists, atheists and secularists alike. The theological quest to find explanations, meaning and understanding for the good life is not so different from the non-theological in some ways. Yet there are different premises and perceptions of the world and life, exploration of which also form part of this analysis.

Natural Law, Theology and the Scope of Science

In essence natural law is reflection on the natural world, experience and the creation in a search for understanding, meaning, the good and how to live the good life. Aristotle himself, like Gazali, Aquinas and others after him, used the word 'contemplation'. In ethical terms the 'good life' encompasses both a life that enables flourishing for the individual and a communal life that enables the common good. Doctrines of just war as justifying the use of force where justice and the re-establishing of peace require it, also envisage a morality of action for the common good.

To varying degrees theological ethics adds to the good life in the temporal world those dimensions of an ethically good life that will also lead to salvation and eternal life. Natural law engages with material nature and its sciences, both in their historical or narrower contemporary definition, and with non-material aspects of creation and humanity such as emotions and intuition. Theologies of natural law also add to these aspects of human experience that of the numinous, the transcendent and glimpses of what they have experienced as the divine.

Contemporary society tends to view philosophy, like theology, as amongst the more metaphysical humanities by contrast with the empirical material, human and social sciences. By contrast Greek philosophers viewed themselves as natural scientists in an ethical and philosophical tradition without the twentieth century division into the two cultures of art and science. Accordingly Greek philosophy, particularly natural law, is simply another aspect of exploring the natural world, alongside speculation about the universe, astronomy, maths and medical and natural science. Each of these areas of knowledge, the metaphysical and the physical, is addressed from the perspective of systematic deduction from empirical observation. Such deduction is located within, but also questions, the frameworks of Greek worldviews about the metaphysical and unseen. Thus there were a variety of views about the Greek gods, differing views about life after death and the relationship of body and soul; Aristotle himself accepted a monotheistic worldview but not the Jewish deity. Regardless of which aspect of knowledge is being considered each area of enquiry is addressed using systematic tools of logic, rhetoric and philosophical disciplines. This systematic method is also adopted and followed by those developing theories of natural law theology.

By contrast the origin of most religious scriptures and genesis of much religious revelation is anything but systematic. Modern philosophical enquiry has tended to highlight this lack of system, perceiving it as a lack of reason. Thus the parameters of philosophical rejection of theology and religion as unscientific are set, both because of a perceived lack of method as well as religion's purported reliance on the non-empirical. From the use of 'supernatural,' to mean greater than and beyond nature, it has come to mean simply the invisible, the unprovable in material terms and often the superstitious. It is fair to say that many sources of religious revelation and foundational theological premises do not follow the patterns of systematic modern scientific reason. Yet examined in the context of the societies in which they were being developed, the earliest sources of religious revelation do demonstrate significant processes of ethical development and contextual reasoning about the world around the societies concerned. The Hebrew scriptures are some of the most systematically developed, through the gradual codification of generations of ethical practice, tradition, narrative, mythos, ritual codes and subsequent codification of their application in *halakhah*. The sources and authors are varied in style, method and aim and so apparently unsystematic in modern terms. However, taken as a whole as a people's developing understanding of their world and how to live faithfully and well in response to the events that beset them, they display a surprising range of reason. Further attention will be paid to analysis of reason in scripture in a later chapter as any exploration of natural law theology requires some consideration of its relationship with scripture.

Possibly of more significant than the methodologies found in scripture and theology, when compared with philosophy, is the difference of foundational premises. The division that has tended to be drawn is that natural law philosophy is based primarily on observation of what is believed to occur in nature, on the empirical. Religious belief is based ultimately on beliefs about the nature of God as the creator and on things that are not materially observable. There is observation, including through modern scientific method, of what occurs in nature, both the wider creation and human behaviour, but such observations are coloured and mediated through belief in God. Yet, as illustrated below many theologians and theological-philosophers have recognized this disparity of premise and method and have developed methodologies for reconciling the physical and metaphysical, the seen and unseen. Perhaps the foremost of those who have pursued rigorous natural law ethical and philosophical enquiry whilst maintaining an authentic and lively life of faith, prayer and philosophical enquiry are Thomas Aquinas and Al Ghazali.

Al Ghazali outlines the 'various philosophical sciences' as being 'six in number', namely 'Mathematics, logic, natural science, theology, politics and ethics'. He uses the word 'science' in its original sense as pertaining to knowledge, rather than the more restricted interpretation of the post-Enlightenment world. He analyses these sciences by reference to their relationship with Islam and the teachings of the Qu'ran. Thus maths and logic are forms of science, reasoning and argument that are objective realities or methodologies that have no bearing on theology. They neither prove nor disprove theological contentions and they therefore have no moral or epistemic connotations for religion. For Al Gazali the only danger of maths is that because it provides a coherent and precise system of thought it may delude people by its simplicity so that they look for such simplicity and coherence in religion and find the latter wanting. This is an interesting contrast with some modern approaches found particularly in Christianity, which try to prove theological premises, for example the design of the universe and altruism or sacrifice, through mathematical or genetic science.[1] It may be argued that some of these attempts tend to suggest that Al Gazali was right.

Of the natural sciences, in which physics receives a special mention, Al Ghazali lists investigation of 'heavens, heavenly bodies and all that is beneath the heavens and causes of changes, transformations and combinations...' Effectively the whole panoply of how nature works although he distinguishes the exploration of non-human nature from medical sciences which examine the human body using similar methods of observation and deduction. Both natural and medical science are related to God as they are 'in subjection to God...An instrument in the hands of its maker'. He therefore states that it is no purpose of religion to reject science save

---

[1] e.g. Intelligent Design – http://www.intelligentdesign.org/whatisid.php; Meyer SC. *Signature in the Cell: DNA and the Evidence for Intelligent Design*. HarperOne, 2010 (Meyer 2010); King MS. *God v Darwin: The Logical Supremacy of Intelligent Design Creationism Over Evolution*. CreateSpace Independent Publishing, 2015 (King 2015) & Genetic arguments for altruism Coakley S. *Sacrifice Regained: Reconsidering the Rationality of Religious Belief*. Cambridge University Press, 2012 (Coakley 2012).

insofar as it conflicts with a few points of religion, as he outlines in his book 'The incoherence of the philosophers'.[2]

Al Ghazali then goes on to talk of theology, which he sees effectively as a higher branch of knowledge than the natural sciences. His theology and metaphysical enquiries are the benchmark by which other forms of truth, based on experience and observation of the natural and medical worlds, are assessed. It is not that other forms of science are rejected, far from it, they are explorations of the creator's creation. In fact Al Gazali's criticism of those who reject natural or mathematical science is repeated on several occasions in his discussion of these branches of philosophical enquiry. His argument is that it is 'no condition of religion' to reject such forms of enquiry unless or insofar as they are incompatible with religion. For Al Ghazali therefore religious revelation and theological enquiry are the higher sciences providing the benchmark against which observation and experience of the natural and material creation is assessed. However, observation, exploration and rational analysis of experience in the world that God has created is also an essential part of theology and the search for a faithful ethical life.

Al Gazali's appreciation of theology as the benchmark of the search for wisdom means that for him religious revelation is distinct from other forms of philosophical enquiry. This distinction is made to the extent that theology is not so much superior to other approaches to wisdom but foundational to and definitive of the search. Of the Greek philosophers he is most taken with Aristotle and part of his objection to the Muslim philosophers Ibn Sina and Al Farabi is that they have, he argues, been misled into heresy by Platonist philosophy about resurrection and dualism of body and soul. He also criticizes their view that God knows universals and not particulars[3] and accuses them of confusing Greek philosophy with Islamic revelation, seeking to limit religious

---

[2] Al Gazali. *The Incoherence of the Philosophers: A Parallel English-Arabic Text.* Trans: Michael E. Marmura University of Chicago Press, 2002 (Al Gazali 2002); Griffel F. *Al Gazali's Philosophical Theology.* Oxford University Press, 2010. pp. 101–103, 111–122 (Griffel 2010); Montgomery Watt W. *The Faith and Practice of Al Gazali.* Allen and Unwin, 1953 & ONeWorld Publications, 1995, pp. 17–26 (Montgomery Watt 1995).

[3] Montgomery Watt, op. cit., p. 38.

revelation to coherent systems of thought and philosophy. In discussing approaches to wisdom, of which exploring nature, theology and ethics is part, Al Ghazali outlines different classes of seeker,[4] not simply a binary of those who believe and those who do not. Instead there are varying degrees of approximation to truth or wisdom, from scientists and mathematicians, to philosophers and those who understand part of the truth, then those with a sense of a monotheistic God and the believers in the book, with ('true') Muslims at the pinnacle. Thus he argues the *mu'tazilah*[5] are not infidels, as alleged by some, as they do not wholly reject faith.[6]

For Al Ghazali religious revelation goes beyond the limitations of philosophy based on the observable and limited by the intellect. Having spent some years teaching he withdrew from all his public responsibilities and his family to pursue mysticism as the true source of revelation and wisdom. He argued that seeking God wholly, not just with the head but also with the heart as the true seat of all life, is where true religion lies. Yet the foothills to that mystical quest, namely exploration of all that is in and under the heavens as natural science is still compatible with and part of the journey to God, which has good in and of itself. The true believer however also observes the religious practices and disciplines of Islam as a means of attaining that higher wisdom. It is significant that another of Al Ghazali's criticisms of Ibn Sina is that he liked a glass of wine, albeit for medicinal purposes. It is no surprise then that his return from mysticism to teaching was prompted by a call 'to tackle the problem of this lukewarmness in religious matters'.[7]

Gazali's world is therefore one in which all creation is caught up in God, according to revelation in the Qu'ran and sunnah. This premise engages with all aspects of the creation as revelation of God with cognitive understanding and exploration as part, but not all, of that quest. Yet the over-arching ethical imperative is to prioritize that search

---

[4] Montgomery Watt, pp. 26–66.
[5] Rationalist philosophers.
[6] Montgomery Watt, op. cit., p. 38.
[7] Montgomery Watt, op. cit., p. 80.

for the knowledge of God according to the pattern of a fairly strict observance of an ascetic Islam. This is not submission to deontological commands but a reasoned understanding of creation and life that adopts what is helpful from natural law but is grounded in an over-arching theism as its ultimate *telos*. It is also worth noting that this theism is not an unreasoning departure from empiricism as Gazali's experience of God through contemplation of creation is also very real. Like many others who experience a significant sense of the divine or the transcendent, Gazali made radical changes in his life and priorities as a result of his experience. It is this impact that can counter a narrative that religious belief is entirely metaphysical, unreal or superstitious, with consequences for theological ethics and public contribution.

In many ways Thomas Aquinas' approach to the interface of nature with theology and religion is similar to Al Ghazali. He draws a clear distinction, as does Augustine before him, between philosophy and theology. Philosophy is identified as the exploration of creation through understandings of nature and reason that are open to all. Theology, literally talk-about-God, requires an understanding of creation grounded in a belief in God, recognizing that God's existence cannot be proved philosophically or materially. Although his cosmological proof argues that creation is evidence of God's existence and nature he recognizes that this recognition of God in creation nonetheless requires the eyes of faith. Aquinas defines the distinction of natural philosophy and theology as the division between the natural, open to all by power of natural reason and the supernatural, apprehended only by faith. The end of a naturally ordered life is human happiness in the sense of flourishing. The end of supernatural order is happiness as unity with God in eternity.[8] Aquinas also classes virtues such as justice and courage as natural virtues, expected of all. By contrast faith, hope and charity, based in scripture, are seen, in Aquinas' analysis, as supernatural virtues.[9] It might be objected that faith, hope and charity are perfectly open to those who do not have a

---

[8] Aquinas T. *Summa Theologica Prima Secunda Questions 1–5*. Beloved Publishing LLC, 2014 (Aquinas 2014).

[9] e.g. Faith is based on Paul's definition in Hebrews 11.1 – Eberi JT. *The Routledge Guidebook to Aquinas Summa Theologica*. Routledge, 2015, pp. 192–202 (Eberi 2015).

religious faith but this is not Aquinas' meaning by the distinction. It is rather that justice and courage are natural in the sense that they are instinctive, whilst faith, hope and charity or altruistic love, made known to Christians by revelation in scripture, are virtues that do not necessarily come naturally to humanity; they are therefore above nature or supernatural modes of ethics.

The effect of Aquinas' philosophy is to create a two-tier but not entirely dualistic system. There is a distinction between the natural and the supernatural but there is also both overlap and continuity. The natural and supernatural overlap as the hand of God is seen within the natural world through the eyes of faith.[10] Continuity proceeds from observing the natural world and use of natural reason, to the supernatural and use of reason in relation to theological and faith-based experience. The fact that Aquinas uses scriptural justification for classing faith, hope and charity as supernatural virtues also indicates the role of revelation in that supernatural reason and reflection. Thus, whilst recognizing the distinctions, Aquinas also seeks to unify faith, scripture and natural philosophy into one system of seeking wisdom and God.

Nature and Theological Ethics Without the Greeks

Technically speaking 'natural law' is used to refer to that understanding of philosophy and ethics derived from Greek philosophy and the *Nichomachean Ethics*[11] in particular. Similarly natural law theology is the systematic theology based on natural law philosophy.[12] In practice however, ethics derived from observation of and assumptions about

---

[10] Aquinas T. *Light of Faith*. Book of the Month Spiritual Classics. New York: Sophia Institute, 1993 (Aquinas 1993).

[11] Aristotle. Ed. Tredennick H. *Nichomachean Ethics*. Penguin Classics, 2004 (Aristotle 2004).

[12] Note however that whilst theological ethics draws on and interrogates the thinking of Aristotle, it is not co-terminous with it. Both Gazali and Aquinas interrogate, draw from and use what helps from classical philosophy but also distinguish where theology parts company. See e.g. Stump E. *The non-Aristotelian Character of Aquinas Ethics: Aquinas on the Passions*, pp. 91–106 of *Faith, rationality & the passions*. Ed. Coakley S. Blackwell, 2012 (Stump 2012).

nature appear in a variety of religious traditions as well as informally in much common parlance and contemporary debate. Whether it is in discussions about sexuality and gender, bioethics or euthanasia, appeals to what is 'natural' occur regularly. The ways in which nature is applied or appealed to in theological ethics is diverse. There is a variety from the philosophical systems of Al Ghazali and Aquinas to the illustrations, parables, exemplary stories and ritual prayers seen in the various sources of revelation that ground religious practice. Assumptions made about nature and the ways that they are employed are therefore worthy of reflection, both as regards methodology but also when considering the substance of conclusions about particular aspects of nature.

Even those who are overtly suspicious of natural law and the fallible, self-deluding human reason that interprets the world ethically, nonetheless have to engage with humanity and natural phenomena in any reflection on the world in which they live. Karl Barth actively rejected natural law and its liberal rationalist tendencies yet his theology engages with all manner of natural phenomena and scientific theory. His exploration of gender in Volume 54 of the Church Dogmatics[13] provides an illustration of how Barth juggles natural science, his interpretation of scripture and experience. Although bound by adherence to scriptural revelation as the living word of God Barth circumscribes and limits his understanding of gender hierarchy as far as he can.

Rather than adopting purportedly scientific arguments for male intellectual superiority over women, so as to bolster scripture-based understandings of male headship, Barth rejects the scientific arguments as inconsistent with his experience. He argues that science cannot limit the diversity of womanhood and female intellectual capacity, something he had experienced via his fellow researcher Charlotte von Kirshcbaum. He limits his interpretation of scripture to a symbolic order rather than one that limits women's role. Thus Barth maintains his utter respect for scripture whilst engaging with natural science in what some have

---

[13] Barth K. *Freedom in Fellowship: Man & Woman,* pp. 109–231, *Church Dogmatics Study Edition.* T&T Clark, 2010 (Barth 2010b).

interpreted as a surprisingly progressive way.[14] He allows reasoning from his own experience to take precedence over poor science and to circumscribe rather than contradict his understanding of scripture.

Yet Barth's conclusions remain unacceptable to most liberal or feminist theologians as incapable of allowing his reasoned rejection of unsatisfactory science to operate in the same way in relation to scripture. Even though other Biblical passages, for example Jesus' treatment of women,[15] Paul in Galatians[16] and the role of women in the early Church,[17] contradict a Genesis-based gender hierarchy, Barth maintains a conservative interpretation of revelation in relation to Genesis 2 that contradicts the general trend of his reason. Thus although Barth rejects natural law theologies based on essentialist interpretations of gender complementarity[18] his ethical endpoint as regards gender on the basis of scripture is not dissimilar to conservative natural law arguments about gender complementarity. This is not to defend such positions but to give more detail as to their reasoning and how they might be engaged and challenged.

Nature and Scripture

There is much about nature in religious scriptures with which theological ethics must engage, as scripture remains an important source of revelation for all traditions. Thus all the major religious scriptures include references to and accounts of creation.[19] From such accounts of creation flow observations and understanding about the natural order.

---

[14] Sonderegger K. *Barth and Feminism*, pp. 258–273 of *The Cambridge Companion to Karl Barth*. Ed. Webster J. Cambridge University Press, 2000 (Sonderegger 2000).

[15] e.g. Mary in John 12: 1–9; Mary Magdalene in Luke 7: 36–50 and John 20: 11–18; the woman at the well John 4: 1–30.

[16] Galatians 3: 28.

[17] e.g. Phoebe the deacon, Romans 16:1.

[18] The official position of the Roman Catholic Church and also found in Islam and Judaism.

[19] e.g. Genesis 1 & 2 of the Bible; Sura 21, 41 & 79 of the Qu'ran; the *Agannah Sutta* in Buddhism and the Puranic account of creation in the *Rig Veda*. *Hindu Mythology, Vedic and Puranic*, by WJ Wilkins 1900, pp. 343–344 (Wilkins 1900).

Interestingly one Christian account of the beginning of creation, and Christ's place in creation, at the start of John's Gospel draws not on the Hebrew tradition but on Stoic philosophy of the word. Again the overlapping influences of different accounts and explorations of creation are evident. The fact that there are diverse accounts of nature and creation within the scriptures of the same tradition is further testimony to open-ended searches for meanings or ways of expressing that search, rather than a single definitive understanding.

Other aspects of life and experience covered in Abrahamic scriptures – and religious scriptures more widely – include grappling with sexual relationships, the creation and preservation of life, justifications for the use of violence and war and tales of nations seeking to live with each other. Yet framings of war are often considered in the context of preserving good in the balancing act against evil. Other dynamics of the natural and ethical in scripture include the challenges of subjecting the particular of family to the demands of leadership, truth and justice.[20] Justice for the poor, distribution of resources, explanations of disparities in fortunes, attitudes to wealth and how bad things happen to good people are also regular features of religious scripture and tradition. They explore the natural in terms of what is ordered and natural in God's creation and lead to questions of order for a good life, both personal and communal.

Dharma and Nature

The *dharmic* traditions also have various accounts of nature and creation set out in their diverse mythology and scriptures. Lipner lists narratives that draw on the imagery of 'dismemberment of a primeval figure, sexual union . . . Measurement, . . . proliferation from a seed or development from a womb'. He also suggests that there is a stronger 'ontological continuum between the creative Spurce and its products' than in the Abrahamic traditions. The Vedic speculation about Aktri or the

---

[20] Examples include the story of Arjuna in the Gita being set against relatives Menski W. Hinduism In *Ethical Issues in Six Religious Traditions*. Edinburgh University Press, 2007, p. 26 (Menski 2007); & Jesus dividing families Matthew 10:34–39.

normative inner essence of particular beings bears a resemblance to the Platonic ideas of the 'forms' but seems to have developed separately. There is a sense that word and creation are intertwined and it is performance of word and ritual that also creates the natural.[21] Rambachan also argues that the natural sources of *advaita Vedanta* draw on arguments that have a proximity or resemblance to natural law philosophy,[22] although in some ways the cosmic at-one-ness of the *advaita* philosophy goes beyond the androcentric approach of Greek-derived natural law.

The coverage of these ethical issues in scripture and some commonality of legal codes are taken to support arguments to justify a universal natural law. For example, the seven Noahide laws, the basic minimum for humanity not just Jewish peoples, covered respect for God (do not deny or blaspheme the divine), do not murder (respect life), do not engage in incest, adultery or homosexual relationships (respect marriage), do not steal (respect property), do not eat live animals and establish courts and legal systems. These standards and the fuller Ten Commandments, with its similarity to the Jews' neighbouring precursor, the Hamurabi code, reinforces for some arguments for universality. Observations of nature also ground arguments for common or universal rights and justice in other traditions. Robert A Yelle suggests a parallel between the Jewish oral Torah and the legal traditions of early Hindu codes in the *Dharmasastra*.[23]

In Islam Sura 49:13 observes that God made all humanity male and female and of many tribes, tongues and nations and yet all originate in Adam, the first man. Accordingly principles of equality and dignity are established leading to respect for justice, others' property, life and honour. Similar principles are seen in Sikhism, which intentionally sought equality and justice as a reaction against the caste system

---

[21] Lipner J. *Hindue: Their Religious Beliefs and Practices.* London: Routledge 2010 at pp. 59–66 (Lipner 2010).

[22] Rambachan A. *A Hindu Theology of Liberation: Not Two is Not One.* Albany: State of New York Press, 2015, pp. 3–4 (Rambachan 2015).

[23] Yelle RA. 'Hindu Law as Performance' pp. 183–192 at p. 190. In *Hinduism and Law: An Introduction.* Cambridge University Press, 2010 (Yelle 2010).

prevalent in Indian society. All traditions also have codes that govern sexual and property relationships. The centrality to ethics of nature, experience, reasoning and regulation that are found in most cultures' ethical codes and religious scriptures is further reinforced by the appeal to nature for moral lessons in narrative and illustrative forms. Examples include Jesus' use of agricultural and natural imagery in his parables or the poetic inspiration of nature in the Gita. So far so universal.

Universalism or Not?

Yet analysis of the detail of these texts, codes and narratives reveals differences that at once undermine carefully constructed arguments for human universals. Thus well before contemporary arguments about whether those in same-sex relationships could validly or ethically be called married, marriage took many forms. The Bible alone features polygamy, concubinage and marriages of convenience or expediency as well as monogamy and in the New Testament exhortations to celibacy. The fact that there are references to homosexuality also evidences its place in human experience even if ethically contested. Similar diversity is found across other scriptures and contemporary societies; for example much of the world is monogamous but in several Muslim States[24] polygamy remains legal and is also recognized in Mormon understandings of Christianity.

Relating to Creation; Engagement or Withdrawal

Besides the differences of application or detail in ethical codes the ethics of how faiths engage with the natural also varies significantly. Formal natural law theology's affirmation of nature as God's order determining the purpose of things and therefore their ethical orientation has been

---

[24] e.g. Pakistan, Yemen.

explored above. Both the Greek and Abrahamic faiths understanding of nature is androcentric with humanity as part but at the pinnacle of creation. The operation of natural laws within the *dharmic* traditions is more complex. On the one hand the Vedic texts provide for an engagement with the natural, cosmological order, through ritual. Ritual chanting is practised as a necessary means of respecting and preserving good Kharmic forces. In addition to the ritual engagement with Kharma personal actions and behaviour can also generate good or bad Kharma both for the individual in this life, with consequences for their reincarnation into a future life and in relation to previous acts of themselves and others. There is a sense that *dharmic* ethics, in the form of actions for good or bad, not only has implications for the individual in terms of their current well-being or eternal salvation but also has general cosmological impact.[25]

Most Hindus, particularly historically those of the lower castes less bound by *Brahminic* purity, seek engagement with the world, recognizing the ethics of *kharmic* consequences but living in the material world of human achievement, family, sexuality and full human potential. This sense of engagement in the pursuit not only of fullness of life but also equality and justice is also seen strongly within the partially *dharmic* tradition of Sikhism. Yet there is a division in the *dharmic* traditions between these ways of *pravritti* or engagement with the world and the ethics of *nivritti*, detached self-denial and withdrawal from the world. The perception of Hinduism, following the higher class, *Brahmanic* traditions, has tended to be of the latter *samsara* tradition, oriented to liberation or *moksha through detachment*. It is the latter, detached tradition that is also predominant in the Buddhist search for the liberation of *nirvana*. In this construction, rather than embracing the world and creation, the material is seen as unreal, illusory and simply the process and precursor to liberation.[26]

Whilst the *dharmic theologies* present a more holistic or pantheistic approach to nature and creation than often seen in the more

---

[25] Lipner J., op. cit.
[26] Lipner J., op. cit., pp. 199–272.

androcentric Abrahamic traditions, the parts of the tradition oriented towards *samsara* also relativize and therefore distance themselves from creation and the material in favour of withdrawn contemplation. Although in some ways this very different treatment of nature again militates against universalism some parallels can be found for example between the Hindu tradition of *samsara*, Al Gazali's withdrawal from teaching and Christian monastic contemplation contemplation of God. The traditions of affirmation and engagement with the world found most particularly in Christian incarnation, Jewish *halakhah*, Muslim *sharia* and Sikh struggles for justice, tend in the opposite direction. All of which means that the only real universality throughout these traditions is the spectrum from engagement with nature and the world to contemplation and withdrawal from such engagement.

Academic natural law theologians differ in their assessment of the degree to which universality is possible. Whilst continuing to argue for a natural law universalism David Novak, using as an example the Noahide laws, concedes that universal principles are translated into detailed application through particular traditions and are therefore positive rather than wholly natural or universal law.[27] By contrast John Finnis disagrees, arguing that the generic human goods of life, which he defines as life (including procreation), knowledge, play, aesthetic experience, sociability and friendship, practical reasonableness and religion are found in all cultures and therefore establish a universal benchmark in which to ground rights.[28] Yet even these display the bias of those with a certain lifestyle, as aesthetics and play may not seem so essential to those struggling to meet basic levels of material need.

These differences of approach across and within traditions, both as to fundamental orientations to creation and the particulars of ethical application, as demonstrated above by marriage, illustrate several of the major weaknesses of natural law philosophies. These challenges to natural universalism are seen in whichever part of the theological or non-theological

---

[27] Novak D. *Tradition in the Public Square: A David Novak Reader*. Eds. Rashkover R & Kavka M. SCM Press, 2008, pp. 113–144; 154–162; 213–230 (Novak 2008).

[28] Finnis J. *Natural Law, Natural Rights*. Clarendon Law Series. Oxford, 1980, pp. 81–94 (Finnis 1980).

spectrum they are considered. Firstly, the degree of diversity across faiths, cultures and nations belies natural universalism at any more detailed level than simply a common quest for understanding of the world and the life as human beings. The one universal is that in order to live all human beings must inevitably engage in some way with the creation of which we are a part, even if only to relativize and withdraw from it but this is a very generic benchmark of experience.

Secondly the degree of diversity and varied understandings both of premises and reasoning across traditions undermines any theory based on a common or universal reason, save at the level that all but a minority of human beings have the capacity to think. As noted in the previous chapter[29] when considering the history of *dharmic* development there has been a western imperialistic tendency to privilege the style of systematic reasoning from Greek philosophy and its Christian developments. This is acutely felt in some quarters as shown by the following comments:

> The moral deficiency of those who subscribe to non-Christian religions is a well-established – and still endemic – theme in Western culture.... Modern secularism, although it purports to transcend the bias of particular religions, has not abandoned this theme and it survives and reproduces through other, ostensibly non-religious secular tests.[30]

> The poetry of ancient law, as we have seen in the case of ordeals and kharmic punishments in Dharmasastra, also reinforced the idea that law reflected the natural order of the cosmos. Various currents of thought that we refer to for convenience as the 'Reformation' and the 'Enlightenment' combined in European culture to discredit such views.[31]

Thirdly there is the epistemic problem that what all human beings actually observe will be different depending on experience, standpoint

[29] Lipner J. *Hindus: Their Religious Beliefs and Practices,* 2nd edition. Routledge, 2010, p. 2 at fn 64.

[30] Shah Prakash. 'Judging Muslims' In *Islam and English Law: Rights, Responsibilities and the Place of Shari'a,* Ed. Robin Griffiths Jones. Cambridge University Press, 2013. pp. 144–156 at p. 144 (Shah 2013); Balagangadhara SN. *The Heathen in His Blindness: Asia, the West and the Dynamic of Religion.* New Delhi, 2005 (Balagangadhara 2005).

[31] Yelle RA., op. cit., pp. 191–192.

and assumptions. There is a classic illustration of two people standing close to and trying to describe an elephant, offering very different descriptions depending on whether standing at the trunk or tail end. This is where differences of position in society, culture, place in the world socially and geographically, of gender, race and the many other diversities of humanity and creation, affect the premises, understandings and approaches to reasoning in ethics. Thus epistemic difference also undermines universalist assumptions about reasonableness. This is particularly acute in relation to faith, theology and religion, the epistemic and empirical basis for which has been undermined by western scepticism about religious experience and practice.

Gender and sexuality are particularly good examples of epistemic misunderstanding in which theology, philosophy and science have all tended to be explored from the perspective of white, western males. The lack of contribution to knowledge from women until very recent decades has led to significant ethical assumptions that ignore the reality and knowledge of life of those about whom others research and develop ethical speculation. The same goes for failure to encompass as equal the perspectives of those with disabilities, people of colour, in poverty and those who identify as LGBT or I. Whilst in contemporary debate religions, often rightly, receive a bad press over the ethics of gender and sexuality religious epistemology has not been the only conservative or even regressive force. Barth's analysis and rejection of 'scientific' research about women referred to above is a case in point. It was only in 1925 that women in Britain were legally seen as capable of owning property, taking care of their children without male guardianship or voting. Underlying the opposition to womens' rights were 'scientific' theories about women having smaller brains and the need to preserve them from intellectual exertions that would affect fertility amongst other myths.[32]

Fourthly, even if people see or experience the same things they can draw radically different conclusions or theories from them. This latter

---

[32] Darwin Charles. *The Descent of Man and Selection in Relation to Sex.* New York: D. Appleton and Company, 1896 (Darwin 1896).

point, known as the naturalistic fallacy, points out that just because something 'is' does not mean to say that it is essential to its nature that 'it is' or that certain consequences or conclusions are drawn from it. To an extent the differences of epistemic standpoint and consequential theorizing may overlap in giving rise to the naturalistic fallacy. The naturalistic fallacy gives rise to differences that are not limited by any means to religious belief or theological assessment. Examples of such differences are many and various. One example that is fundamental to ethics is the construction or understanding of human nature. Hobbes viewed human beings as irretrievably selfish, competitive and in need of ethics and law as a means to restrain conflict and enable peaceful co-existence both at individual societal and international levels. In some ways this is not so different from Luther and Calvin's dim view of fallen humanity, suffering from 'utter depravity' in Calvin's memorable phrase and unable to save themselves by human reason or without God's grace.

By contrast, other secular thinkers, for example Rousseau, Kant, Bentham and Mills had a more optimistic view of human nature and its capacity for ethical self-governance by human reason. Yet amongst these thinkers there is still a spectrum of view about human nature, from Rousseau's belief that humanity is born innocent but corrupted by the pressures of society to Kant, Locke and others' views that human reason, without religion, could establish a perfect, peaceful rationally ordered society. Whilst Hobbes' pessimism about humanity is shared by Calvinism the more positive belief in humanity of most post-Enlightenment humanism reflects the optimism of liberal and natural law theologians from Erasmus during the 15th CE flourishing of humanism to Niebuhr, Schleiermacher, Novak, Ramadan and many others in contemporary theological circles.

Changes in Science over Time

Another major difficulty with assumptions from nature, whether from natural law theology, philosophy or the other codes of law and practice reviewed above is the changes of both epistemology and naturalistic assumptions over time. This is at the core of the perceived challenge for religion of holding onto theological authenticity, timeless truths and ethical codes in a changing world. It is in fact a challenge for all societies regardless of whether religious or not as old truths, ways of doing things and thus the ethical codes that frame a society or a part of it, change. The advances in understanding that scientific exploration gives change entire worldviews. For example the realization that the world was round rather than flat and that books could be mass-produced by printing, caused revolutions in terms of human self-understanding and democratization.

Science in the twenty first century is probably more mathematical, calculated and far more detailed, than in the time of Aquinas and his predecessors in natural law theology. Yet those natural law philosophers such as Sahdia Ben Gaion, Ibn Sina, Gazali and Averroes who were also scientists and physicians were on the same journey as contemporary scientists, of exploring aspects of the natural world with a view to aiding human flourishing. Although Aquinas might be seen as not a scientist and 'just' a philosopher the distinction is misleading given the different levels of technical scientific development in his time. As a philosopher Aquinas was clearly engaged with the empirical world, using his observation of that world to explain and illustrate wider transcendent questions. Thus whilst his arguments about God as the 'prime mover' do not bear analysis from the perspective of modern physics and laws of thermo-dynamics, they do reveal close observation of causation and illustrative experience from natural science.[33]

Modern natural law theology is inclined generally speaking to accept modern science and scientific methods and observations. In some cases this has led to modifications of view of a particular moral issue. However, one problem of some contemporary religious approaches to science in natural law theology is inconsistency. There are examples that suggest that changes or developments of scientific understanding are accepted insofar as they boost an existing argument or position but are

---

[33] Te Velde Rudi. *Aquinas on God: The 'Divine Science' of the Summa Theologiae.* Ashgate, 2006. pp. 48–54 (Te Velde 2006).

rejected insofar as they do not fit. Inconsistent logic and application of natural law can arise in order to hold onto what is perceived as the unchanging and therefore authentic position of particular religious beliefs at the expense of the science underlying it. An example of such inconsistency is the Roman Catholic Church's teachings on abortion and homosexuality respectively.

Of all religions the theology of the Roman Catholic Church remains the most dogmatically wedded to natural law theology. The Roman Catholic argument against abortion is that human life begins at the point of conception and that therefore any abortion after that point in time is the taking of life and morally on a par with murder. However, this has not always been the Roman Catholic position. Aquinas himself believed that life began at 'quickening' the point at around 3 months of pregnancy, when the soul was believed to enter the foetus in the womb and the foetus became a human being, protected from abortion. To a degree this followed Aristotle's understanding (though with a less sexist dynamic) in which the soul entered a male foetus at 40 days and a female at 90. The change of church view arose because medical science can now identify what it argues are indisputably human features from just a few weeks and a genetically new human being from conception. Accordingly not only is abortion wrong but so too is any interference with the embryo, as medical science confirms what the church takes to be the start of human life at conception. Thus the church's application of modern science to its natural law ethics means that its teaching on abortion has altered the period of protection to an earlier point in the pregnancy.

By contrast, the church's position as regards homosexuality remains largely unchanged. Homosexuality is seen as wrong because it contravenes the natural law *telos* of sexual intercourse as being oriented to procreation and therefore inalienably heterosexual. Since the fourth century CE, when Augustine defined the *telos* of sex as procreation, societal and scientific understandings of sex and sexuality have developed significantly. The Church of England's Book of Common Prayer recognized companionship and mutual support as ends of marriage, in addition to procreation, as early as the sixteenth CE. More recent science has recognized sexuality as a spectrum from straight to gay with a far greater diversity of what is natural. Social science has also noted the socially constructed nature of both gender and sexuality. Yet despite its acceptance of modern understandings of the beginnings of life the official position of the Church has been reluctant to accept modern understandings of sexuality.

Thus homosexuality remains 'intrinsically disordered' according to the Catechism.[34] A similar natural law process of reasoning applies to the continued Roman Catholic prohibition of contraception.[35] Whilst defending natural law as a valid basis for ethical norms Roman Catholic natural law theologian Jean Porter has raised these inconsistencies in approach to developments in science. She argues for the development of natural law premises and conclusions in line with developments in the scientific thinking that underlies understanding of human beings and what is in fact natural.[36] Porter remains out of step with her church and other Roman Catholic natural law theologians such as John Finnis and Germaine Grisez.

Conservative ethical views about sexuality are not limited to the Roman Catholic Church. Many faith traditions and indeed, whole societies as noted by Grace Davie,[37] retain conservative ethical views about sexuality because of naturalistic assumptions, arguably fallacies, about gender difference and the purpose of sex. Hesitancy about change in such matters is witness to the deep sensitivity but also deeply intuitive nature of much thinking in this area of ethics. Simply ignoring such conservatism will not make it go away; serious engagement is needed, seeking to understand but also challenging inconsistencies. The ethics of gender is a good example of where reason differs and what one person interprets as conservative and problematic, another may affirm as a positive expression not only of their faith but also of how they wish to

---

[34] The Catechism of the Roman Catholic Church Para. 2357–2359, 2393 & 2396 all state that homosexual activity is intrinsically disordered,' and offends against chastity. http://www.vatican.va/archive/ENG0015/__P86.HTM.

[35] Para. 2370 Catechism, op. cit.

[36] Porter J. & Wolterstorff N. *Natural and Divine Law: Reclaiming the Tradition for Christian Ethics.* Eerdmans Publishing, 1999 (Porter and Wolterstorff 1999).

[37] Sociologist Grace Davie argues that churches and religious groups' conservatism about societal changes in gender roles is a proxy for unease in society at large about such changes; Davie G. *Religion in Britain: A Persistent Paradox.* Wiley-Blackwell, 2015. pp. 177–196 (Davie 2015).

live and express their gender. This is particularly the case for arguments over headscarves and veiling, which exist both within as well as across traditions.[38] Whilst enforcing scriptural prescriptions for example about hair length,[39] or maternity as the salvation of women,[40] is unacceptable many women choose to wear longer hair and want to be mothers.

Caste and Class versus Equality and Human Rights

Another significant change in understandings of nature, science and society is modern human rights and the associated aspiration towards equality of all peoples. The endorsement of this aspect of moral discourse is evidenced by the fact that the Universal Declaration of Human Rights (UDHR) is the most translated document in the world.[41] The United Nations Convention on the Rights of the Child (UNCRC) is signed by all but two states.[42] Both suggest universalism as regards aspects of ethics that relate to protecting humanity and rights. The development of human rights, arguably with input from natural law as grounding human dignity and reason, is particularly interesting. Human rights both draw on natural law concepts and yet depart significantly from the context and premises of the societies in which natural law theories and theologies were first developed. Alasdair MacIntyre's scepticism about the potential for universal human rights simply by virtue of humanity or human dignity[43] has grounded some dissent in modern human rights discourse, from a number of perspectives. MacIntyre's traditionalist arguments against human rights are in the same sort of

---

[38] see e.g. Ahmed L. *Women and Gender in Islam.* Yale University Press, 1992, pp. 144–168 (Ahmed 1992); Roald AS. *Women in Islam: The Western Experience.* Routledge, 2001, pp. 254–294 (Roald 2001).

[39] 1 Corinthians 11:14–15.

[40] Following Genesis 2.

[41] 467 translations by 2016. http://www.ohchr.org/EN/UDHR/Pages/Introduction.aspx.

[42] www.unicef.com.

[43] McIntyre A. *After Virtue: A Study in Moral Theory.* Duckworths/University of Notre Dame Press, 1990/1984, pp. 68–69.

trenchant terms as Bentham's condemnation of human rights as 'non-sense on stilts'. Yet, the natural law influence on the Universal Declaration on Human Rights is discernible from its language. The convention is grounded, according to the preamble, in 'recognition of the inherent dignity and... equal and inalienable rights of all members of the human family' as 'the foundation of freedom, justice and peace in the world.' Rights are a reaction to 'barbarous acts which have outraged the conscience of mankind' (notably the Holocaust) and aspire to 'a world in which human beings shall enjoy freedom of speech and belief and freedom from fear and want.' To ensure they are respected without 'rebellion against tyranny and oppression.... human rights should be protected by the rule of law.' There are also three references in the preamble to 'fundamental human rights,' along with 'the dignity and worth of the human person' and 'equal rights of men and women.'

The first Article draws on natural law philosophy in assuming that: 'All human beings are born free and equal in dignity and rights..... endowed with reason and conscience...' (Article 1). Further rights in support of this assumption include entitlement 'to all the rights' of the Declaration, 'without distinction of any kind' (Article 2), 'the right to life, liberty and security of person' (Article 3). 'No one shall be held in slavery' (Article 4) nor 'subjected to torture or to cruel, inhuman or degrading treatment or punishment' and 'Everyone has the right to recognition... as a person before the law', to be 'equal before the law....' and with 'equal protection of the law.'

Modern assent to human rights as a universal language, via international conventions, has led to claims not only that human rights' are compatible with religious worldviews but also that they derive from theology. Links are asserted with the natural law theology of Christianity,[44] the egalitarianism of early Christian communities and Christian and Jewish recognition of the dignity of all human beings as

---

[44] Porter J. From Natural Law to Human Rights: Or, Why Rights Talk Matters. *Journal of Law and Religion* 14, 1 (1999–2000), pp. 77–96 (Porter 1999–2000); Wolterstorff N. *Justice Rights and Wrongs*. Princeton University Press, 2009 (Wolterstorff 2010); Finnis J. *Natural Law and Natural Rights*. Clarendon.

made in the image of God regardless of creed.[45] Islamic sources also argue for grounding in human rights from natural law theory and scripture[46] and the Sikh tradition claims early development of equality and rights because of its arguments against caste.[47]

Yet MacIntyre has a point, in arguing that natural law is not the natural precursor to human rights, because the world of Aristotle's Nichomachean Ethics, like the world of Aquinas and the caste-shaped Indian sub-continent, did not share the modern aspiration to equality of all peoples. Observation of nature indicated that the world was not equal and that there were clearly different classes of people, or rather men; women barely featured in ethical classification save as objects contingent upon the men in their lives, whether fathers, husbands or owners if slaves. Thus he says of politics that it: 'appears to be of this nature; for it is this that ordains which of the sciences should be studied in a state, and which each class of citizens should learn and up to what point they should learn them;'[48] and

> to judge from the lives that men lead, most men, and men of the most vulgar type, seem (not without some ground) to identify the good, or happiness, with pleasure; which is the reason why they love the life of enjoyment. For there are, we may say, three prominent types of life – that just mentioned, the political, and thirdly the contemplative life. Now the mass of mankind are evidently quite slavish in their tastes, preferring a life suitable to beasts. . . . A consideration of the prominent types of life shows that people of superior refinement and of active disposition identify happiness with honour; for this is, roughly speaking, the end of the political life.[49]

---

[45] Rushton R. *Human Rights and the Image of God.* SCM Press, 2004 (Rushton 2004).

[46] A An Na'im. *Islam and Human Rights: Selected Essays of Abdullahi An-Na'im.* Ed. Mashood A. Baderin. Routledge, 2010 (An Na'im 2010); Glahn B, Emon AM & Ellis MS. *Islamic Law and International Human Rights Law.* Oxford University Press, 2015 (Glahn et al. 2015).

[47] Some argue that Sikh approaches to human rights are more radical than the UDHR, see for example: http://sikhmissionarysociety.org/sms/smsarticles/advisorypanel/gurmukhsinghsewauk/sikhismandhumanrights.html.

[48] Aristotle. *Nichomachean Ethics* I (ii) *The Object of Life.* Penguin Classics, 1976, p. 64 (Aristotle 1976).

[49] Aristotle. *Nichomachean Ethics* I (v) *The Object of Life.* op. cit., p. 68.

So enfranchisement in the Athenian *polis* was limited to the political classes who understood about honour and virtue beyond mere pleasure. Similar distinctions have been drawn in many societies and historically pertained in all developed nations. Hindu caste is perhaps the best-known class system in religious circles and scriptures. Rights and responsibilities are assigned by birth not personality, gifts or equality of worth or opportunity. The Hindu conception of the social order is that people are different, and different people will fit well into different aspects of society. Social order or social class according to *varna* forms the framework of moral duties according to their role, not birth. The caste system dates from the Aryan invasion of India around 2,000 BC. It divides society into four main groups plus those below that order altogether who are the *dalits* or untouchables.

The *Brahmins* are the prophets, priests and those who reflect, who become the intellectual and spiritual leaders or philosophers, religious leaders and teachers of our society. The *Kshatriyas* are the leaders, nobles or rajahs, warriors and administrators, equating to the protectors of society, today the politicians, police and military. The *Vaisyas* are seen as the producers, craftsmen, farmers and today the manufacturers and merchants of society. The *Shudras* are the unskilled labourers or labouring class, maintenance and manual labourers.[50]

The caste system in Hindu tradition is one of the most notorious non-egalitarian systems. However, all societies religious and otherwise have had class-based societies, based on perceptions that such distinctions were naturally and divinely ordained. A quick review reveals how endemic class or caste was, from the various ruling classes e.g., princes and kings for Aquinas, political leaders and emperors for Aristotle, tribal warrior leaders for Mohammed and both warrior leaders (*ksatrya*) and priestly leaders (*brahmin*) in Hinduism. Judaism had priestly leaders (*Levites* and *Cohenim*) and from the book of Samuel kings beginning with Saul, David and Solomon, until deposed by exile and giving way to the *Sanhedrin* or other non-religious leaders. Below the ruling classes each society had other classes, business people or merchants, court

---

[50] Lipner J., op. cit., pp. 126–147, *Caste and its realities.*

functionaries, labourers, peasants, servants and slaves and those, like the *dalits* found in Hinduism, who were untouchable and outcast. Each class had their own objects and purposes appropriate to their class and their place in the communal narrative, save that the *dalits*, like the Jewish shepherds and tax collectors in Jesus' time, were beyond the law and ethics. Similarly in most societies the prostitutes, slaves and others outcast were beyond the law and outside the expectations of the ethical code, as well as outside its protection.

These narratives and the roles developed for different classes or groups, framed the ethics and ethical virtues to be developed and observed by particular classes of people. Thus the ethics and virtues, rights and responsibilities, to be expected of a leader were very different from the ethics and virtues expected of a peasant and the ethics of the outcasts and slaves were deemed non-existent. These systems were not only natural but were reflections of the divine creation and therefore divinely ordained. A notable example that developed in Christianity was the divine rights of kings in which kings ruled of right relatively unchallenged as it was believed they were ordained of God.

It is this narrative or contextual aspect of cultural distinctiveness that causes some theologians and philosophers, following MacIntyre, to doubt the universality of natural or intrinsic human rights. The prevalence of class or caste across so many societies suggests that equal rights and equality are far from natural. MacIntyre queries the extrapolation of universal human rights from natural law as flawed. Nature and traditional natural law do not guarantee equality between human beings, human societies have rarely been equal and nothing in nature can indisputably justify treating all humanity as equal. Nor is there any intrinsically justifiable argument from nature that all should have rights or any naturally or universally provable set of rights that should pertain to all human beings. Contemporary universal adoption of natural law human rights therefore uproots natural law from its original context and applies it to a radically different setting. Ethics developed for and determined by a stratified society cannot, according to MacIntyre, sit well with communities asserting egalitarianism. Above all simple assertion of allegedly natural human rights is ineffective in a global village without common understandings of what constitutes the substantive human goods being protected. The argument against natural law human rights is therefore that assumptions of natural human equality, dignity and rights are at odds with observations of nature and the original framework of natural law ethics.

Observing the Nature of Class

The fact is that in considering even contemporary human societies and the global village, a dispassionate, alien observer could be forgiven for not immediately being struck by equality and respect for rights. Observation of what appears to be the natural state of most societies still reveals significant inequality between people and classes. Historical inequalities based on class, status and role that were justified as out-workings of nature and ethics through allegedly 'natural' caste or class hierarchies, are no longer accepted. At least they are no longer officially accepted in most societies nor in the forum of international opinion and UN conventions. In theory all receive equal protection of the rights guaranteed in the Declaration and all have equal opportunities. Yet levels of inequality in the world are growing. Theoretical equality of opportunity and equal rights to vote and other civil freedoms are little use if in fact economic and social inequality cripple life chances and opportunities.

The World Bank indicates that in the UK approximately 25% of the country's wealth is owned by 10%, whilst the bottom 10% of earners own only 2.5%.[51] An October 2014 Credit Suisse study also claims that the top 1% now own nearly half of the world's wealth.[52]

Oxfam reports, 'the gap between rich and poor is widening. In 2013, seven out of 10 people lived in countries where economic inequality was worse than 30 years ago, and in 2014 Oxfam calculated that just 85 people owned as much wealth as the poorest half of humanity. . . . The

---

[51] http://data.worldbank.org/indicator/SI.DST.FRST.10 NB many other indices for the UK poverty gap are not completed within the World Bank data – at 06 December 2015.

[52] Jill Treanor (13 October 2014). Richest 1% of people own nearly half of global wealth, says report. *The Guardian*. At 06 December 2015 (Treanor 2014).

majority of the world's poor now live in middle income countries – there are more people with incomes under $1.25 a day living in India than in all of sub-Saharan Africa.[53]

The World Institute for Development Economics Research[54] states that the richest 1% of adults alone owned 40% of global assets in 2000, which suggests that the divisions are growing worse. The *three* richest people in the world possess more financial assets than the poorest 48 nations combined. The combined wealth of the '10 million dollar millionaires' grew to nearly $41 trillion in 2008.

The IMF has stated that widening income inequality is the defining challenge of our time. In advanced economies, the gap between the rich and poor is at its highest for decades. Inequality is more mixed in emerging markets and developing countries (EMDCs), with some countries experiencing declining inequality. However, pervasive inequities remain in access to education, health care and finance.[55]

Thus inequality and economic discrimination continue, despite the reduction in impact of caste and class systems. It is economic factors more than any appeal to caste or any other understandings of class as religious or natural that are now responsible for inequality. Whilst traditional or natural law understandings of class or caste-based difference are no longer accepted, alternative justifications, based on economic power, prevail. There is another argument that the application of natural law as the universal guardian of an egalitarian human rights is not incoherent so much as it ignores or masks situations of significant inequality and the lack of human rights that continue to exist.

Yet unlike the arguments over gender and sexuality, for the most part religion and theology adapted to moves for greater class equality, the abolition of slavery and other time-bound caste-based ethics in their

---

[53] Oxfam 2014 and 2015 http://policy-practice.oxfam.org.uk/our-work/inequality – at 06 December 2015; Wearden, Graeme 'Oxfam: 85 richest people as wealthy as poorest half of the world'. The Guardian; Larry Elliott and Ed Pilkington. New Oxfam report says half of global wealth held by the 1%. *The Guardian*.

[54] https://www.wider.unu.edu/article/what-inequality.

[55] https://www.imf.org/external/pubs/ft/sdn/2015/sdn1513.pdf.

religious scriptures.[56] Natural law too accepted a change in its understandings of humanity as class-based, as did theologies based on natural law. The experience of discovering indigenous peoples with conscience and innate human dignity, recognizing the exploitation of slavery and post-Holocaust reflection on the barbarities of Nazism and Stalinism all in their times brought about recognition of a need for equal protection of all individuals on the basis of their humanity. Thus experience and changed understandings of class and slavery in the world around them have led to changes of theological ethics such that there is no suggestion that exceptions to equalities be made for race or class. Although to some degree contested in a few places the acceptance of human rights and changes of theology to accept equality, at least aspirationally, are a major contrast to the holding onto naturalistic understandings and scriptural interpretation of sex and relationships.

The broad ranging appearance of class and caste in societies across the world is no more sufficient than for example marriage to ground incontrovertible evidence of universalism. Yet the common acceptance of both class and caste in earlier societies and the stand against them across faiths in modern societies is another example of experience in ethics and human rights changing the views of religious communities. The changes provide further examples of both theological development over time and inconsistency of approach towards change, with which to challenge religions over areas of ethics where more time-bound views are retained. The fact that faith-based groups such as the Vatican and Muslim states want places at the table, for example at UN debates, is further testimony to the acceptance of common discourse over rights, even where conclusions differ on some issues. It is also a further forum in which to affirm what theological discourse can add to debates as well as to challenge over areas of continued disagreement.

The abandonment of attempts to justify rights as universal or developed from one understanding of natural law or reasoning gives way to recognition of rights, law and ethics as applied, developed and shaped as positive law. The development of positive law in democratic societies gives even more justification for ensuring that all possible viewpoints

---

[56] with rare exceptions like apartheid.

should have a place at the table to negotiate and share contributions to developing rights. Whilst resisting any argument that rights are inherent or somehow natural MacIntyre[57] and others such as Hauerwas who reject natural rights, do acknowledge a place for negotiation of common ground and rights as the ground on which to meet.

Interestingly MacIntyre does accept the dimension of natural law that grounds contemporary virtue ethics, despite the different context of the virtues involved. This is due to a view of ethics that emphasises growing into virtue and being schooled in habits of virtue so as to develop good decision-making in an ethically good life. In this framing of ethics such schooling occurs only in the context of particular communities with a more homogenous consensus about what is good. The process of developing of habits of virtue and the sort of society that develops people with habits of virtue is more important than the particular historical virtues.

It is arguable that human rights and a culture based on human rights do not need to abandon this concept of virtue ethics. If based on common respect, engagement in mutual understanding and a search for common ground that can build on but transcend particular faiths, theologies, philosophies and traditions, other virtues will grow. Just as the development of virtue in classical ethics is a process of growth, so too the development of a commonly agreed global ethics is a process. It is a process that requires mutual respect, agape, humility and a common search for truth and integrity. Within such a process religions and theologies can add important things to the dialogue, from the richness of centuries of experience and ethical reflection. Theology also has a communal memory and experience of developing ethics to encompass new and different temporal and cultural situations. There are also historical examples of the openness of theological and philosophical exploration developing common ethical minds and processes from Spain to Arabia. The search for a degree of unity amongst the theologians and philosophers is therefore entirely possible.

---

[57] Bowring B. *Misunderstanding MacIntyre on Human Rights* Analyse & Kritik 30/2008 (© Lucius & Lucius, Stuttgart) pp. 205–214, Bill Bowring (Bowring 2008).

The dominance of sciences, natural, medical, social and technological as means of exploration and development in contemporary life lends itself to philosophies and theologies based in the exploration of natural law. All dialogue involving such sciences also needs to remain open and alive to the naturalistic fallacy and varied understandings of what seems reasonable. Such flaws of reasoning are not particular to religion, as illustrated by the more sexist dimensions of the 2016 US elections. If changes to theologies of race and caste can be achieved so too can development of ethics around gender and sexuality.

From the centuries of theological reflection however religion can also bring additional things to the table. The grounding of rights in the sanctity and gift of all human life, whether based in theologies of the image of God or recognition of the divine in all being, is a corrective to the contemporary naturalistic fallacy of worth based in economic productivity and consumer choice. The theological traditions of law and ethics as protection particularly of those most vulnerable to exploitation also reinforce this view of rights as a respect for each individual rather than the 17th CE protection of landed or state rights. The holistic nature of theological exploration and theological anthropology also bring all aspects of human experience into play as rights are discerned but within the framework of a search for truth. Yet there is sufficient recognition in the development of theological laws of the need for specific, detailed application to encompass positivist development of contemporary codes of rights, ethics and virtues.

Theological ethics and ethics in general is always a dialogue between the experience of things or objects, other people and life in its fullness. Those experiences are varied and differ with perspective. Even in the relatively homogenous, elitist circles of the societies in which Natural Law theory developed, competing ethical theories made for a far from unified community. The societies in which Natural Law Theory and Theology developed were diverse in views and theories and ethics was forged in that dialogue. Yet dialogue alone or the communicative ethics envisaged by Habermas is not enough; ethics also needs material application and substantive goods around which to focus. It is this application that engages with experience to evaluate what is good. The common grounds or language for substantive goods in today's global village are sciences of all varieties. To a significant extent they always have been, as is seen in the development of natural law and theology. Far from being alien from or inimical to theology and faith natural and theological science were – and still are – part of the same spectrum. They may now be approached in different ways but that common exploration and sense-making as part of ethics remains.

In addition this search for sense-making may be more contemplative and less functional or reductionist in its orientation than some modern applications of science. Exploring the world has intrinsic value, an importance in itself. This appreciation of the value of nature for itself is also extended to the value of human life for itself, as a gift not a functional or economic entity. It is this sense of life as a gift that undergirds natural law theology's commitment to value and respect for human rights with all human life as gift. This also means that human worth cannot be dictated by the market or material worth as rights are grounded in intrinsic not functional, producer or utilitarian worth. In addition to this sense of gifted worth in all humanity, natural law theology brings to its understanding of rights not a vindication of man and man's property but a protective intent. This protective dimension is based in ideas of equality and sanctity as made in the image of God. It is an understanding of the natural as part of the sanctity of all creation, which is not to be exploited rather than doing what comes naturally, which may be more brutal as Hobbes feared. It is these distinctive features and added ideas that Natural Law Theology and religious reflections on nature, human gift and its protection, can bring to the ongoing conversations about what is best for humanity, common ethical frameworks and the development of human rights as part of that ethic.

4

Utilitarianism: A Modern, Godless Ethics?

As illustrated in the previous couple of chapters, natural law and virtue ethics have a long historical association with theological ethics. Aquinas and Augustine are often included in collections covering the development of western ethics[1] and several contemporary theologians who write about natural law do so from a faith-based perspective.[2] The same sort of link or overlap between theology and philosophy is much less obvious or easy to come by in the field of utilitarian ethics. In some instances a connection is actively avoided, so that for example *The Cambridge Companion to Christian Ethics*[3] has no chapter on utilitarianism nor does the *'Blackwell Companion to Christian Ethics'*.[4] Both publications view classical, natural law philosophy and virtue ethics, rather than modern philosophy as the appropriate heritage for theological ethics.

---

[1] e.g. Russell B. *A History of Western Philosophy.* Routledge, 2004, pp. 289–448 (Russell 2004); Kenny A. *A New History of Western Philosophy.* Oxford University Press, 2007. pp. 253–296;

[2] e.g. John Finnis, Germaine Grisez, Jean Porter, David Novak, Elizabeth Anscombe.

[3] Gill R. *A Cambridge Companion to Christian Ethics.* Cambridge University Press, 2012 (Gill 2012).

[4] Hauerwas S & Wells S. *Balckwell Companion to Christian Ethics.* Oxford: Blackwell Publishing, 2004–2006 (Hauerwas and Wells 2006).

© The Author(s) 2017
C. Shelley, *Ethical Exploration in a Multifaith Society*,
DOI 10.1007/978-3-319-46711-5_4

From another trajectory, those theologians and faiths that ground their ethics supremely in revelation would turn to scripture and other revealed sources rather than any secular philosophy.

The reasons for antipathy between religion and theology versus utilitarianism are not difficult to find. The first and probably most significant reason for the stand-off is that the construction of Utilitarianism as a discreet ethical theory in the 19th CE was a key move in seeking to rid ethics of God and religion. The theory argues for an ethics based on the (allegedly) simple principle of 'utility' defined according to the calculus of weighing harm versus pleasure, seeking to maximize the latter and minimize the former.[5] The assumption is that what promotes utility is what produces the most benefits for the largest number of people. There is also an assumption that utilitarianism can apply to all people, regardless of belief, without positing particular sets of moral rules or assumptions about ethical goods, rights or wrongs. The theory built on Enlightenment principles of empirical rationality, personal and ethical autonomy and egalitarianism. God and theology were neither needed nor wanted, being blamed for disagreements that caused major European conflict, such as the Thirty Years war. Such disputes were ultimately irresolvable, so the argument went, because their appeals to the metaphysical and transcendent could not be proved. Religion and classical philosophy were also criticized by Bentham and others as being principally responsible for promoting asceticism, which is singled out as contrary to utility, according to the definition of utility as pleasure.[6]

Overlaps and Distinctions

Yet the diametric opposition is not as clear-cut as Bentham supposed. As can be seen from the work of Al Gazali, Aquinas and other theological ethicists who engaged with Aristotle's philosophy and natural law ethics,

---

[5] Jeremy Bentham. *Utilitarianism and Other Essays*. London: Penguin Classics, 1987, p. 65 (Bentham 1987).

[6] Bentham J., op. cit., p. 70.

some theologians have no difficulty working with non-religious material and universal premises. It is also arguable that, to the extent that both utilitarianism and natural law theology are consequentialist, they are in the same area of ethics or even that utilitarianism is a sub-set of natural law.[7] The strength or extent of this contention will be considered along with other ways in which theological ethics and utilitarianism may overlap or reach consensus. Concepts of good and pleasure are examined in detail, as are those of harm, utility, virtue as a contrast with utility, empiricism versus the unprovable, the public as provable versus the private and this life versus the after-life. Exploration of these concepts should enable an assessment of whether utilitarianism really is so opposed to theological ethics, whether it is simply a process that is incorporated into other ethics and an appreciation of its strengths and gaps in ethical terms from the perspective of theological ethics.

It is conceded that religious understandings of ethics built on natural law ethical theory and developed its principles to encompass the supernatural within the empirically natural. In that respect theology remains alien to utilitarians and their worldviews remain formally separated by significantly different premises and assumptions. Yet, as seen in the discussion of natural law and as explored below, it is also clear that to an extent utilitarianism reacted against a caricature of religion rather than engaging with religious reasoning and worldviews. In addition, consideration of earlier natural law theory and theological ethics in several traditions also reveals that aspects of utilitarianism have been around in and adopted by religious traditions centuries before Bentham and Mills coined the phrase or developed their theory. These earlier intuitive applications of utilitarian rationale are assessed along with a couple of religious approaches to ethics that have adopted variations of a utilitarian calculus.

---

[7] As argued by Lisa Sowle Cahill in *Teleology, Utilitarianism and Christian Ethics*. Theological Studies Sage Publications, December 1981, Vol 42, pp. 601–629 (Cahill 1981).

The Utilitarian Vision

In theory utilitarianism promoted an age of tolerance, encompassing and enabling not only a broad spectrum of goods but self-determination in how to live and choose ones own goods and ethical values, provided that no-one was harmed. It was assumed that free and autonomous human agents choosing their own goods and avoiding harm to others would be the most effective way to promote the overall good of society. In particular, peace was promoted as more useful than strife and dissension. If difficult choices had to be made then the choice that generated the most overall good and/or created the least harm was the choice to be preferred as the means of maximizing good and the best use of resources, within society as a whole. The state, whose power was relatively unquestioned and whose government was elected by a property-owning minority, would make those decisions.

At first sight, like assumptions about ethics derived from natural law, the theory has a great deal to commend it intuitively; who would not want more pleasure and less pain? In fact, despite the utilitarian rejection of natural law theology the two have in common the consequential goods of happiness or pleasure as indicative of human flourishing.[8] As a means of ordering society utilitarianism, like appeals to nature, retains a strong influence on the construction and values of contemporary western nations, if not the majority of the global village. As a way of enabling a diversity of lifestyles, ethical choices, religious and other beliefs, a liberal utilitarianism seems ideally suited. This utilitarian diversity, it is argued, is also what underlies the economic system of free market capitalism. The argument, which is generally attributed to Adam Smith's *Wealth of Nations*,[9] is that in a society where people choose

---

[8] Neo-liberal Roman Catholic theologian Michael Novak defends free market capitalism on the basis of JS Mills liberalism as a development of Thomist natural law theology; see e.g. Long Stephen D. *Divine Economy: Theology & the Market.* London & New York: Routledge, 2000, pp. 13–29 (Long Stephen 2000); Roman Catholic Lisa Sowle Cahil also regards utilitarianism as a sub-category of natural law teleology – LS Cahill – Teleology, utilitarianism and Christian Ethics – Theological Studies 1981 – tsj.sagepub.com.

[9] Wordsworth Editions: World Classics 2012. Ed. Spencer Mark G, Griffith Tom.

their own ethical and material goods, the markets enable exchange of goods, gauging value according to the popularity of particular goods and maximizing them through free trade. In consequence producing the goods that will satisfy the desires and needs of the nation will employ the optimum number of people in the labour to produce the goods and so enable the labourers to earn their living.

Smith now known as amongst the first economic scientists was actually a professor of philosophy and part of the movement known as the Scottish Enlightenment. His Enlightenment ambition, though never realized, was to develop a complete 'Science of Man' effectively based on a rationalist enlightenment analysis.[10] Whilst often adopted by free market utilitarians Smith's lesser-known 'Theory of moral sentiments'[11] includes two chapters that to a degree critique the Humean argument for the 'beauty' of 'utility'. He is also deeply critical of the veneration of wealth and despising of the poor. Yet within contemporary western society the rhetoric of free trade and the value of utility is widely accepted and Smith's thesis has tended to be championed by neo-liberal free-marketeers. The question is whether utilitarian free trade really does deliver the goods and pleasure that utilitarianism promises. Statistics that illustrate the increasing wealth gap both between and within nations[12] suggest that the free market and its utilitarian analysis do not necessarily work. It might be argued that the utilitarianism of the free market is balanced by its application as a means of distributing finite, and in much of the world declining, public or common resources. In such situations utilitarianism may indeed be the best or even the only way to allocate goods fairly. An interesting example is the work of NICE[13] in the UK, which aims to evaluate the maximum effective impact of clinical treatment and use of resources. It is a process that takes for granted, in modern bureaucracies, the level of infrastructure required to allocate public resources at societal level and to consider whole populations.

---

[10] Phillipson Nicholas. *Adam Smith: An Enlightened Life.* Penguin, 2010 (Nicholas 2010).
[11] Smith A. *Theory of Moral Sentiments.* Penguin Classics, 2010 (Smith 2010).
[12] See above Chapter 3, 'Observing the nature of class.'
[13] National Institute for Clinical Excellence.

Theology and Utilitarianism

In addition to the questions raised above by Smith some of the sharpest critiques of utilitarianism, possibly inevitably given Bentham's original arguments and criticism of religion, have come from religious sources. One objection is that in practice autonomy and egalitarianism were limited to those with the power, money and station in life to exercise them; arguably that is still the case today. If the primary way to determine value in a diverse society is through the market, so that value is set by what people will pay for, those things that are most valued are likely to be available only to those with the most money. Whilst, in theory, the market is self-correcting the timescale for such corrections tends to leave significant losses in its wake for many. The reality, as economic statistics show, is that even if the free market does vindicate utilitarianism (which is contested) far too many other factors come into play in human society to enable genuine egalitarianism or fully free exchange of goods and benefits. A simple example of how the principle of utility determined by mere economic value fails to enable equal access to significant goods is that 'the law, like the Ritz hotel, is open to all'. The emphasis on pleasure, materialism and the empirical also deepens an economic trend that pays far more to stars of entertainment than to nurses, doctors and teachers.

It is on this basis, as much as its atheism, that the general theological trend has been opposed to and critical of utilitarianism and often of the liberal capitalism with which it is linked. John Hughes' exploration of the theology of work critiques utilitarianism in both its liberal capitalist and Marxist applications to economics and social science. He opposes to this a theo-aesthetic of work as fulfilment of gifts, life and human flourishing, drawing on both the romantic traditions of Ruskin and Morris and Roman Catholic metaphysics.[14] Hughes' critique also draws significantly on the work of John Millbank, Catherine Pickstock and others in the movement known as Radical

---

[14] Hughes J. *The End of Work: Theological Critiques of Capitalism.* Wiley Blackwell, 2006 (Hughes 2006).

Orthodoxy.[15] The key arguments are that utilitarianism is simply an economic and bureaucratic process rather than an approach to ethics, which in its ultimate logic leaves the supremacy of choice to those with the largest army.[16] The supposed rationality of utilitarianism is also spurious as in the ultimate analysis its parameters of pleasure and pain are subjective and based on sentiment and opinion rather than objective ethical foundations. Thus normative concepts are limited if not impossible and again, anarchy and the powerful prevail.

Another, related strand of the critique of liberalism and utilitarianism comes from those such as Barth and Hauerwas who argue for an entirely revelation-based ethic. Their analysis is that ethics for those of faith must be located in revelation and God, as revealed supremely for Barth and Hauerwas, in religious scripture because appeal to any form of reason is suspect. If natural law theology's reliance on liberal reason is suspect for such writers then utilitarianism with its location in human desire and pleasure must be even more suspect and prone to self-serving delusion. Whilst a few Christian commentators, notably the neo-liberal Thomist[17] Michael Novak, defend free market utilitarianism as compatible with Christianity, for the most part theological ethicists take a more critical view.

Suspicion or rejection of utilitarianism can also be found in Islam, on the basis of incompatibility with Islamic principles of ethical right and Shari'a.[18] Judaism would also have little time for utilitarianism in any form because of the prior ethical authority of the Torah, although most would not go so far as the website 'Torah Philosophy' in suggesting that utilitarianism is psychopathic![19] Nor are the *dharmic* faiths generally seen as compatible with utilitarianism both because of the claims of *dharma* as

---

[15] Millbank J, Pickstock C & Ward G. *Radical Orthodoxy: A New Theology.* Routledge, 1998 (Millbank et al. 1998b); Blond P. *Post Secular Philosophy: Between Philosophy and Theology.* Routledge, 1997 (Blond 1997).

[16] Donovan O. *The Desire of the Nations: Rediscovering the Roots of Political Philosophy.* Cambridge University Press, 2006 (Donovan 2006); Kirwan M. *Political Theology: A New Introduction.* Darton Longman & Todd, 2008 (Kirwan 2008).

[17] Novak M. *The Spirit of Democratic Capitalism.* Madison Books, 1990 (Novak 1990).

[18] Al Hassan Al Aidaros, Faridahwati Mohd S & Kamil MD. Idris. Islam and Ethical Theory. *International Journal of Islamic Thought,* 4 (December 2013), pp. 1–13 (Al Hassan et al. 2013).

[19] http://www.torahphilosophy.com/2011/09/atheist-ethics.html.

an ethical way and the search for *liberation (moksha)* as something beyond this-worldly pleasure.[20] An example is that whilst some have suggested that Hindu reformer Ram Moham was utilitarian in his approach, his motives and inspiration were drawn clearly from the Vedas and his vedantin spirituality.[21] For the most part therefore the atheism and this-wordly material emphasis and analysis of utilitarianism is alien to religious faith, even if some parallels can be drawn by theological ethics.

What Is the Good?

Much of the difficulty with utilitarianism from a theological perspective but also from a general ethical perspective is that its materialistic empiricism, at least in its crudest form, precludes discussion of non-empirical or immaterial experience and value. This was outlined above to a degree when considering the relationship of utilitarianism to the growth of capitalism and the drawbacks of the market as a prescriber of value. Linked to the issue of how value is determined is the question of how the pleasure that is central to utilitarianism is constituted or defined. Although Bentham does list several types or causes of pleasure and pain the lists are comparatively random, subjective and distinctly middle-class in their assumptions.[22] Simple pleasures include for example sense, wealth, skill, amity, good name, power, piety, benevolence, relief, expectation and even malevolence. The pains are largely seen as their opposites. Quantifying pleasure or happiness also relies on the subjective factors of intensity, fecundity and purity of pleasure correlated with the likelihood of pleasure resulting from particular actions.[23]

Whilst this breadth of possibilities for subjective interpretation of pleasure provides the benefits of diversity in a multicultural, multifaith

---

[20] Bradley Dr M & Bendorf M. *Utilitarianism, Deontology, Hinduism, and Buddhism on the Nature of Moral Right and Wrong.* http://bendorfm.com/essays/PR202Essay1.htm. Accessed 28 May 2016;

[21] Lipner J. *The voice of scripture as veda and 'veda' in Hindus; their religious beliefs and practices.* op. cit., p. 79

[22] Mill JS and Jeremy Bentham, op. cit., pp. 29–97.

[23] Mill JS and Jeremy Bentham, op. cit.

society it is also far more of a problem than its original promoters realized and remains a problem in contemporary society. The difficulty is the lack of any objective framework or criteria by which to determine what constitutes 'goods' or what is harmful. The critique, that the hedonic calculus lacks any overarching or purposive framework by which to determine what is good, is particularly acute from natural law theorists. Although also consequentialist, natural law at least purports to have an objective evaluative mechanism. If the natural law determination of 'the good' by reference to teleology is contested (and also arguably subjective to those framing what is 'natural'), the lack in utilitarianism of any common concept of human anthropology is even more problematic. Where there is no objective evaluative framework of human goods, with 'value' ascribed only to arbitrary financial 'value' anarchy, the might of the most powerful, is ultimately the result. Those who suffer most from anarchy are inevitably the most vulnerable and in a market-based values system, the poorest. Joseph Fletcher, another Christian theologian, sought to develop a utilitarian approach through his situation ethics, substituting love for pleasure.[24] Yet his arguments and the construction of love are just as problematic as pleasure in trying to establish some common measure of 'good'.

Mills and Pleasure

Recognizing the limitations of Bentham's approach to ideas of pleasure Bentham's successor, student, chronicler and first critic, John Stuart Mill argued against any concept of pleasure that was reductionist of what it is to be human. In considering the issue of human goods Mills' warning against reductionism is epitomized in the phrase 'Better a dissatisfied human being than a contented pig.'[25] To a degree his cautions about reductionism have been justified, even vindicated, by traits in the

---

[24] Fletcher JF. *Situation Ethics: A New Morality.* Westminster: John Knox Press, 1997 (Fletcher 1999).

[25] Mills actually wrote 'if the sources of pleasure were precisely the same to human beings and to swine, the rule of life for one would be good enough for the other...' Mills JS. *Utilitarianism.* London: Penguin Classics1987, p. 279.

contemporary economy. Is it arguable that Mill's argument that utility is not a mere pleasure machine foresaw the challenges of a society in which the GDP garnered by the sex industry, celebrity and various entertainments significantly outranks the rewards for teachers, medical staff and other essential caring services?

Mill sought to expand understandings of 'pleasure' in a utilitarian framework by considering the higher pleasures such as art and intellectual enquiry, human fulfilment and social goods.[26] His consideration of utilitarianism advocated significant practical application in social and governmental contexts. The development of distinctions between rule-based and act-based utilitarianism also sought to add correctives to a situation in which the collective good could be classed as outweighing an individual life. Despite Mills' refinements of the theory generally speaking utilitarianism, particularly in its more crude forms, remains unsympathetically received within religious frameworks. This is especially obvious when contrasted with the popularity that natural law theology has found. It is notable that even though he sought to develop Bentham's understanding of pleasure to ensure that it acknowledged the 'higher' powers or aspirations of human endeavour and culture, Mill's scheme also remains fairly subjective and culture-bound in its articulation.

Religion and Pleasure

For many religious traditions the 'pleasure principle' is not only too simplistic an approach to human goods and flourishing, it is also – intentionally from Bentham's point of view – at odds with aspects of faith traditions that commend various forms of abstinence or asceticism. The latter are often linked to those faiths that also have understandings of suffering or pain that do not sit well with the utilitarian principle of simply reducing or avoiding situations that cause pain. This is not to endorse crude caricatures of faith, such as those promoted by Nietzche[27]

---

[26] Mills JS., op. cit., pp. 278–294.
[27] Nietzche FW. *The Genealogy of Morals.* Dover Publishing, 2003; Nietzche FW. Ed. Tanner M. *On Good and Evil.* Penguin Classics, 2014 (Nietzche 2014).

or Richard Dawkins,[28] as belief in a cruel, punitive God keeping a vigilant watch on mere mortals and their peccadillos. Nor is it to justify simplistic explanations of pain and suffering as a form of good because they are God's way of making humanity grow up, the sort of analysis that was castigated by CS Lewis as making God a vivisectionist.[29] It is however, to recognize that many faiths have a more complex relationship with the challenges of suffering and pain than allowed for by a utilitarian framework.

These alternative approaches include the recognition that much pain in the human condition is inevitable and the result of human finitude or attachment to the goods of this world as ends in themselves. This means that the context for and attitude to suffering amongst those of faith differs from utilitarianism. In response to the inevitabilities of suffering inherent in mortality aspects of Christianity embrace the love of God as a means to cope with suffering. At their most ascetic the *dharmic* faiths regard all attachments in earthly life as the source of suffering rather than pleasure, which is not necessarily about rejecting them but relativizing them against the expanse of those things beyond our finitude. Such attachment will inevitably disappoint as, for the *dharmic* faiths, the material or this-worldly is illusory. For the Abrahamic faiths, particularly Christianity, this world is only a temporary home. Thus the promises of eternity and the transcendent, which Bentham saw as useless, are far more real than the material for many faiths.

A good example of the search for the good in theological terms is the following from a letter by a Sikh father to his son, which would resonate with many religious traditions:

'Dearest Jaskirat,.... When you leave the university and face the world.... You must not merely question what you call the significance...of your own life.... In our efforts to be practical individuals, we want to imbibe only what is of utility and significance...The search for significance in everything is a curse for the present century. The first step in your

---

[28] Dawkins R. *The God Delusion.* Boston Houghton Mifflin, 2006 & Black Swan, 2007 (Dawkins 2006).
[29] Lewis CS. *The Problem of Pain.* Williams Collins, 2015 (Lewis 2015).

questioning of the 5 K's should be to be free of this yoke of significance. . . .
It is a pity . . . to reduce Sahib Guru Gobind Singhji, to our own mundane
level of thinking and view all his actions in light of practical animal
utility. . . . The Kanga, the Kesh, the Kara, the Kirpan and the Kachha
were all delicate gifts of love and beauty. . . . A way of total love. . . . unique
for the Khalsa;'[30]

Yet the division between theological ethics and utilitarianism is not so
straightforward as either some theologians or some secularists would like
to claim, particularly as there are some significant overlaps with natural
law theory. It is arguable that these overlaps indicate that some of the
conclusions to which utilitarianism comes may be inevitable in corporate
or governmental contexts.

Assessing the Hedonic Calculus: Pleasure or Good, Harm and Evil

First however, it is necessary to explore further how pleasure or the good
is constituted or defined. As noted above it is problematic that utilitarianism lacks any objective framework or criteria by which to determine
what constitutes 'goods' or what is harmful. Whilst the breadth of
possibilities for subjective interpretation of pleasure provides the benefits
of diversity in a multicultural, multifaith society it is also far more of a
problem than its original promoters realized.

   The critique, that the hedonic calculus lacks any overarching or purposive framework by which to determine what is good, is particularly
acute from natural law theorists. Although also consequentialist, natural
law at least purports to have an objective evaluative mechanism. If the
natural law determination of 'the good' by reference to teleology is
contested and subjective to the extent that what are 'natural' purposes is
defined by those with the power to frame what is 'natural', utilitarianism
lacks any common concept of human anthropology. Where there is no
objective evaluative framework of human goods, with 'value' ascribed only

---

[30] http://www.sikhs.org/nosymbol.htm.

to arbitrary financial 'value' anarchy, which most harms the poor and vulnerable, is ultimately the result. Whilst natural law has the consequentialist pragmatism of utilitarianism, it also includes additional factors such as objective parameters for defining the good, concepts of justice to protect minorities and concepts of the mean to avoid excess.

The Ends of Ethics

One of the mistakes made by the original coiners of the theory of utilitarianism, Bentham in particular, about religion and religious ethics was to assume that it was primarily ascetic, self denying and abstinent. However, as seen in previous chapters, theological ethics based on natural law should primarily be affirming of both this life and the after-life. A true appreciation of those religions that adopt natural law ethical premises involves embracing creation and material as well as spiritual flourishing. There may have been a limited appreciation by the Enlightenment of the fact that natural law theology aims for flourishing and happiness as the breadth of natural law theology and ethics had been reduced into either casuistry or absolutist dogmatism. An understanding of theological ethics as primarily abstinent, kill joy, rule-bound and life denying might also have been a valid assumption from the puritanically protestant or the conservatively catholic. Yet to the extent that both natural law and utilitarian ethics evaluate ethical actions and decisions according to their capacity to generate positive goods as ends or results they are similarly consequentialist. Ethical goods are defined and evaluated by an end-point analysis of what is good.

Where the two differ in ethical terms is in their construction of what is seen as good and how that conclusion is reached. For utilitarianism what is good is what is useful in creating pleasure or reducing harm, which enables a wide range of goods to be considered but fails to define what is understood by good or pleasure. By contrast, as seen in the previous chapter, the 'good' in natural law is defined by particular, generally single, understandings of the purpose of something or some act. Thus, if sex is for procreation that purpose determines the goods towards which sex is ordered and the conditions required for sex to be ethically valid. Equally importantly are the anthropological assumptions of natural law theory, whether by Aristotle's own understanding or the faith-based versions of natural law theology. The end of humanity is contemplation; there is an anthropology of a human being in the image of god or created for the highest mental contemplation of how the world works and what life is about. That is quite a distance from the utilitarian focus on the far more material concept of pleasure.

As explored in the previous chapter the difficulties with natural law theory are that many things or acts have more than one possible end and the naturalistic fallacy confuses what is, with what ought to be, in ethical terms. The more complex and interventionist society becomes in terms of its use of material science, the more estranged it is from what is or is not 'natural'. Utilitarianism avoids some of these limitations of natural law theory. The more diverse range of ends and consequences encompassed by the utilitarian umbrella of 'pleasure' may reflect better the diversity and possibilities of creation and be closer to the diversity of creation seen in Hindu narratives than the western tradition's more limited and didactic understandings of natural goods.

It could be equally argued that whilst 'pleasure' permits of a wide range of goods, the concept, as recognized by Mills, risks being reductionist. There also seems to be a tension between the fact that 'utility' and natural law would seem to involve some element of objective assessment about what is useful or good, whilst pleasure is a more subjectively defined good. Religion is an interesting illustration. Bentham objected to established religion but he recognized that religious services and practices are pleasurable to some. There are many people whose religious observance is the centre of their lives in part because it delivers certain forms of pleasure and fulfilment. For some it may be the pleasure of singing together and the peacefulness of praying; for others pleasure can lie in the duties of service, the beauty of the ritual, a sense of belonging and so on. Thus religion itself provides an illustration of the variability and subjectivity of pleasure as a measure of good and pleasure and therefore in utilitarian terms, utility. The positive benefit of utilitarian diversity is illustrated by English law's protection of entirely opposing views, for example those within a tradition who wear religious clothing and those who choose not to.[31] Everything is fine, so the utilitarian mantra runs, provided that it does no harm.

Do No Harm

Yet what is overlooked is that conceptions of harm and what is harmful are related to ideas of what is good for the persons or lives in question. It is only by having some idea of who or what the human being is, both in the particular and generically, that what may be good or harmful to humanity or particular individuals can be assessed. Whilst accepting that a diversity of goods may generate the goods of tolerance, mutual acceptance and peace, a lack of consensus about where the boundaries of harm lie is more problematic. The construction of pleasure in a reductionist sense or the simplistic numerical preference of one perspective over a minority are similarly problematic. A practical example is that utilitarianism would endorse the pleasurable and noisy carousing of clubbers leaving a club at 4am over the objections of the minority sleeping in flats above the club.

Both secular and religious differences illustrate that what is harmful is not necessarily commonly agreed. To give one example, some parents favour corporal punishment to discipline their children, arguing that failure to use such methods harms the child, in some cases citing scripture that 'to spare the rod is to spoil the child'.[32] However, support for corporal punishment is not confined to believers in the Bible; there are Muslim and secular supporters for the same viewpoint. Conversely, opponents of corporal punishment are also found amongst the Christian population and other religious traditions, as well as constituting the secular child protection norm in the UK. These differences over corporal punishment illustrate that 'harm' is not so easily defined, even in one country or one religious community. When it is recognized that there are many other issues in the UK and even more across different world cultures and communities that raise similar differences, the problems of 'harm' as a criterion for ethical determination become readily apparent.

---

[31] *Re Begum ex p Denbigh High School [2005] UKSC 15.*
[32] Proverbs 13:24, 19: 18, 22:15, 23: 13–14.

Yet it tends to be assumed in western society that harm, like 'good' or 'pleasure', is a self-evident concept. Examples include the concept of 'significant harm' in UK child protection law and the norm to 'do no harm' in the Hippocratic oath. What is harmful is not only contested as between different cultures and worldviews but also varies with context. Thus what constitutes 'harm' is not as commonly agreed as often assumed, leading to serious definitional shortcomings in utilitarianism. Whilst 'goods' or pleasure may be matters of subjective preference when it comes to 'harm', particularly harm that requires correction or protection, subjective preference is inadequate. To return to the example of corporal punishment; if harmful, it requires some restraint. Similarly protection for children from parenting that views blood transfusions or homosexuality as sinful, require criteria to define harm rather than simple assertions defined by a dominant majority about what constitutes harm.

One model for defining human anthropology and therefore what requires protection is the framework of human rights. For some these are a pragmatic consensus-based framework for universal norms, respected by secular and religious alike. For others, particularly some critics of utilitarianism,[33] rights are just another example of suspect utilitarianism, conceiving them as protecting individualist preferences. Although it is fair to critique the United Nations Declaration of Human Rights (UNDHR) as predominantly reflecting a western civil libertarian perception of human rights, to say that it is no more than subjective utilitarian choices ignores the search for consensus about human protection. If a multicultural, multifaith society is to find sufficient common ground ultimately to live and grow together, some means of agreeing common human anthropology is needed to undergird common ethical values and norms. It is for this reason that human rights, in its contemporary, protective, post-Holocaust understanding, has significant ethical force. Yet the fact that there are differences of interpretation across cultures does need to be recognized

---

rather than taking for granted that rights are agreed, any more than other utilitarian or positivist ethical lists.

Part of the objection of orthodox critics to both rights and utilitarianism is that ethics are culturally produced and therefore that the universals sought by utilitarians are unachievable. Such critics also argue that conceiving of universal ethical rules, whether utilitarian or Kantian deontology, incoherently uproots ethics from the cultures and traditions that produced them.[34] The theological anthropology suggested as an alternative to utilitarian and other attempts at universal ethics is virtue ethics, arguing for an ethics of human character within particular communities not action-oriented universal ethical rules. As identified when discussing natural law, virtues are not alien from theological ethics and derive from both scriptural and philosophical sources. Yet most theological ethics do also seek universals and answers to common problems; a view of the world grounded in a universal divinity will inevitably be dissatisfied with ethics that stop at particular cultural boundaries. To the extent that they aspire to universalism, at least at the level of universal ethical principles, most theological ethics are closer to utilitarianism than its critics. Yet the differences as well as overlaps remain.

Good, Pleasure and Sex

A significant dimension of the utilitarian reaction against religion and abstinence, both on the part of Bentham and Mills and critics of religion to date, focuses on the ethics of sexuality and sexual pleasure. Insofar as natural law perspectives, reinforced by religious ambivalence about sex, have limited sex to procreation natural law has also been reductionist. That reductionism is compounded by the privatizing of religion, over-identifying religion and religious morality with sexual morality and setting up an opposition between secular utilitarianism and religious worldviews that persists to today. Changes to the law in many countries over the past few decades around abortion, homosexuality, same-sex partnerships and most

---

[34] Millbank J, Hauerwas S, MacIntyre A & Anscombe E., op. cit.

recently same-sex marriage, have brought these areas of life more prominently into the public sphere. Some religious groups have engaged in this public battle, pinning their religious identity to a counter-cultural sexual morality, which has simply accepted the false reductionism constructed by a similarly reduced utilitarian calculus.

To a degree it is true that natural law constructions of sexual ethics and the legacy of St Augustine and St Paul has led in some church traditions to a narrowly procreative purpose for sex.[35] However, in many other religious traditions and even in Christianity the pleasurable, enjoyable and companionate aspects of sexual relationships as well as the procreative are also recognized. Besides procreation the Anglican prayer book and Canon Law recognize the wider purposes of relationship in marriage, including mutual companionship and satisfying the 'natural affections'. For Judaism, Hinduism and Islam marriage and sexual enjoyment, love and companionship as part of a good marriage are assumed as the norm. Marriage in these traditions is often at a younger age than the average in western or Christian society as there is no tradition of prolonged celibacy pending marriage, encouraging young people instead to face the inevitable and indulge their 'natural affections'. It is notable that whilst polygamy may be sexist (depending on the value that women place on husbands) one key principle of Islamic polygamy – and marriage generally – is that husbands recognise their wives' entitlement to enjoy sex. That enjoyment of sex and recognition that women are entitled to its enjoyment, is a stark contrast with western, Greek and Christian fears about sex as irrational and assumptions that 'good' women are too 'nice' for it.

What does remain distinct between religious and most utilitarian understandings of pleasure in relation to sexuality is that religious constructions generally view sex as best expressed within committed relationships, generally marriage. By contrast a strict utilitarian construction of sex can divorce questions of sexual activity and pleasure

---

[35] e.g. the Roman Catholic Church, see Moore G. *The Body in Context: Sex and Catholicism.* Continuum, 2011 (Moore 2011).

as a human need from longer-term decisions about relationships, marriage and children. The fact that a 2005 court case[36] has effectively endorsed this distinction is an interesting reflection of societal changes around sexual relationships. The distinction is drawn in a case about the capacity to consent to marriage of a Muslim woman with both learning difficulties and a mental illness. In holding that the woman in question had capacity to consent to sexual relationships but not to the longer-term and therefore more serious commitment of marriage, the court effectively endorsed a distinction between sex for pleasure and marriage as a life commitment.

It is not that the religious perspective rejects enjoyment and goods other than procreation but it holds to a position that true flourishing in human relationships requires love and commitment. The move to mutuality in relationship and marriage is also believed to be best protected by equal expectations about relationship, commitment and mutual growth in love and life through that commitment. It is fair to say that this understanding of relationships and commitment is not limited to those whose belief is shaped by religious conviction. However, there does remain a dividing point between those who do not countenance sex outside marriage and those whose ethic encompasses sexual experimentation and shorter-term involvement. Ironically the homosexual community, castigated for utilitarian attitudes towards sex as mere promiscuous pleasure, is now involved in moves to greater recognition of commitment in sexual relationships through civil partnership and same-sex marriage. Further ethical complexities of religious versus secular constructions of sexuality are considered in a later chapter. However, this exploration suffices to show that the Benthamite critique of religious abstinence in defining utility, pleasure and the good is over-simplistic.

---

[36] Re SA. (Vulnerable Adult) [2005] EWHC 2942, [2006] 1 FLR 867 – adult with mental health diagnosis and learning disabilities held to have capacity to consent to sexual relationship but not more serious longer term commitment of marriage.

Life and End of Life

Another area in which most theological ethics, including natural law theology, differs significantly from the predominant utilitarian view is that of the ethics of life. It is here that the individual autonomy of utilitarianism is in significant contrast with the understandings of much religious belief. This is a fundamentally different worldview not so much a deontological command as ways of understanding life. Yet again however, there is a spectrum of belief.

Some more liberal religious ethicists have followed the utilitarian path of seeking to divorce religion from ethics in the public square. An example of this approach is Richard Holloway's 'Godless Morality'. In discussing euthanasia and IVF, Holloway adopts a somewhat Benthamite position, only able to conceive of religion as unthinking deontology and therefore rejecting it from public conversations about IVF, euthanasia and life issues.[37] It is true that in relation to approaches to the inevitable pain and suffering of human existence theological ethics is most distinct from utilitarianism. Besides beliefs that their creation by God means that human beings never have complete autonomy over their lives, there is an acceptance of pain, suffering and growth as inevitable aspects of mortality. There is a possibility for example of living grief well rather than simply railing against it.

Yet Holloway's rejection of theology from the debate on the basis of its alleged deontology ignores the range of ethical arguments from religious communities and their experience. Again the perception of theological ethics as entirely revelation based and therefore not engaging with the realities of life and experience could not be further from the truth. Far from being based solely on the sanctity of life theological perspectives on life and opposition to the end of life in euthanasia are also significantly about concerns, based in experience, of imbalances and abuses of power. In addition to arguments that life is sacred, which are not necessarily exclusive to religion, are arguments about protecting the

---

[37] Holloway R. *Godless Morality: Keeping Religion Out of Ethics*. Canongate, 2004 (Holloway 2004).

frail or elderly. In a society where pleasure and happiness are the ultimate objectives and pain and suffering to be minimized, the person who is suffering can feel alien, unwanted, un-useful. It is to protect those who may be feeling un-useful or burdensome that many religions are wary of euthanasia and oppose pressures in that direction, affirming that human life has a dignity and worth even when there is suffering.

There is also the argument that simply searching for pleasure and avoiding pain is again reductionist and misses important aspects of human experience and maturing. The solidarity of going through hardships together can forge something more solid than happy times alone. The lessons learnt from finding that you can survive particular challenges, from living without something for a while and facing adversity head-on, can engender greater resilience and appreciation. Above all the relativizing of particular attachments, towards not an absolute but an open-ended acceptance of both the inevitable and the unexpected, can provide far greater holiness and grounded contentment than searches for simple material pleasures.

Life and After-Life

Any consideration of life issues and ethics in theological context also has to engage with another significant difference between theological ethics or religious perspectives and utilitarianism, which is beliefs in an after-life. These differences have a number of implications. One is that belief in an afterlife changes the perspective of the timeframe over which pleasure and pain are assessed. For those who believe that one life, on this one earth, is all that there is or will be and that its end will be simple death and bodily disintegration, will evaluate good and harm according to a one-life, this-life calculus. However, the majority of religious faiths include an aspect of their belief that looks beyond this material life to the transcendent, whether conceived of as an eternal heaven or a kharmic wheel. For many the transcendent can be glimpsed from within this earthly, mortal life but for most significantly includes something beyond by way of continued existence into an afterlife.

More critically for ethical conduct is that not only does religious belief promise a longer-term, even eternal perspective over which to assess pleasure and pain but beliefs about that future life are related to ethical conduct in earthly life. This is a further dimension of religious belief that is anathema to utilitarians and has attracted major criticism. On the one hand an afterlife is a promise that cannot be proved and is therefore irrational and holds out false hope. Of more concern, it can also hold out false and abusive threats of hell to believers.[38] Such hopes can also distort behaviour, leaving believers, particularly the more wealthy or powerful ones, to ignore injustice and promise instead rewards in the hereafter or 'pie in the sky when you die'.

In most cases the other-worldly dimensions of religious belief simply provide additional incentives for what is considered good conduct in a particular religious community or culture, rather than alternative motives for doing them. Such an analysis led William Paley, one of the rare theological utilitarians, to interpret and defend the hedonic calculus in the context of eternal life. Yet for Kant, this dimension of theology is unacceptable in ethical terms as it makes good ethical conduct self-seeking rather than doing or being good for the sake of good itself. This reflects Kant's opposition to much of utilitarian ethics on the basis that for Kant duty and objectively right ethical conduct is more important than consequences, pleasure or reward.

For others, like Bentham and Mills framing conduct around the uncertainty of promises in another, unprovable, life is pointless because incapable of proof. Yet for those who have a religious belief and conduct their lives according to eternal as well as temporal timeframes the awareness of the afterlife is very real. In extreme situations such consequences in another life can be a powerful source of motivation for conduct and ethical decisions. This is not only a perception of the contemporary major religions but was also an important factor in ancient Greek ethics, for whom the immortal gods were profoundly unethical as there was no eternal sanction.

Yet in practice whilst there is awareness of the afterlife there is more to faith than a simplistic utilitarian calculus of pleasure-now

---

[38] Bentham J. An Introduction to the Principles of Morals and Legislation. In *Utilitarianism & Other Essays*. Penguin Classics, op. cit., p. 95; Dawkins R. 2007, op. cit. pp. 317–387.

versus harm-in-eternity or abstinence and altruism now in return for eternal life and salvation. William Paley's eighteenth century extrapolation of Bentham's theory to a utilitarian Christianity with the pleasure in the afterlife[39] was widely rejected, suggesting that such simplistic calculus does not bear much on the reality of faith. Insofar as the fear of eternal sanctions or hope of reward does apply it relates not to everyday decisions but to major issues. An example is Jehovah's Witnesses refusal of blood transfusions as contrary to an interpretation of the Bible that each person's blood is their unique source of life, so that accepting a blood transfusion jeopardizes eternal salvation. Observant Jehovah's Witnesses will seek alternatives to transfusion but ultimately will risk death by refusing transfusion rather than forfeit eternal life.

Paradoxically, so far as utilitarian calculus with an eternal dimension does operate in religious practice its over-simplification can lead to dangerous and extreme distortions of religion. The Jehovah's Witness example is one minority perspective. Another illustration of simplistic utilitarian thinking, disowned by all reputable Muslim scholars, is the alleged Islamic belief that to kill the infidel through suicide bombing will earn the *jihadi* eternity in paradise. A similarly distorted utilitarianism in a religious ethical argument is the phenomenon of pro-lifers killing heads of abortion clinics. This misguided utilitarian identification of a religious or sacred cause with the greater good argues that life begins at conception and that killing an abortionist is justified in the interests of saving greater numbers of foetal lives by preventing abortions. The argument carries little sympathy, even amongst the pro-life community.

The *jihadist* and anti-abortionist distortion of the concept of eternal life and of foetal versus abortionists' lives, tends to be found in groups who believe that belonging to particular sects and causes will ensure that the believer is saved. This tends to lead to counter-culturally distinctive ways of observing the faith at odds not only with secular premises but also the mainstream of their religious communities. Such exclusive certainty or 'sacred' religion, seeks homogeneity, self-identity and purity,

---

[39] Paley W. *The Principles of Moral and Political Philosophy.* Liberty Fund Inc, 2003 (Paley 2003).

bolstered by an absolute ethical and sacred order. This is opposed, in an analysis by Fasching, Dechant and Lantigua,[40] to the 'holy', which is characterized by faith not certainty or absolutes, in which the holy and secular are complementary. The former, sacred understanding of religion, rather than the latter sense of the holy, is likely to reflect the sort of narrow religion castigated and rejected by Bentham. This is one of the instances in which theological ethics does differ from simple religious faith, as theology is faith seeking understanding not exclusive religious certainty.

The reality is that for all faiths the relationship between ethical conduct during an earthly life is not in any event so straightforward. Theology does not give rise to a simplistic or mechanistic utilitarian calculus. Such mechanistic analysis is contradicted in the Abrahamic faiths by the concept of God's mercy, so that eternal condemnation or reward cannot be predicted. Similarly in most faiths there is a sense that truly holy conduct goes beyond mechanistic morality, requiring observance of the spirit not the letter of the law. To live a life with reference solely to the promise of eternal life or better *kharma* rather than observing the law or ethical codes for the love of God, love of the law, love of neighbour and love of creation, also misunderstands the point of theologically ethical conduct. Thus Paley's utilitarian calculus cannot realistically be applied to Abrahamic understandings of judgement and salvation. For the *dharmic* faiths the calculus is never just one of personal salvation in an after-life but one of cosmic *kharmic* consequences of which the state into which one is reincarnated is just a part.[41]

For traditions who believe in a specific all-creating deity, following examples laid down in lives and scriptures, heaven or eternal life is the gift of a loving creator not a reward earned by believers. To do good and avoid evil, in the terminology of Thomas Aquinas, is the end of good reason and the common life. It is the way to

---

[40] Fasching DJ, Dechant D & Lantigua DM. *Comparative Religious Ethics: A Narrative Approach to Global Ethics*, 2nd edition. Wiley-Blackwell, 2011, pp. 4–19 (Fasching et al. 2011).

[41] Lipner J. *Hindus: Their Religious Beliefs and Practices*. Routledge, 2010, pp. 259–272 (Lipner 2010).

human flourishing in this life rather than simply being 'good' for 'pie in the sky when you die'. Similarly observance of the Torah in Judaism is about living according to the law of God in this life rather than in expectation of *shamaim* (the heavens) or avoidance of *sheol* (hell) afterwards. Therefore neither the simplistic utilitarian critiques of religious approaches to the afterlife and ethics nor the opposition of sacred and holy drawn by Fasching et al are as clear-cut as the ease of explanation suggests. Fasching et al acknowledge the need to beware of stereotypes that divide believers into extremist versus moderate. In practice the relationship between conduct in this life and salvation in the next, as part of a faith community, is a good deal more sophisticated, as is theological ethics.

Just War, an Essentially Utilitarian Argument

Whilst real or perceived differences between religious and utilitarian understandings of life undergird different ethical frameworks, as explored above, there are also well-accepted aspects of religious understanding and scripture that effectively adopt a utilitarian calculus. Such examples of 'utilitarianism' pre-date the Enlightenment framing of utilitarian theory and illustrate that some ethical dilemmas may be irresolvable by other than what is effectively utilitarian analysis. It is interesting to compare theological rules in personal ethical decisions over life issues, such as abortion and euthanasia, with the more corporate or state-based decision-making involved in war.

The most obvious example of utilitarian analysis in theological ethics is Just War theory. The overarching ethical issue in war is that it tends to kill people, thus breaching the command 'thou shalt not kill' in Natural Law's first precept, the Ten Commandments and Kant's principle maxim, not to take life. In the *dharmic* traditions war breaches the command not to kill based on *ahimsa*, do no violence, which applies not only to violence against human beings but also to destruction of the wider creation. Proceeding originally from the natural law tradition Just War theory finds grounds for the waging of war as exceptions to the primary precepts of preserving life and peace. The grounds for declaring war or *ius ad bellum*, are:

(i) War must be the last resort after other means to resolve the conflict have been exhausted.
(ii) War should be for just cause, not self-aggrandizement, enrichment or imperialism.
(iii) Just war can only be declared by a legitimate ruler or state. Contemporary international law only accepts declarations of war by duly recognized nation states. In theory this means that the Vatican, as a UN recognized state, could declare war but Palestine could not, raising its own ethical and political questions.
(iv) The purpose as well as the cause of war must be just, with the primary aim of re-establishing a just peace.
(v) War must also have a reasonable prospect of success and not simply inflame the situation or perpetuate animosities. Success is consequentially defined as peace and longer-term stability. Only peace justifies the inevitable killing involved in war, even though precise consequences are hard to predict.
(vi) Pursuit of Just War, as for self-defence, must be proportionate to the threat posed and created.
(vii) War must also be conducted so that innocent non-combatants are not harmed. Modern tactics and weaponry lead to civilian as well as military casualties so this principle now accepts civilian casualties as a secondary consequence or 'double effect' of war.

Just War also includes ethics for *ius in bello*, the conduct of war. Proportionality applies on the battlefield; shooting a soldier who is unarmed or defeated is unethically disproportionate. *Ius in bello* reiterates that no action should be taken against non-combatant civilian targets like hospitals and schools, subject again to policies of double-effect. There should be no desecration or exploitation of conquered peoples and prisoners must be treated humanely, principles now set out in the Geneva Convention. Yet, as for *ius ad bellum*, the utilitarian calculus of double effect means that civilians or prisoners of war may be harmed as collateral damage for the greater good.

The first and fourth to the seventh justifications for war as numbered above, are essentially utilitarian. The doctrine of double effect is the epitome of a utilitarian position justifying loss of some life for the greater good. Modern weapons mean that war causes civilian casualties to an extent not possible at the time that the major religious scriptures were written (or even as recently as the 1914–1918 war in Europe) and Just War theory was originally developed. In most faith traditions, even those like Buddhism that are mostly perceived as pacifist, there is a utilitarian line of reasoning that justifies use of force or war, even at the risk of life, in the interests of the greater good.

Religious scriptures all have things to say about war, violence and preservation or restoration of peace in one form or another. All consider compromises of principle as regards the sanctity or preservation of particular lives against the greater good of the whole. Most traditions have ethics that justify the taking of life and use of violence in self-defence; the Qu'ran specifically advocates self-defence in Surah s.22:39 and 22:40. Just War theory advocates self-defence as a just cause for war. As self-defence does not protect third parties threatened by unjust regimes and oppression all traditions have narratives that go further than self-defence and support the taking up of arms to restore peace and protect innocent third parties. Thus a utilitarian calculation, temporary loss of peace and possible loss of life, is justified by the longer-term good of restoring peace with justice.

The Sikh concept of *"dharam nibhaona"*, involves a duty to maintain *dharam* (equivalent of *dharma*, the way or just order) and counter war and violence caused by lust and greed. It is a clear contrast with quests for pleasure in the cruder versions of utilitarianism but using force to restore peace and justice is essentially utilitarian rather than deontological in analysis. The Guru Granth Sahib urges Sikhs not only to seek reconciliation but actively to correct what undermines peace and harmony, across and between nations. "A true warrior is one who fights for the downtrodden, the weak and the meek.[42] Seeking justice is a permanent duty

---

[42] Bhagat Kabir, Guru Granth Sahib.

not just defence under fire of war. As a *dharmic faith* Sikhism recognizes the limits of war and generally promotes peace and reconciliation so the duty to use force to correct injustice is similar to just war theory.

The Sikh view that where there is injustice there is no peace is reflected in other worldviews. Christian and Jewish ethics point to passages from the prophets like 'let justice roll down like waters'[43] to indicate that true peace is not simply the absence of war. *Shalom* in Judaism comes from God and that will only be fully realized when there is justice and harmony not just between peoples, but within individual communities. In Islam *jihad* can also mean combatting injustices of ignorance and poverty and justifies intervention to defend the oppressed. The Hindu story of Arjuna goes further. As in Sikhism unjust breach of the natural order raises duties to re-establish right order. In Hinduism the duty, placed on the Kshatriyas warrior class applies even if that means taking up arms against ones own relatives and friends. Arjuna is told by Krishna that his *dharma* or divine mandate to protect the greater good prevails even over personal considerations.[44] Despite texts suggesting pacifism Christianity also includes texts stating that in the cause of the Gospel Christians should be prepared for conflict even with family members.[45]

A utilitarian position that killing may be justified to end war does not necessarily make such a course theologically right. For Dietrich Bonhoeffer, involved in planning Hitler's assassination, taking life was clearly contrary to the commandment forbidding killing. Bonhoeffer believed that assassination was the right course to rid Europe of Hitler and end the 1939–1945 War. He nonetheless recognized that assassination breached the sacred protection of life and that he would have to account for the decision before his maker, taking the risk of eternal damnation if wrong. This contrasts with the

---

[43] Amos 5.

[44] Werner Menski. Hinduism. In *Ethical Issues in Six Religious Traditions*. Edinburgh University Press, 2007 at p. 48; Lipner J., op. cit., pp. 159–160 (Menski 2007).

[45] Luke 12:53; Matthew 10:35.

absolutist, unreflective utilitarian defence of assassination by *jihadists* and anti-abortionists considered earlier.

Yet theological support for what is effectively utilitarianism in just war is not the only religious perspective on war. Most traditions include alternative groups arguing for pacifism not just peace. Ghandi's interpretation of *ahimsa* (non-violence) as peaceful resistance to oppression, Christian doctrines of turning the other cheek and Buddhist absolutism over *ahimsa*[46] are examples of theological non-violence counter-cultural to the utilitarian just war position. Other theologians, as some secularists, acknowledge reluctantly that some just force may be needed to establish peace but reject its extrapolation to justify nuclear deterrence, in the case of modern weaponry and warfare.[47]

The Common Good

The essence of Just War theory is that good order and justice requires some form of government with powers in the last resort to ensure the common acceptance of that order. The Noahide commandment to establish courts and justice in the land is an early example of this ethical principle in the interests of a greater good. More systematically developed ethics of the common good and communal justice are found in traditions whose context required public ethics for governance not just personal or communal ethics for minority communities. The Holy Roman Empire in Christianity and the Ottoman Empire in Islam are cases in point. As with any governance compromises of strict or deontological principle for the greater good are necessitated by the realities of ruling for a whole community. Smaller minority communities, such as the Jewish or Sikh diaspora, may have been able to adhere more closely to strict religious principle simply because they had only themselves not an empire to order. Yet minorities forced to live under occupation or pogrom also had to find pragmatic compromises.

---

[46] Fasching, Delchant and Lantigua, op. cit.

[47] Hauerwas S. *The Peaceable Kingdom: A Primer in Christian Ethics.* SCM Press, 2009 (Hauerwas 2009). Biggar, N. *In defence of war.* Oxford University Press, 2013 (Biggar 2013).

Where utilitarian analyses and governance for the greater common good fall down is in the vindication of minority rights. If a minority can be accommodated within the global greater good, without prejudicing the wellbeing of the whole, utilitarian calculus is willing to preserve that minority. In this respect the diversity of goods that is possible in utilitarian liberalism is an ethical positive. Yet where minorities are seen as undermining the whole, utilitarianism also justifies imposing what is seen as a greater homogenous good. Thus Aquinas would impose the death penalty for criminals who undermine law, just war would sacrifice innocents if it will end the war earlier and utilitarian calculus would sacrifice minorities for the welfare of the majority. It is this tendency that has led to the totalitarian disasters of Stalinism and Nazism and underlies contemporary restrictions of religious dress in France and Turkey in the interests of homogeneity. Such totalitarianism is not just a secular phenomenon; the same utilitarian tendency was seen in religious history, for example the suppression of Jewish and Muslim minorities in 15th CE Catholic Spain. It also underlies Aquinas' view, contrary to current Roman Catholic teaching, that capital punishment to rid society of criminal elements is justified in the interests of the Common Good.

The theology of holiness, or openness to other ways of being, seen in the pluralism of *dharmic* faiths or the 'live and let live' *millet* courts of the Ottoman Empire are possible correctives to this tendency. So too are theologies of peace with justice, rather than peace as the absence of war through imposition of a homogenous concept of pleasure. Further questions that now challenge utilitarianism and indeed all contemporary ethics include what is the unit within which to calculate the greatest good in a global society and religious communities that are often international? Who, when seeking to live out the Golden Rule, promote justice and tackle global poverty, migration and peace keeping, is my neighbour? Much enlightenment thinking assumed a strong and self-contained state; contemporary utilitarianism, like contemporary theological ethics and religious communities, have to consider global neighbours. Thus the involvement of many Christians in opposing apartheid South Africa, of Muslim solidarity with Palestine and of many faiths' commitment to tackling worldwide poverty, debt and refugee crises.

Such analyses might seem alien to the utilitarianism of Bentham and the protection of property, land and peace between Hobbesian nations. Yet modern utilitarianism, exemplified by the global ethics of Peter Singer[48] or Heather Widdows[49] amongst others, takes a worldwide perspective and holds strongly that our neighbours are found across the world. On issues of tackling poverty, environmental degradation, war and political or market oppression, some religious ethics and a socialist utilitarianism may not be so far apart. They would find much in common in relation to feeding the stranger, tackling poverty and seeking international justice. Those at the more libertarian end of both the utilitarian and theological spectrum, such as Michael Novak[50] might disagree with these interpretations. Such disagreement tends to confirm that politics, economics and ideology are more accurate measures of division in today's world than religion.

Divisions along political and socio-economic, rather than religious versus secularist lines, can also be seen domestically in relation to the welfare state. Contrary to the Benthamite and Marxist critique of religion as ignoring poverty for 'pie in the sky' when you die, religious groups provided healthcare, welfare and education for centuries before the welfare state, drawing on millennia of Biblical authority about providing for those in need, particularly widows, orphans, the ill and the alien. Recognizing the limitations of such charitable provision Archbishop William Temple[51] invoked theology to support the welfare state, possibly also coining the phrase. Concepts of the welfare state also owe something to the theology of the early church in Acts as an example of from each according to means, to each according to need. Similar theologies are found in all major faiths. Jewish scriptures are the precursors of Christian theology on poverty;

---

[48] Singer P. Famine, Affluence and Morality. *Philosophy and Public Affairs* 1, 3 (Spring 1972), pp. 229–243 (Singer 1972).

[49] Widdows argues for a 'global public goods' rather than rights-based analysis which is essentially utilitarian ie dealing with migration and treating refugees reduces global health risks. Widdows H. & Marway H. *A Global Public Goods Approach to the Health of Migrants.* Public Health Ethics, 2015, pp. 1–9 (Widdows and Marway 2015).

[50] op. cit.

[51] Temple W. *Christianity and the Social Order.* Shepeard-Walwyn Publishers, 1984 (Temple 1984).

Islamic *zakat, langar* in Sikhism and alms-giving in the *dharmic* faiths all testify to this worldly imperative of religious social concern. In that the safety net of the welfare state seeks to share goods and maximize human freedom through reducing poverty, 'want', sickness and unemployment, it is utilitarian in the best sense of the word. Faith-based contributions have continued to support and defend welfare principles, for example in the 1980's *Faith in the City* report and the Catholic church's social theology of the Common Good.

Alongside theologies tackling poverty by giving and sharing all religions include teachings on wealth and its use, again emphasizing the common good. This is supported by recognition in all faiths that wealth does not wholly belong to us but that all we have comes from God or fortune as much as our own efforts. Theologies of detachment and awareness of the eternal also reduce the risks of absolutizing material wealth. Judaism, Islam, Hinduism and Sikhism have no difficulty with business success provided that greed, possessiveness and exploitation are avoided. The injunction to share is a positive holistic gift, not deprivation. Bentham's critique of Christian poverty as virtuous, even where unchosen, is legitimate but ignores the call to relieve unjust poverty and the balancing choice of renunciation implied in the hard saying that it is impossible for the rich to get to heaven. The value of theological teachings on wealth is that they do not elevate the material or capital to an absolute; observation of Sabbath and holy days, time for worship, community, study and family, value goods and life other than wealth. Natural law traditions of justice as the mean also temper risks of excess, unquestioning acquisition and pleasure seeking. Thus religious teachings have much to offer as correctives to the risks of homogenizing materialist market utilitarianism and much in common with utilitarian visions that seek to tackle poverty through the common good.

Conclusions

As can be seen from the discussion of just war, use of force to establish peace and relief of poverty utilitarian calculus in the interests of the common or greater good was not new when Bentham and Mills began their ethical exploration in the nineteenth century CE. Aspects of utilitarian calculus are seen in Greek ethics, branches of natural law and scripture, particularly when dealing with larger scale and communal decisions. Yet to be compatible with theological perspectives pleasure versus harm is better substituted by deeper concepts good versus evil, fuller and not simply material understandings of human wellbeing and flourishing.

Theological insights and ethical codes can add moderating correctives to the more crude forms of liberal materialistic utilitarianism based on attitudes to wealth, abstinence and the relativizing of the material. Where theology must continue to part company with utilitarianism is in recognizing that human beings do not have total control or autonomy over their lives, cannot wholly determine the creation of life or the natural incidence of sickness, health and death. The recognition in religious communities of relationship, human inter-dependence and fallibility also highlights the limitations of human autonomy.

Human finitude, self-serving delusion and fragility mean that we cannot always assess the best thing for ourselves or for others. Totalizing human visions without a sense of openness to the other, to the transcendent or to the hereafter seem always to have failed because of this human tendency to self-destruction or sin. To date neither political visions of left or right, the power of trickle down from the market, the research of material science nor human-led religious communities have managed to deliver the utilitarian dream of perfect universal peace or happiness. Nor can utilitarian rules alone develop an agreed rational or universal definition of harm or good. Therefore whilst there are more overlaps with theological ethics than Bentham might have conceived there are still differences to be negotiated and neither perspective has completely satisfactory answers.

5

By Whose Authority? What Gives Ethics Their Power?

The interplay of secular and theological reasoning in natural law and utilitarian theories suggests that it is foundational premises and worldviews that affect ethical conclusions rather than the presence or absence of reasoning. One significant factor in those differing premises and worldviews is the authority behind them. This chapter considers the various forms of authority that ground premises and worldviews underlying secular and theological ethics. Nick Adams suggests that reasoning in relation to theology is strange not because of the reasoning but because the knowledge is 'strange' as God is so 'unlike anything at all' and therefore unknowable.[1] Yet the situation is more complex than the experience versus strangeness that Adams suggests as some people do claim experiences of God in prayer, in apprehension of creation or events of life and in scripture. However, Adams' comment highlights the fact that epistemic authority in theological ethics is more contested than any other form of knowledge and is at the core of tensions between theological and non-theological ethics.

---

[1] Adams N. Confessing the Faith: Reasoning in Tradition, pp. 209–221 In *The Blackwell Companion to Christian Ethics,* Eds. Hauerwas S & Wells S. Oxford: Blackwell Publishing, 2004 at pp. 212–213 (Adams 2004).

© The Author(s) 2017
C. Shelley, *Ethical Exploration in a Multifaith Society,*
DOI 10.1007/978-3-319-46711-5_5

Authority encompasses epistemic authority, the knowledge base and source texts or premises from which reasoning proceeds and procedural authority, which lies in the juridical or constitutional framework that determines what or who is authoritative. In many instances it can be difficult to disentangle the epistemic authority arising from interpretation of a text or tradition from the process and person of the interpreting authority. In a multicultural, multifaith society the sources of authority and consequently ethical assumptions that people live by are inevitably diverse, a diversity expanded by the progress of the global village. Yet as the examples given in earlier chapters indicate there are some ethical commonalities in terms of traditions' assumptions, conclusions and ethical paradigms.

The development of theological and religious ethical thought is influenced by the society around it but traditions or parts of traditions respond to those influences differently. The exploration of authority within particular religious traditions can highlight their distinct character and complexity but also potentially enable a transcendence of differences on the basis of better understanding. This is significant for relationships both between and within communities, the resolution of communities' internal differences and for anyone charged with making strategic or professional decisions in a multicultural context.

Authority has both internal and external dimensions. The internal forum for authority is the concept of conscience, which is informed by personal and social experience, intuition, preference, emotions and commitments in caring and other relationships. The internal forum is also identified in western enlightenment terms with the space for spiritual experience. Living according to conscience may be equated with personal autonomy but the two are not necessarily the same. Conscience is inevitably informed and shaped by communal as well as personal influences, relationships perceived by some secularists as being particularly problematic in religious belief and practice. In a society that at least in theory, values personal autonomy it is appropriate to explore the interplay of conscience and autonomy and the weighting of individual versus communal conscience in interpreting ethics and faith.

External authority comes in a variety of guises. The ethical authority of law is a significant external forum in British society generally and within several religious traditions. Yet law and its relationship to ethics varies widely. Law and ethics are therefore evaluated as applied in both secular and religious paradigms. The relationship between secular or state law and the religious laws and legal fora of specific communities is also examined by assessing their accommodation in English law. The role of communal authority, through law and otherwise, is also considered, for example as mediated through religious and community leaders, communal decision-making processes and less formal or transparent channels. Authority, particularly as exercised at communal level, also raises issues of power. These are illustrated through considering ethical issues in relation to power, gender and minorities, analysing how these issues are acknowledged or addressed in various ethical paradigms and worldviews. One dimension of this exploration is the concept of idealized ethical stances and community identity,[2] paradigms by which religious communities idealize the upholding of their values by contrast with wider society. The reality is often that each community is closer to the other than they think. As previous chapters also illustrate, the challenges of juggling differing sources of authority and allegiances in a multicultural society are not new; they are perennial and vary with the role, status and power of particular groups in relation to wider society. This requires consideration of theological and practical ways in which religious authority is negotiated alongside 'alien' authorities and traditions, be they secular or from other religious faiths.

Another important authority for theological ethics is religious scripture, which includes not only the written text but the oral traditions that preceded the writing and continue to be used in exposition and interpretation. Yet scriptures and their interpretive sciences are so significant that they warrant a separate chapter. Accordingly the sixth chapter will consider scripture as a source of ethical authority both for religious traditions and more widely in cultural contexts. The challenges of scriptural authority are to a degree intertwined with the authority of leaders and others entitled to interpret scripture, both posing challenges for contemporary society. However, the detail of scriptural authority

---

[2] Roald AS. *Women in Islam: The Western Experience.* Malmo: Routledge2001 (Roald 2001).

merits separate treatment so this chapter focuses on the sources of authority by which scripture and tradition are mediated, interpreted and norms formed.

Defining Authority

Before thinking specifically about religious authority the subject of authority in general is considered; authority is as diverse in its operation and interpretation as its sources. Definitions use words like: *power – jurisdiction – command – mastery – dominance or dominion – rule – sovereignty – influence – leverage* which in practice means that authority, in any sphere, can include:

(i) The power or right to give orders,
(ii) The power to make the decisions underlying those orders
(iii) The power to enforce decisions and obedience
(iv) Authority as the right to act in particular ways, for example to make an arrest or carry a gun
(v) Charismatic or inspirational authority arising from influence of character rather than organizational authority given by a role
(vi) Authority earned through example and respect
(vii) Representative or delegated authority
(viii) An institution representing 'the authorities'

Whether given through status, role, earned, assumed by charisma or empty, in the case of an ineffective authority, authority can be exercised in enabling or oppressive ways, directly or on a representative or dele-gated basis. Whilst some forms of authority have legal or contractual force others are exercised on a more voluntary basis in which people allow an authority to have power over them. The latter includes for example peer group, work and community cultures. Whether con-sciously or not, all human beings are subject in greater or lesser degree to some forms of authority, simply by living as members of a society, even a society such as contemporary Britain which is reputedly less tolerant of authority and more autonomously focused. Examples are myriad from the police, legal system and law-makers, bosses at work, teachers at school, parental and familial influences, peers, as well as religious authorities for some.

An understanding of authority is important in ethics because of its impact on worldviews, premises and the degree of autonomy to heteronomy in ethical discernment, from daily life to more long-term decisions. It is also significant because it is generally associated with power, whether over people's lives at work or home, power over decisions and conduct, for leaders in corporate settings power over resources and often power over societal perceptions. How theology and religious authorities affect individuals within communities, the communities themselves and individuals from those communities in wider society, has also raised concerns about the interplay of religion and authority over the years. Legal constraints on religious authority include preventing abuse of position by public officers and personal undue influence in preparing a will. Broadcasting regulations, limits on confessional faith in education and healthcare and statutes against 'undue spiritual influence' in elections[3] all constrain exercises of religious authority in public life. Theological authority is seen as having a power beyond other influences because deriving representative or delegated authority from the divine, with implications for ethics and salvation, is perceived as more powerful or open to abuse than secular authority.

Authoritarian Religious Vocabulary?

Ways in which authority is exercised vary from top-down, mandatory forms seen in the operation of law, to authority in the sense of being able to demand accountability. Authority in religious circles tends to be perceived as the top-down model but also contains much that is mediated via the believer's own prayer and conscience. The original Jewish word for obedience is heard in the prayer known as '*the Shema*', 'Hear O Israel, the Lord your God is one God...'[4] The Hebrew *Shema* became '*ob audire*', 'listen to' in the Latin Bible, the

---

[3] In the 1883 Corrupt & Illegal Practices Act, now s.115, 1983. Representation of the People Act.
[4] וְשָׁמַעְתָּ יִשְׂרָאֵל יְהוָה, אֱלֹהֵינוּ יְהוָה.אֶחָד

Vulgate, and then 'obedience' in English. Thus obedience to God's authority is not a servile jumping to order but rather about listening and discerning, a discernment that is relevant to leaders in their exercise of authority but also to all believers in following their faith.

In the New Testament a more top-down, imperative authority begins to be used alongside obedience; 'ob audiere' becomes 'auctoritas', particularly in the letters of St Paul. By a similar process the word *mitzvot*, which in Judaism means rules for living in harmony with God and neighbour, takes on the more imperative tone of 'commandment' in the Christian tradition. The Jewish sense of *mitzvot* as rules for harmonious life with God reflects a similar sense to observing the *vedas* in Hinduism and Buddhism. Additionally, the authority of practice and observance in Judaism and the *dharmic* faiths is more important than the authority of credal belief that obtains particularly in Protestant Christianity. Yet for both Judaism and Christianity the authority of commandments and listening to God is set in the context of love, for God and neighbour. Any exercise of 'authority over' should be a liberating, God-ward request, mindful of the fact that the person leading and the person led are neighbours bound to love God and each other. The word 'Islam' also conjures up unhelpfully top-down authoritarian images of God and leadership, as Islam means 'submission'. Yet, as in all the monotheistic faiths, the believer consents, through voluntary submission, to follow God.

The reality is that for everyone, not just those in faith communities, there are elements of submission to external authorities, the force of law generally being the most objective and non-negotiable. Reflection on authority can help evaluate which aspects of decision-making and moral impact are given most power, both personally and within society or communities more generically. It is in the interplay of factors involved in ethics and decision-making, both as particular moral quandaries and patterns of virtue, that tensions for individuals and communities can arise, particularly between secular or religious authority. Most people are influenced by more than one form or source of authority so this interplay and tension is not limited to those from faith communities. Yet issues of authority and who exercises it are particularly important when thinking about theological ethics because of the sense and power of the divine. The contested nature of God, and those who mediate the divine means that religious authority matters not only to religious communities but also to their engagement in wider societal debates, as noted above.

Yet personal conscience, informed by experience in all areas of life as well as by religious teaching, remains important within faith. The requirement of personal assent to faith and its practice places emphasis on the role of conscientious discernment to inform right personal practice. In turn the authority of conscience draws on reason, intuitive and emotional influences and the power of experience as mediated in prayer. Beliefs about the consequences of actions include immediate reward or punishment as well as longer-term concepts of salvation, eternal life, heaven, reincarnation and release by *nirvana or moksha*. Conscience in some religious communities may be exercised more heteronomously, in the sense of attention to community views, than some secular contexts yet religous faith also assumes personal responsibility for decisions.

Assumptions and Habits

The assumption of western society, education, philosophy and western or natural law religious traditions, is that in making rational conscience-based decisions, human beings have and exercise their agency according to free will. Even in those traditions that do not follow or actively reject natural law the concepts of judgement and consequences for life beyond death, which are found in all major religious traditions' meta-ethical frameworks, require the personal responsibility for action that is implicit in free will. In reality the weighing of factors and options, authorities and ethical rules involved in decision-making is shaped not only by freely-willed reason but also by the habituated assumptions that generate feelings and intuitions about particular issues and ways of life. In addition, there is that aspect of being human that knows what the rational or right thing to do might be but continues, following old unhelpful patterns, to make the wrong choice and do the unhealthy or unethical thing. St Paul was acutely aware of this dimension of humanity when he wrote 'I do not understand my own actions. For I do not do what I want, but I do the very thing I hate. . . . I do not do the good I want, but the evil

I do not want...'[5] Problems with free will were recognized at a metaphysical level by Hume[6] and are substantiated by sociological theorists like Bordieu whose theory of *habitus* recognizes that early experience, upbringing and formation lay down more deterministic elements in decision-making.[7] Habituation, alongside elements of free will, is assumed by the theory of habituated action and character in virtue ethics. The reality is that history, upbringing and culture determine free will and choice to significant degrees, casting utilitarian and Enlightenment ideals of wholly rational, blank-slate choice in an unrealistic light. However, habituation, history and various external forms of authority do not wholly displace individual responsibility in making decisions both day to day and in the larger vocational and familial decisions that face everyone.

The complexities of free will, conscience and individualism versus external or heterogenous authority become more significant in a multicultural and multifaith society with communities who express scepticism about secular assumptions of individualism and autonomy. For many faith communities discarding the wisdom of religious leaders and community elders is folly. Ignoring God is not possible and acting with disregard for relationships and communal values or expectations is also seen as unwise. In such communities the ethical stance and worldviews surrounding authority are both more communal and theologically focused than western assumptions. The reality is more mixed but the assumption of self-reliant autonomy is not universal as a model for ethical authority. In practice nor is it wholly the reality for most societies; the opposition of heteronomous religion to autonomous western reason is an example of idealization. Many peoples' consciences in secular society are influenced by heteronomous factors such as advertising and peer group culture, which are just as powerful as religious

[5] Romans 7: 15–20.

[6] Analyses of Hume's on necessity and freedom see:
https://plato.stanford.edu/entries/hume-freewill/; Botterill G. *Hume on Liberty and Necessity.* http://www.philosophy.dept.shef.ac.uk/papers/Botterill2002.pdf.

[7] Swartz DL. *The sociology of Habit: The perspective of Pierre Bordieu.* http://www.bu.edu/av/core/swartz/sociology-of-habit.pdf.

authority, although more diffuse and taken for granted. An interesting example is coca cola, a brand with global reach. Some young westerners may be forbidden by parents from drinking it because of its impact on dental and dietary health. Within the Jewish community the Beth Din had to rule on whether Coke was kosher before Jews could drink it. However, the influence of coca cola's global advertising affects all communities.

What Is Distinctive about Theological Authority?

Theological ethics derives its distinctive foundations and purpose from religious revelation in various forms including personal and communal prayer and worship, religious texts and law, customs, narrative traditions and ritual. These authorities are mediated via the religious community exercising authority in various ways, most obviously through religious leaders who have traditionally held significant authority. The scope and function of leadership varies within and between traditions; the role and authority of Roman Catholic priests differs from most priests in the Anglican Communion and is different again from priests in the Hindu tradition. In Judaism, Islam and Protestant Christianity the authority of law or scripture outweighs human authority, although human interpretive agency of leaders or scholars is required.

Religious Leadership

Religious leaders have been castigated by secular theorists as problematic and accused of holding 'the faithful' in subjection undermining personal autonomy.[8] Yet the profile and operation of religious leadership is a

---

[8] Allegations of 'undue spiritual influence' recently resurfaced in the trial of Lutfur Rahman for electoral fraud although exhortations over decades by the Roman Catholic church to vote for anti-abortion candidates and the Hindu Council to oppose legislation on caste by voting Conservative at the 2015 General Election went unnoticed. See Giles Fraser. http://www.theguardian.com/commentisfree/2015/apr/29/lutfur-rahman-tower-hamlets-mayor-verdict-undue-spiritual-influence; http://www.lawandreligionuk.com/2015/05/04/spiritual-influence-and-the-law/;

complex and variable phenomenon. A recent survey[9] suggests that even amongst members of faith communities respect for the views of religious leaders is on the wane, replaced by aspects of faith that favour personal conscience. Having said which, most religious communities still have leadership structures and set some store by their leadership. In addition, wider society continues to call on religious leaders to contribute to enquiries and comment in the media. Accordingly reflection on the nature of religious authority mediated through leadership remains relevant. Religious leadership varies depending on where authority is grounded and how leadership is exercised; the anti-nomian charismatic leader is radically different from the scholarly interpreter, the shepherding pastor and the holy inspiration. The following illustrative rather than exhaustive analysis considers leadership styles and the basis of their authority, providing some insight into the ways in which religious leaders affect both their own communities and in some cases wider society.

Professional Religious Leaders

Leaders with a full-time paid professional roles, as found in the Church of England have, because of its established place in national life, tended to set up certain expectations of religious leaders. For example the Muslim community has taken the route of professionalization in developing courses on Muslim chaplaincy. Historically the parish priest has been a local leader, living in their parish community with the Bishop as regional religious superior. They are professional in the sense both of professing a vocation or calling, and exercising significant autonomy in that calling. They exercise formal authority on behalf of the Church in trusted community roles; vicars with their churchwardens have not only been trustees of Church property, but also many foundation Church schools and parish charities. By the law of the land vicars are expected to be available for baptisms, weddings and funerals for all living in their

---

[9] Woodhead L. *Religious leaders don't represent religious people – 20 August 2013.* http://www.publicspirit.org.uk/religious-leaders-dont-represent-religious-people/.

'patch'. In response to other providers of welfare and educational services the Church has increased professionalization in training, through placements, competencies, job descriptions and CPD, with less 'pure' theology in the curriculum. The aim is an authority based in study and professional credibility in the wider secular sphere as well as for the faithful in Church.

Roman Catholic priesthood shares features of professional authority with Anglican clergy but with double the theological and philosophical training. The vow of celibacy adds the authority of someone set apart by a distinct commitment. However, Catholic priestly celibacy can undermine authority through perceived removal from everyday relationships,[10] by contrast with the Hindu *sant* who raises a family before renouncing the world for contemplation. Within their Church Roman Catholic clergy constitutionally have greater authority than their Anglican counterparts; Roman Catholic priests make decisions alone, whereas Church of England clergy share responsibility with lay Church Wardens and Parochial Church Councils.

Scholarly, Holy or Wise Leaders

By contrast with the professional leader oriented to the society outside their religious community the scholarly leader is oriented primarily towards the faithful. The authority of the Jewish rabbi comes from their deep study of Torah and Talmud and their application in practice. Most religious leadership involves teaching authority but the Rabbi is teacher before anything else although some also have legal authority in the Beth Din.

All religious leaders are also supposed to be holy but the specifically holy leader is the contemplative guru to whom people turn for wisdom based in prayer, lifestyle and experience rather than scholarship. A classic example is the Buddha but monks, anchorites and Hindu *sants* are also examples of such authority. This authority is generally exercised individually; the seeker finds help from their guru or spiritual director in a private voluntary arrangement. However,

---

[10] And more recently through child abuse scandals.

the spiritual director can exercise significant influence over their direc-tee. A good director is aware of this and sees the role as enabling rather than directional; the less aware are a concern.

The forms of leadership above carry some credibility in wider society as authority is based on reason, training, experience and practical man-agement. The following leadership styles are more likely to be limited to the religious community; their grounding in revelatory experience, ritual and inheritance, rather than reason and training is less accessible to non-religious audiences.

Ritual Expertise

Aspects of religious leadership that are primarily concerned with ritual and chants such as found in *dharmic* faiths, are generally seen as having authority only for particular religious communities. Such authority requires an understanding of the premises of the faith and worship and the transcendent focus of worship may be seen, even by members of faith communities, as having little to do with ethics. Yet for Hindus rituals with cosmic ethical implications are of the essence of Vedic observance.[11] Recent developments in Christian theology, inspired by virtue ethics, echo the view that worship and ritual are essential to ethics through forming the faithful in virtuous habits and values.[12] Although ritual priestly leadership carries little authority outside the faith, where the rituals performed are not understood, it can carry significant weight within faith communities, for whom exclusion from worship constitutes a major penalty. For those, like Hauerwas, who base theology in the virtue ethics of Alistair MacIntyre, a lack of weight in wider society is irrelevant, the key thing is to be true to revelation and the charism and ethics of the tradition.[13]

---

[11] Lubin T. et al., op. cit., pp. 191–192.

[12] See e.g. Hauerwas S & Wells S. *Blackwell Companion to Christian Ethics*. Oxford University Publishing, 2010.

[13] Hauerwas S. *A Community of Character*. Notre Dame University Press, 1982.

Charismatic Leaders

Religious leaders whose authority derives primarily from charisma are best contrasted with those selected, trained and ordained through top down organizational process. Many appointed under formal, professional routes are charismatic and annointed at ordination; yet whilst charisma enhances their leadership it is not the exclusive basis of appointment. Charismatically appointed leaders draw their authority from a sense of special access or anointing by God. Examples include Pentecostal churches whose leaders are appointed by the acclamation of followers as blessed by God with holy gifts of prophecy, tongues and healing. In practice spiritual charisma is generally accompanied by personal charisma and psychological influence alongside divine endorsement. Such extrovert leadership often generates a group psychological power that supports the authority of the charismatic leader. Charismatic authority is associated with charismatic Christian movements but is also found in other traditions. For example Gokkai Buddhism draws on the charisma of contemporary leadership and its historic monastic founder, Nichiren.[14]

The Hereditary or Anointed Leader

Some traditions include an anointed or hereditary priestly or leadership class like the Jewish levitical priesthood and the Hindu Brahmin caste. The Tibetan Buddhist election of a child as the Dalai Lama provides another example of hereditary, anointed leadership. This approach seems most at odds with modern, secular understandings of equality. Yet paradoxically the Dalai Lama commands significant respect as a world religious leader and Queen Elizabeth, Governor of the Church of England and head of state, is respected for her faith-based service.

---

[14] John Woolf (Ed.). *Global Religious Movements in Regional Context.* Ashgate, 2002. p. 45 & pp. 109–156 (John 2002).

Lay Leadership

In addition to specific leaders many faith communities operate collectively through the church or the Muslim *Ummah*; some operate judicially through courts such as the *Beth Din, Shari'a courts or Canon Law*. The interaction of individual and collective leadership can be complex. For example, in Christian episcopal traditions leadership, for temporal and spiritual matters, ultimately lies with the priesthood of Bishops, the overseers. In the Anglican Church this is tempered by lay and ordained joint responsibility in the Parochial Church Council and Synods; however ultimately Bishops can override synodical processes. In other traditions whilst the rabbi, imam or Hindu priest is called upon as the religious spokesperson, management of Mosques, Synagogues and Temples is vested in lay management committees, which also carry significant authority. Legal interpretive authority in Judaism lies with the rabbis who are members of the Beth Din but in Islam legal scholars (*alim*) do not need to be imams. This mix of authority places de facto and de iure restraints on those with spiritual authority but lay leaders can be cowed by powerful religious leaders and vice versa. The balance of power is also influenced by the authority to appoint leaders, which may be top down, for example from the Bishop, or, bottom up from the community or congregation itself. Conflicts arise where the two forms of authority fail to collaborate.

Although analysed distinctly, styles of religious leadership overlap and are inevitably influenced by personal characteristics and interpersonal dynamics, as well as the framework of the religious body in which the authority is held. Leadership is also exercised through different functions; a Christian minister is likely to carry authority through preaching, personal pastoral encounters and strategic as well as spiritual leadership of the community. By contrast an imam traditionally only exercises the ministry of preaching and leading prayers although more pastoral duties have arisen in some communities influenced by Christian pastoral ministry. Authority exercised in one context may also vary from another; a strong ethical line stated in a sermon or public statement may be moderated or nuanced in the exercise of pastoral ministry and application to the dilemmas and heartaches of a specific member of the community. Similarly good spiritual direction is tailored to the character of the person seeking guidance.

The problem for the societal perception of theological ethics and religious authority is that the public statements are those that come to public attention. This can give a distorted picture of the clarity, force or cohesiveness of theological ethics on particular issues and thus of the force of religious authority. It is a fair comment that within the faith community the symbolism and charisma of religious leadership may carry more force than leadership in the secular sphere because of belief in the divine origins of such authority. Yet religious symbolism and authority can also still carry weight in wider society thanks to mass media whose presentation relies on traditional symbols and assumptions. Yet such presentations fail to recognize the complexity and variety within and across religious communities and the nuanced and highly skilled ways in which religious authority is exercised in practice in most cases.

Historical Leaders

The authority of contemporary religious leaders also draws on and interprets historical religious leaders, including the original founding figures – all fathers – for example Jesus, Mohammed and Buddha and later interpreters of religious tradition. Historical figures take on authoritative ethical stature either during their own lifetime, like Ghandi or Martin Luther, or their full authority becomes canonical after their death. Examples of the latter who have shaped traditions, texts and ethics, include St Paul, Augustine, Al Gazali, Maimonides, Sankara and Manu. The vast majority of such foundational figures and authoritative leaders are male. Whilst there are female saints in Catholic tradition and amongst the Hindu pantheon they tend to be secondary to the men. Insofar as they are authoritative women tend to be role models for particular understandings of good female behaviour, for example the Catholic saints who sacrifice life in holding onto virginity. Within Judaism there are no foundational figures other than God, who though above gender, is nonetheless typically referred to as Father.

Authority, Ethics and Gender

The power and authority of religious leaders lies in their purported superior knowledge of the religious tradition, their authority to interpret it and their holy, ethical example. This authority shapes the faith community, what constitutes orthodox belief and in some cases who is deemed in or out of the community. Yet even the holiest and wisest of religious leaders is limited by their background and experience as are even the founding fathers of religious traditions; Jesus challenged by a Syro-Phoenician woman reacts, at least initially, in a highly defensive even rude way.[15] Whilst making significant sacrifices of wealth and expectation Buddha's example will always be limited by the fact that he had such a background to renounce.[16] Ethics around gender and sexuality provide a good illustration of this dynamic. The fact that most religious leaders are male, even in contemporary society, means that religion has been skewed by patriarchal and male-oriented assumptions. This is compounded by the fact that most foundational and historical religious leaders are also male and male terms are generally used for the monotheistic God.[17] Even *dharmic* faiths, which do not have such explicit scriptural statements about gender, nonetheless tend to conservative gender roles, so that female Buddhists cannot become *Bodhisattva*

---

[15] Mark 7: 25–30 & Matthew 15: 21–28.

[16] Some suggest that this explains the appeal of the humbly born Nichiren, over Buddha as the founder of Nichiren Buddhism and the Soka Gokkai movement *Global Religious Movements in Regional Context.* op. cit. pp. 109–156.

[17] Themes explored in a range of feminist religious writing including, e.g. Welchman L & Hossain S. *Honour Crimes, Paradigms & Violence Against Women.* London: Zed Books, 2005 (Welchman and Hossain 2005); Soskice JM & Lipton D. *Feminism & Theology.* Oxford University Press, 2003 (Soskice and Lipton 2003); Roald AS. *Women in Islam: The Western Experience.* Malmo Sweden: IMER Routledge, 2001 (Roald 2001); Plaskow J. *Standing at Sinai: Judaism from a Feminist Perspective.* London: Harper One, 1991 (Plaskow 1991); Esposito J & De Long Bas N. *Women in Muslim Family Law.* Syracuse University Press, 2001 (Esposito and De Long Bas 2001); Awde N. *Women in Islam.* London: Bloom & Bennett, 2005 (Awde 2005); Badawi L. *Women in Religion.* Eds. Bowker J & Holm Continuum, London, 2000 (Badawi 2000); Pui Lan K. *Introducing Asian Feminist Theology.* Bloomsbury, 2000 (Pui Lan 2000); Radford Reuther R. *The Development of Feminist Theology: Becoming Increasingly Global and Interfaith* **Svenska kyrkans forskardagar, Uppsala 12 September 2011.** https://www.svenskakyrkan.se/default.aspx?id=863846.

and there are no female Hindu *sants*. Although not all women are called to be religious leaders the fact that men predominantly carry the authority and power to interpret and define religious ethics within and outside the faith community has led to what can be styled sexist interpretations in a number of respects.

Religion is by no means unique in its sexism; male theorists dominated secular philosophy until the later 20th CE and at least some religious 'mothering' of women derives from Greek dualism. In the UK women could not vote or care for their children following divorce until 1925. Western 'scientists' claimed that women had smaller brains and inferior intellectual capacity until well into the 19th CE. Yet in the past few decades, as society has changed and domestic law and international conventions have articulated women's rights, religion is portrayed as retaining comparatively conservative understandings of gender as complementary. The dynamics are complex but gender politics and ethical arguments about relationships, marriage and family remain a major arena for ethical disagreement in contemporary society across the world. The place of the Vatican and some Muslim states at the UN negotiating table, promoting what is often referred to as a conservative religious agenda, has helped to fuel disagreements and discredit religious voices. Legitimate concerns are raised about the influence of religious communities and male religious leaders in relation to women's role, early and forced marriage, FGM, lack of contraception and various other forms of violence by which women are abused, vulnerable and unable to their realize full potential.

In practice however, boardrooms, University Councils, the medical, political, legal and other professions still reveal male-dominated leadership in most sectors. Pay rates demonstrate that equality remains some way off and domestic violence happens in all sectors of society. The focus on religious communities and statements from male religious leaders that perpetuate a conservative ethical agenda are a useful diversion from critical questions about gender equality in secular society. However, the fact that secular society at least aspires to equality contrasts significantly with some religious communities that continue to promote an ethics of gender complementarity. As usual however, the picture is diverse. Many strands of theological ethics adopt a feminist ethical stance, often based on liberation theology, enabling a range of female voices to challenge male-dominated theological interpretation.[18]

At the other end of the spectrum however, there seems to be some evidence that as patriarchal structures have begun to change within wider society, in some religious communities there appears to be a conservative backlash. Examples include the rise of 'male headship' evangelical Christianity and women wearing the *niqab* rather than *hijab* in Islam. The causes of this actual or perceived backlash include the phenomenon of faith communities clinging for identity to countercultural ethical identities as much as ethical standards. This is the case for both diaspora faiths and some parts of the Christian community defending its identity against perceived decline. For many communities the burden of this countercultural identity falls on women as the exemplars of religious purity and idealized gender roles. For women themselves there can be strengths in identifying with these ideals and creating a clear role within that ethical framework, as mothers and home-makers, declaring their faith in their clothing. Yet locating religious counter-cultural identity in the ethics of private morality, gender and family arises from western or secular privatization of religion as much as religious communities' own norms. The process of privatizing religion began at least as long ago as the private law courts of colonial India. In imposing its own understanding of Hindu personal law on the Indic population[19] British colonial rule distorted the community's own laws and reinforced the power of the community leaders in that sphere of life. The phenomenon has been reiterated in various forms over the decades, whether formally or informally and remains a factor in contemporary religious identity, ethics and politics.

---

[18] e.g. Alehossain A. *Islamic Liberation: Theology for Women.* Grin Verlag GmbH, 2014 (Alehossain 2014); Radford Reuther. *Liberation Theology: Human Hope Confronts Christian History and American Power* (1972) (Radford Reuther 1972); *New Woman/New Earth: Sexist Ideologies and Human Liberation* Harper Collins, 1989 (Radford Reuther 1989); Bianchi & Reuther. *From Machismo to Mutuality: Essays on Sexism and Woman-Man Liberation* (1976) (Bianchi and Reuther 1976). *Religion and Sexism: Images of Women in the Jewish and Christian Traditions.* Simon & Schuster 1974.

[19] Lubin T, Davies DR & Jayanth KK. *Hinduism and Law An Introduction.* Cambridge University Press, 2010. pp. 1–16 (Lubin et al. 2010); Rocher R. *Creation of Anglo-Hindu Law.* Lubin et al., op. cit. pp. 78–88.

Grace Davie suggests that the countercultural ethics of religious communities actually acts as a reactive surrogate for unease with ethical changes over gender and sexuality in wider society.[20]

Where such roles and ethical norms are accepted voluntarily there is an argument for religious freedoms to be respected and protected. After all female members of Christian religious orders wore veils for many generations without controversy. Problems arise where roles and norms are adopted either because forced or for want of knowing about alternatives. The most vulnerable are women in communities where norms from male religious leaders are accepted and reinforced by family, school and the wider community. It is in the latter context that norms can be presented as non-negotiable rules revealed by the community leaders, with risks of forced marriage, FGM and other abusive practices that do not reflect religious teaching or any form of theological ethics. The lack of alternative viewpoint or of tools for ethical reflection contrary to community norms is problematic from the perspective of liberal freedom and human rights but may be justified by the faith community arguing that the leader's authority should be put before self. It is only if this assumption and dynamic is tackled on the basis of faith and theology's own tools that change can be enabled to happen. Yet the 2010 Equalities Acts further reinforces the power of religious leaders over their communities by providing exemptions from the Equalities Acts so that where it would be offensive to religion, gender equality in religious leadership is not required.

Female Authority: Alternatives to Patriarchy

Yet, as explored by various feminist theological ethicists, male religious leadership and the gender discrimination assumed by exemptions to the Equalities Acts are not inevitable interpretations of faith or theological ethics. There are Biblical texts that make gender distinctions and suggest that women should not speak in a Christian Church[21] or that women

---

[20] Davie G. *Religion in Britain Since 1954*. Sage, 1994.

[21] 1 Corinthians; see also Galatians 8, for a statement of equality. The letter to the Galatians carries more authenticity as Pauline than does 2 Corinthians the authorship of which is doubted.

must join their husband's family and submit to them post-marriage. However, there are also contradictory texts; the account of woman's creation from Adam's rib in Genesis 2 is at odds with the far more equal account 'male and female He created them' in Genesis 1. Throughout the Hebrew Bible female characters play a pivotal role in Israel's story; Judith who protects the nation by cutting off Holofernes' head,[22] Deborah the judge, Esther the Queen and so on. It is also clear that there were key women members in early Christian communities; Phoebe who held a deacon's role[23] and Lydia the dyer of cloth baptized, with her household, by Paul.[24] There are also historic female faith leaders outside scripture, two of the most striking examples being Mohammed's wives. Kadijah taught Mohamed all he knew about business and Ayisha was instrumental in keeping his legacy alive after his death, even reputedly on the battlefield.

Examples of female leadership are however in a minority and there are difficult or at least contradictory passages in scripture, about women's role in general and in specific issues. Some Qu'ranic passages can be interpreted to require absolute obedience from a wife, a husband's right to enforce obedience and even female circumcision.[25] Similarly Biblical passages set out requirements for wives to obey husbands, stay quiet in church and keep their hair covered. Both the Qu'ran and Biblical scriptures also contain arguments for punishing adulterers[26] and condemning homosexuality as 'abomination'.[27] Yet, as noted there are other contradictory texts and no credible Muslim authority defends the practice of FGM, nor does any Abrahamic faith use scripture to justify domestic violence. As society has developed, communities dispersed and found themselves

---

[22] Book of Judith NRSV Apocrypha.

[23] Romans 16: 1.

[24] Acts 16.

[25] For a detailed analysis see Roald AS. *Women in Islam.* op. cit., pp. 150–165; 237–253.

[26] Qu'ran 24:2; Deuteronomy 22:22.

[27] Leviticus 18: 22; Qu'ran Surah 7: 80–84.

in alien lands, theological ethics and scriptural interpretation have developed to re-evaluate the tradition in new times.[28]

Conservative interpretations of scripture and theological ethics about gender and family are not inevitable but culturally conditioned both from within faith communities and through wider society. This is highlighted by the fact that neither Hinduism or Buddhism nor the Sikh faith has passages similar to the Abrahamic texts that specify gender roles or condemn homosexuality. Nonetheless conservative ethics are found in all such communities around marriage, religious leadership and homosexuality, suggesting cultural as much as theological conditioning. The fact that negotiations about religious accommodation are conducted predominantly with male religious leaders, has led to religious exemptions from the Equalities Acts.[29] Whilst such exemptions are limited to religious leadership, the impact is to perpetuate conservative theological ethics affecting whole communities.

Leaders and Communities

The ways in which leaders influence their communities and the inter-relationship of religious, cultural and secular authority for members of faith communities and their ethics are also complex. In some instances there are clear mechanisms for ruling on the interpretation of ethics and religious law; examples include Islamic *fatwa, Shari'a* court decisions, rulings of the *Beth Din* in Judaism and Roman Catholic encyclicals and canon law. Whilst reservations are expressed from time to time about the role of religious, particularly *Shari'a* 'courts', research has found that they do have some transparency.[30] In many cases the relationship of power, leadership and ethical authority is less clear; charismatic leaders claiming personal access to God's authority are rarely subject to accountable processes. Yet even in more ordered religious communities

---

[28] The next chapter provides further analysis of scriptural interpretation.

[29] Equalities Act 2010 Schedule 23.

[30] Douglas G, Doe N, Gilliat-Ray S, Sandberg R & Khan Asma. *Social Cohesion and Civil Law: Marriage, Divorce and Religious Courts.* AHRC & Cardiff University.

charisma and communal culture can take on an authority despite the existence of more formal processes, principles and theologies. The powerful preacher, charismatic musician and inspirational mentor carry significant influence whatever community they come from.

It could be asked whether the authority and ethical influence of religious leaders is necessarily so different from secular figures. The power of celebrity role models, politicians, the media and advertising moguls carries significantly more influence than most religious leaders. The phenomenon of Jimmy Saville's abuse at the BBC and other institutions illustrates that abuse of charismatic authority and fear are not limited to religious communities that have failed to tackle child abuse. Ultimately however, religious authority depends on claims to divine and eternal sources of authority rather than simple celebrity, which gives an added dynamic to theological power. This is particularly the case where belief in divine authority mediated by anointed leaders makes it difficult to question or hold such leaders to account. Ideally divine authority and holiness should inspire to the highest standards of leadership and integrity; yet such leaders are not immune from the maxim that absolute power corrupts absolutely. These difficulties are compounded in communities that place a high value on unity, stigmatizing or demonizing those who ask questions. Generally the more counter-culturally isolated a community the more problematic this dynamic but demonization of individuals occurs in apparently mainstream religious communities.

Religious leaders and jurists, in ruling on particular cases, generally operate in an executive fashion even where there are more communal or democratic forms of decision-making authority. Yet the Christian theology of the church as Christ's body, inspired or animated by the Holy Spirit, exemplified by Paul's first letter to the Corinthians, argues that the church should value all its members' gifts. One challenge is that the unit conceived as church varies from local congregational gatherings, particularly in Protestant, Pentecostal and other free churches, to worldwide hierarchical structures like the Roman Catholic and Anglican Churches. Thus the operation of the Holy Spirit and ethical direction varies from local membership with autonomous authority to the international accountabilities of the Roman Catholic Church. Yet in some instances federated church bodies such as the Evangelical Alliance can make more authoritative statements as they require members to sign up to specific understandings of the faith and so can command more common acceptance than traditions for whom authority is determined by hierarchical structures.

The Muslim ummah operates from an ideal of a general supra-congregational consensus binding on Muslims worldwide.[31] Yet unlike the Anglican and Catholic Churches there are neither supra-congregational structures nor any equivalent of a Bishop, let alone a Pope; each imam's authority in formal terms is limited to their congregation. Nor is there any central governing or decision-making body, although as for some free churches there are umbrella bodies such as the Muslim Council of Great Britain and the Muslim Parliament. The same dynamic applies to Jewish synagogues, Sikh Gurdwaras and Hindu and Buddhist Temples all of which may federate to a degree but which are legally and operationally separate. Within each tradition there are also distinct groups who do not necessarily recognize each others' authority; for example Orthodox Judaism would not recognize let alone seek to develop consensus with either the Progressive or Reformed movements. The lack of centralizing authority or supra-congregational organization is particularly pronounced in the *dharmic* faiths in which personal ethical autonomy is more pronounced than in Abrahamic faiths, at least theologically and constitutionally, if not in practice due to communal norms.

Normative Authorities

The variable and complex picture of religious authority outlined above, in relation to leaders and communal structures, illustrates why citing particular traditions as standing for specific ethical stances is generally misleading. The role of personal autonomy in understanding and discerning ethics, explored further below, also adds to the complex variety of how faith and theological ethics operate in practice. Yet the

---

[31] Ramadan T. *Western Muslims and the Future of Islam.* Oxford University Press, 2004. pp. 86–101 (Ramadan 2004).

perception is often that religious authority is normative and binding and despite the complexity there are forms of authority that should, according to the theology of particular communities, have normative force. Such authorities operate as normative standards to be considered in applying faith to life if not enforced as absolutely binding on members' consciences.

Legal Systems

As already indicated Islam and Judaism both give expression to the ethical norms of their traditions through formal systems of law derived from canonically recognized scriptures, the Qu'ran and *Hadith*[32] giving rise to Shari'a and the Torah to *halakah*. Canonical scriptural sources have been added to over time through exposition and application leading to four schools of *fiqh* in Islam[33] and various local applications of the Talmud, the principle codified source of Jewish law. In both faiths legal fora can consider cases concerning particular individuals and general rulings, applicable to all the faithful, can be made by legally qualified scholars. Thus law, theology, ethics and practice are closely intertwined. The laws are comprehensive, regulating matters of ethical principle, like the sanctity of life, waging war, regulation of marriage, family and property. They also cover ritual and dietary laws of particular religious importance. Different communities within each faith have varying interpretations of the interplay between religious laws and wider society, including applying laws across different countries in the various Jewish Talmuds, the four schools of Islamic law and more recent developments in western *Shari'a*.[34] Yet there is normative agreement as to the authority of religious law, regardless of regional variations and which particular school, group or strand of the faith is followed. In each case the variations, both geographical and interpretive, are attributed to context rather than theological principle. For example, observing Shari'a in a

---

[32] The sayings of Mohammed.
[33] Hanafi, Hanbali, Shaafi and Maliki.
[34] Ramadan T., op. cit., pp. 62–86.

Muslim majority empire is more straightforward than as a minority in a secular Christian heritage country. Yet wherever they are living for Jews and Muslims law is holy, their key ethical code and a mark of identity. Law is to be celebrated, explored and obeyed.

The Judeo-Muslim view of law contrasts with Christian attitudes, which tend to contrast law with faith and separate law from ethics. Of the Christian churches' approaches to legal regulation Roman Catholic Canon Law is the nearest to the Jewish and Muslim legal systems, in that there is a comprehensive body of law. However, it is not the equivalent of Roman Catholic ethics. In that observing law and order is generally an ethical good, Canon Law has ethical force. It covers the legal dimensions of some aspects of personal life, notably marriage, annulment and laws regulating ministry[35] ordination and religious life. Yet it by no means covers many areas of either general ethical importance nor more specific church and religious ritual, which are found in liturgical rubrics rather than law. Whereas for Jews and Muslims law, ethics and practice are entirely intertwined, Catholic Christianity separates law from wider ethics and practice. Canon Law has a significant impact on those whose marriages break down but Papal Encyclicals, the Catechism and episcopal announcements carry more general ethical guidance. These ethical sources cover a range of issues, from birth control to the dignity of labour[36] and most recently Pope Francis' *Laudato Si*: concerning the environment. They set out ethical frameworks for catholic teaching, drawn from Biblical and theological sources. Yet although they are promulgated via the highest Church authorities, in practice they are inspirational sources for autonomous consideration rather than binding in any enforceable way. This has become particularly obvious in relation to birth control, divorce and abortion where most Catholics make their own decisions, despite occasional episcopal criticism.[37]

---

[35] Catholic Canon Law covers the ministry of all members of the Church unlike Church of England Canons which regulate predominantly access to sacraments and church offices and the ministry of those who are ordained and the few formally licensed lay workers.

[36] Rerum Novarum Pope Leo XIII 1891 and Laboren Exercens Pope John Paul II 1981.

[37] http://www.catholicherald.co.uk/news/2015/04/10/sanctity-of-life-is-top-issue-facing-voters-say-scottish-bishops/; http://www.cbc.ca/news/politics/trudeau-defends-abortion-stance-amid-sharp-catholic-criticism-1.2649810; Byrnes T. *Catholic Bishops in American Politics*. Princeton University Press, 1991 (Byrnes 1991).

In other Christian denominations the division between ethics and law is even more pronounced. Jesus and St Paul's condemnation of law and lawyers[38] influences many Christians. Yet Jesus primarily condemned the abuse of law and legal power to oppress and fetter those put outside the law. Examples of Jesus apparently breaking the law are generally situations of putting substantive obligations to human beings before oppressive interpretations of the law. This includes allowing his disciples to pick corn and heal on the Sabbath[39] and criticizing those who abuse the law of *korban* (temple offerings) to evade the duty of care for parents.[40] St Paul drew a stronger distinction than Jesus between law and spirit, with different nuances. Jesus argued for the spirit rather than the letter of the law. By contrast Paul saw a greater division between the two, arguing that Christians should live by the Holy Spirit rather than the law, in a more voluntarist fashion. Paul is not entirely voluntarist; the letters include expectations of adherence to ethical norms covering communal conduct and responsibility, sharing property, family life, sexual conduct, leadership and teaching. Yet Paul's theology is that a community living in the spirit will instinctively obey God's law without needing the Torah as a code to follow. Ethics are therefore a matter of spirit and truth rather than law. Yet the reality is that no organization can manage without some degree of legal order regulating internal relationships and the interface with law in wider society, such as contemporary charity and planning law. Thus all major Christian denominations have organizational structures and constitutions but they tend to be perceived as separate from the church's teaching on ethics.

The relationship of law, norms and ethics is different again in Hinduism. As noted earlier the lack of central law or norm-making body in Hinduism led to perceptions that Hinduism has no real norms.[41] Yet despite the lack of central authority there is a wide body of ethical and legal norms in Hinduism and other *dharmic* faiths. Underlying principles of ethical conduct are regarded as flowing from

[38] e.g. 'Woe to you lawyers...' Luke 11: 46 & 52.

[39] Mark 2: 23–27 & 3: 1–6;

[40] Korban Mark 7:10–12.

[41] See e.g. Lubin T. et al. in *Hinduism and Law: An Introduction*. Cambridge University Press, 2010. pp. 1–4.

consciousness of the unity of creation, from *dharma*, which is reflected in holy law and principles of righteousness, in some ways similar to the Jewish *tsedeka*. The implementation of law in practice is also various, so that alongside the divine operating principles of *dharmasastra* and the specific revealed codes of the Vedic texts are legal processes of *vyavahara*, judgements of the king (*sasana*) and customary law (*acara*). As in other traditions there are also texts and commentaries that gather together and comment on the implementation of the revealed texts. Possibly the most notable in Hinduism is the *Manusmritti* compiled by Manu in the second century CE. Thus the lack of central canonical authority has not prevented the development of normative codes of interrelated ethics and law.

Religious and Secular Authority

One might have thought that the sources of authority listed above would be quite enough to satisfy those guided in their ethics by religious belief and practice. However, unless living in the rare instances of a theocracy, those of faith have to negotiate the ethical and legal authority of the secular or civic systems and cultures in which they actually live. Even in theocracies, like for example, the Holy Roman and Ottoman Empires and Calvin's Geneva, practical matters of human failing, enforcement and accommodating religious difference need to be negotiated. This means that those with religious faith are also influenced by and have to engage with forms of authority in wider society. These include the law of the land, societal culture, professional norms and codes of conduct all of which require adherence in public life and shape the particular application of religious norms in that context.

The challenge for theological ethics and the religious communities grappling with them is to maintain the authenticity of their faith whilst living in an ever-changing world. This is not a new challenge nor unique to faith communities as all societies experience tensions when new understandings are developed. However religious rhetoric about eternal values, an unchanging God and a source of tradition can make these tensions and adapting to progress particularly difficult. Reference to historical texts is a further factor that compounds such tensions. Many diaspora faith communities also face challenges around maintaining religious traditions and ethics in societies with different assumptions even about basics like which sabbath day to observe.

Religion and the Law of the Land

Despite scepticism about the role of law in relation to faith and ethics and the narratives of the early church that meant Jesus, the apostles and Paul all ended up in prison and worse, most Christians in the UK have a strong ethic of obeying the law of the land, reinforced by Jesus' commandment to 'render unto Caesar' in paying taxes. For some Christians there is also a perception that obedience to civil law is a requirement of their faith because English law is based on the Judaeo-Christian commandments, with some disappointment about changes to marriage and Sunday trading that are seen as altering that picture. Although tracing specific laws to Biblical principles might be stretching the point it is clear that British society has been shaped according to Christian religious practice so that changes to Sunday trading, observance of religious festivals[42] and laws on marriage suggest a distancing from Christianity as the dominant religious code and ethic. The move towards a secular framework without preference for religious calendars leaves Christians in the same position as other religious groups, seeking accommodation rather than automatically entitled to protected religious festivals. Apart from those like the Quakers whose commitment to peace has led to conscientious objection and withholding of taxes the majority of English law poses little ethical obstacle or challenge for the average Christian in terms of how they live their own lives or those of their churches.

For adherents of other faith communities the issues are more challenging as the range of everyday differences from the secular norm are greater. Muslims can usually avoid eating food that is *haram* by not eating meat but Jewish laws of *kashrut* mean that how food is prepared,

---

[42] Especially Easter because of its variable date.

not just what is eaten, is at issue. For other faiths the challenge is whether it has been prayed over or dedicated in particular ways. The Buddhist focus displays a different ethic; whilst generally vegetarian Buddhists, including monks, are advised to focus on the hospitality of the giver and eat the food, even if it includes meat. The relational ethic of gratitude overrides the more deontological ethic of *ahimsa*, embodied in not eating meat. Whilst secular society has found legally speaking that food rules are a matter of policy not law,[43] for religious groups the deontological nature of Torah or Shari'a means that such principles are not trivial or mere matters of taste. The one exception that can qualify such principles is that all divine command is subject to the overriding importance of preserving life, as the gift of God.[44] In a society used to a fair degree of relativism such deontological codes are likely to remain a challenge. Yet for faith communities with such rules, what is worn or eaten is part of a comprehensive ethic. Al Gazali's rules for prayer make clear the authority of such comprehensive religious codes. Similarly the Torah covers all aspects of life, designed to foster an awareness of God at each turn. Although not so evident in Christianity, monastic rules or the Ignatian spiritual exercises also cover all life's details and build into the daily routine a constant turning to God, reminding that the rule is not there for its own sake but is grounded, as all aspects of life, in the divine. The advent of the Human Rights Act and protection of belief and conscience means that comprehensive codes of religious practice and ethics have received more prominence and protection. However, the Act is not only used to seek accommodation of faith communities unused to dividing private from public life but also for non-religious matters of conscience such as vegetarianism, fair trade and peace campaigns. For those for whom faith and issues of conscience are at the core of life all aspects of life have ethical implications not just decisions designated 'votes of conscience' in Parliament.

---

[43] This contrast between theological ethics and civil law is seen in *Re J [2001] 1 Fam (CA)*; the court decided an application for religious circumcision of a son but was not prepared to rule whether he should eat bacon.

[44] Lawton CA. Judaism, pp. 168–215. In *Ethical Issues in Six Religious Traditions,* Eds. Morgan P & Lawton C. Edinburgh University Press, 2nd edition, 2007 at pp. 190–191 (Lawton 2007).

The issues covered above are largely matters of individual religious conscience. A more contentious area of accommodation is that of religious law itself, for example in relation to *Shari'a* courts.[45] In practice religious 'courts' like the Beth Din and Roman Catholic Canon Law tribunals, have operated alongside the civil law in Britain for centuries. However, calls for formal recognition of religious fora, within the wider legal system, have raised significant ethical, legal and philosophical issues. There are fears that such fora will undermine the unity of law and allegiance to British law and governance. Yet British law does accommodate jurisdictions applicable to particular sections of the community, for example professional disciplinary bodies like the GMC and sports regulators. There is an argument for saying that religious legal bodies could be recognized in a similar way in the interests of accountability and protecting the vulnerable as the reality is that members of religious communities continue to turn to religious courts, seeking an ethical jurisdiction that reflects their faith.[46]

Yet for the most part religious practice is to live according to the laws of the land, the classic Judaeo-Christian statement of which is found in Jeremiah 29:7. In Islam there is a growing body of theology oriented towards interpretation of Shari'a and its obligations within a western or non-Muslim context.[47] The more personal nature of Hindu and Buddhist practice, without a co-ordinating authoritative body has perhaps made it easier for these faiths to adapt on a personal level to life outside the country of origin. Yet Sikhs have had to go to court for the right to wear the kara bangle and the turban and Hindus have contested withdrawal from society to observe the status of *sant*. Dealing with accommodation of particular religious ethics and practices via the Human Rights Act means that accommodation of religious ethics can risk being piecemeal and shaping religion according to its own precepts,

---

[45] See for example the debate caused by former Archbishop of Canterbury Rowan William's speech at the RCJ – now recorded in *Islam and English Law*. Ed. Griffiths Jones R. Cambridge University Press, 2013, pp. 20–34.

[46] A further review of Shari'a Courts is due under the Chairing of Mona Siqqiqui.

[47] Tariq Ramadan. *Western Muslims and the Future of Islam*. Oxford University Press, 2005.

as seen in attempts to licence non-Christian religious marriages.[48] However, such an approach is probably most practicable politically and reflects the gradual development of ethics and tradition in most faiths.

Conscience and Internal Ethical Authority

Having considered the range of external ethical authorities to which theological ethics and faith communities have regard, there is a return to the role of personal conscience as the mediator of such authorities. To focus on external religious authorities belies the fact that in all religious faiths, whilst there is communal identity and varying degrees of submission, attention or obedience to external religious authority, there is also personal responsibility and the exercise of conscience. All faiths have some understanding of free will, personal ethical accountability and judgement on how life is lived. For example, even the Roman Catholic John Henry Newman reputedly stated that called to choose between toasting the Pope and conscience he would toast conscience. The fact that neither Hinduism nor Buddhism has a single, authoritative rule-making body or process means that personal interpretation of faith is expected, ideally with the guidance of a guru. Theological authority in the texts and practices is still relevant but the responsibility lies with the individual as to how they are followed. Christianity, Judaism and Islam all posit a day of judgement or reckoning at the end of life and include times for reflection on ethical conduct such as the confession in Christian services and Yom Kippur, the Jewish day of atonement. All therefore assume personal accountability for living out faith and the ethical dilemmas it can pose. This means that for all faiths internal sources of authority and conscience are essential as the means by which ethical authority is understood.

Conscience and the distinctiveness of theological ethics are particularly obvious where someone acts in ways that stand out from the crowd

---

[48] Shah P. *Judging Muslims*, pp. 144–156; Ali SS. *From Muslim Migrants to Muslim Citizens*, pp. 157–175 in Griffiths Jones R. Ed. *Islam and English Law*, op. cit.

by wearing a *hijab*, a Sikh turban or withholding taxes as part of a Quaker peace campaign. However, conscience is also exercised when decisions are made that are not so distinctive but accept the norm. Whilst some of these decisions are made unreflectively there are also examples of active choice to follow the norm, for example in a professional dilemma. Decisions that require an intentional exercise of conscience may beset those of faith more often than those without simply because of faith-based ethics that differ from mainstream norms. For Muslims extending their lunchbreak for Friday prayers or Jewish students torn between completing an assignment or observing Shabbath, conscientious reflection is required. The risk of religious pressure is an issue often raised over Muslim women wearing the veil or gay Christians who opt for celibacy. Yet in most instances the person of faith exercises an active reflective agency, informed by the authorities of their religious community and family, alongside mainstream commitments. Studies such as Stephanie Levine's[49] account of young women growing up in the *haredi* Jewish community in Crown Heights in New York, Mary McClintock Fulkerson's[50] analysis of female agency in traditional Christian communities and various accounts of Muslim women's decisions to veil illustrate an active and positive agency in adopting religious ethics.

This analysis of conscience in religion is not to deny that there are examples of abusive restriction of conscience and autonomy in some religious communities and families. Yet this is also true across society. Domestic violence, child abuse and restriction of expectations in religious communities are not so different from similar phenomena found in other communities. The risk factors to exercise of conscience in religious communities tend to be countercultural isolation and autocratic leadership. Yet communities completely isolated from and hostile to wider society are relatively few, even in the age of ISIS and the factors behind such isolation are not exclusive to religious ethics. Anti-social

---

[49] Levine S. *Mystics, Mavericks and Merry Makers*. New York: New York University Press, 2003 (Levine 2003).

[50] McClintock Fulkerson M. *Women's Discourses and Feminist Theology*. Fortress Press, 1994 (McClintock 1994).

isolationist countercultural ethics are also to be found in non-religious ideologies such as the English Defence League, which also often foster conservative attitudes to gender and sexuality as well as racism.

Conclusion

Whilst sources of ethical authority external to the believer, located both in the community and religious leaders, are significant they cannot operate without conscience. As in any community leadership influence and pressure of community expectation can manipulate conscience or lead to undue influence. However, for the most part if those of faith do follow the normative religious ethic they do so not just because they are a Muslim, a Jew, a Christian and so on, but because in conscience, properly informed, they identify with their faith and believe that this is the way to live it with integrity. It is for this reason that theological ethics supports secular society's protection of personal conscience and integrity as a core aspect of personhood and identity, yet recognizing that conscience is always informed by external as well as internal sources of authority.

6

Authority and Religious Texts

Scripture or religious texts are not the only sources of religious authority, as considered in the previous chapter, yet they are often in significant ways the foundation of other forms of authority. Most religious leaders draw their power from the authority to interpret and apply scriptural principles; in some instances they also derive their constitutional authority or role from scriptural precedent. For some religions, particularly the Qu'ran in Islam, the Torah in Judaism and the Bible in many branches of Christianity, scripture is the most definitive source of religious authority. In Sikhism the Guru Granth Sahib effectively replaced a living Guru with the codified teachings of the first ten Gurus. Even those traditions, such as the *dharmic* faiths, without consensus or an authoritative body to define texts as canonical, have significant religious texts and scriptures. It is worth noting that 'scripture', whilst a useful shorthand signifier is by no means uniform or comparable on a like for like basis across traditions. Whilst western understandings of scripture refer predominantly to the written word, for some traditions scripture also encompasses oral narratives, unwritten traditions of legal interpretation and performative scripture in chants and sung Psalms. Even comparison of the written sources reveals a variety of genres affecting

© The Author(s) 2017
C. Shelley, *Ethical Exploration in a Multifaith Society*,
DOI 10.1007/978-3-319-46711-5_6

interpretation and the ways in which ethical norms may be understood or derived from them. The word scripture will be used in this discussion. Even though 'scripture' might be considered weighted towards particular traditions it connotes the sanctity of the texts in question for believers in a way that is not conveyed by the more academic term 'religious texts'.

There tends to be a perception that religious scripture is about *the* book particular to each tradition. However, very few faiths have just one religious text or book. In fact the only tradition that clearly has one coherent single holy text is Islam. Amongst all religious texts the Q'ran is the most coherent in the sense that it is dictated by one single author or mediator of revelation. Buddhism has a similar dynamic to the extent that all authoritative statements originate with the Buddha but there is less consensus about which texts, derived from Buddha's teaching, constitute the definitive canon. The Sikh's Guru Granth Sahib is comparatively coherent as the teachings of the first ten gurus but also contains hymns from other holy figures in Hinduism and Islam. By contrast Hinduism includes multiple texts and narratives of various authorship. In the absence of an authoritative leader or body to declare which texts are definitive there is no recognized canon. In terms of popular following the *mahabarat,* which encompasses the *Baghavad Gita* and *Ramayana* carry the most authority; yet the brahminical texts and *vedas* are generally considered the purer and higher sources of authority.

Despite references to 'the Bible' and ''the *Tanakh'* or 'Hebrew Bible' Judaism and Christianity also find their sources of scriptural revelation in a diversity of texts. The word 'the Bible' is in fact plural, derived from the Greek *'ta Biblia'* meaning 'the books'. The impression of being one book results from their collection into one approved canon known by the single title. Yet the Hebrew Biblical canon includes twenty-four books and the Christian canon sixty-six, with some variation depending on whether the Apocrypha are recognized. In each case these books vary widely in style, genre and authorship. The fact that the weight of authority, extent of the canon and use of the particular texts varies in most traditions provides some illustration of and explanation for the diversity of ethical stances even within religious traditions. In reading and following such texts there are also varied modes and methods for interpreting scripture, which adds further dimensions to the complexity of deriving ethics from holy texts. The fact that scripture is also not necessarily designed as an ethical guide is another factor.

For all the major religious faiths scripture performs a variety of roles, which includes providing sources of information and ethical guidance but also community narrative and history, divine inspiration and cosmic significance. Scripture may also carry a profound symbolic role warranting venerated treatment. For example the Qu'ran requires strict purity and observance of *wudu* before it is handled, the Torah is reserved in an exalted place in the synagogue and the Guru Granth Sahib has been accorded juristic personality in Indian courts.[1] The challenges posed in interpreting and applying scripture include how literally or metaphorically something was intended, how and in what ways it is inspired, what sort of writing is involved and the context both historically and contemporaneously. In addition, in most instances the original text will need not only to be interpreted but also translated from the original language. All of these exercises will also engage the meta-narrative framework of the interpreter, which can include the interpreter's own agendas and perspectives. All of these interpretive dilemmas add to the complexity of using scripture in ethical debate. Yet the dilemmas of translation in themselves provide fora for ethical consideration. There is an assumption that religious texts are only for those who are members of the faith communities that live by them. However, despite the challenges that interpretation can pose there are aspects of scripture that can affect societies beyond the adherents of the faith. Texts can influence societies by way of inspiration and implicit cultural norms and assumptions.

An Historical Overview of the Texts in Issue

As noted above there is no single obvious or agreed model for what constitutes religious scripture or holy texts, as their origins and development vary from faith to faith. The following historical outline sets out information about the origins, history and nature of the key

---

[1] http://www.thehindu.com/2000/04/03/stories/01030005.htm.

scriptures for the major faiths. This background information will enable a more informed consideration of the place of scripture in theological ethics and the different ways that it can inspire ethical norms. It also illustrates the many differences of approach that make like for like comparisons across traditions and scriptural sources inappropriate in many instances.

Hinduism

Whereas the word 'scripture' is derived from the Latin 'scibere' to write, the equivalent Hindu term '*sabda*' is from the verb to make a sound or call. This illustrates one major difference between Hindu texts and other traditions, which is that the *Vedic* texts are primarily meant to be chanted and the ritual of chanting them has significance for the right ordering of the world. The four *vedas* (from '*vid*' the verb to know), the *Rigveda, Yajurveda, Samaveda and Atharveda*, are the nearest thing to writings with canonical status in Hinduism. The *vedas* are difficult to date but there is evidence that they were being orally composed in north India, the Punjab and Bihar, as early as 1500BCE. The fact that Buddha initially adopted the *vedas* as foundational to his own spiritual search suggests that recognized written texts would have been available by around 500–400BCE. The *vedas* are written in the stylized form of Vedic *Sanskrit* by poets (*rishis*) seeking to convey the most powerfully effective of chants. They are not the passing on of a privileged revelation mediated by a prophet from the divine to the community but invocations to the transcendent deities (*devas* and *devis*) by priests on behalf of the people. They are also grouped to some degree. The *aranyaka* portions of the *vedic* texts, the product of withdrawn contemplation in the woods (*aranya* means woods or wilds) tend to be viewed as more secret, esoteric or elite. These portions lead into the latter part of the *vedic* canon, known as the *Upanishads*, which proceeds by way of exploratory questions and answers about the nature of the universe, its origins and the phenomenon of being and existence.[2]

---

[2] Lipner J. *Hindus*. Routledge, 2010, pp. 27–87.

By the time that the *Vedas* had taken their recognized form the *Brahmana* texts had begun to be written. These are more philosophical prose texts, reflecting on and explaining the origins and purpose of the *vedas*. To the extent that they also set out norms for the proper performance of the *vedas* they operate by way of a sort of commentary. The reflection also muses on substantive philosophical and ethical issues by extrapolation of principles from the *vedas*.[3] However, it is the *vedic* scriptures themselves which remain the roots for understanding the order of the universe. In a more applied mode the *sutras*, derived from the *vedas* provide specific and detailed guidance about aspects of life. For example, the *Grhya sutras* cover domestic ritual and lore. Both the *dharma sutras* and *dharma sastras* contain rules and guidance about the overriding order for life and ethical authority. However, it is the *dharma sastras* which took on legal codification for example in the laws of Manu or the *manusm-ritti*.[4] One slight problem in their interpretation is to distinguish what is original from what was shaped by the interests of colonial administrators in the 18th and 19th CE.

The best-known and most popularly followed texts are the great epic poems, most notably the *Mahabarata*, which includes the *Baghavad Gita* and the *Ramayana*, dating from 400BCE, the written form of which is attributed to *vyasa* or 'the arranger'. Unlike the more formal verses of the *vedas* and prose codes of the *sastras* and *sutras* the epic poems are narratives, for the most part featuring mythical characters. They act as inspirational example and narrative truth, often flagging up the paradoxes of human life and ethical decisions, rather than providing clear or binding norms.[5] The stories have enjoyed contemporary popularity with mass productions in India and screenings on the BBC appealing to audiences of non-Indian background.

[3] Lipner J. *Hindus*. Routledge, 2010, pp. 47–62

[4] Lipner J., op. cit., pp. 47–87; Olivelle P. Dharmasastra: A Textual History. In Lubin T et al. *Hinduism and Law: An Introduction*. Cambridge University Press, 2010, pp. 17–57 (Olivelle 2010).

[5] Lipner J., op. cit., pp. 148–172.

Buddhism

To the extent that some would argue against distinctions being drawn between the various Indic traditions,[6] Buddhism and therefore the Buddhist scriptures, are simply part of the wider corpus of *dharmic* texts. Yet there is evidence of distinct teachings, particularly about caste and animal sacrifice, that the original peoples termed Hindus rejected as anti-*vedic* and overturning *dharma*. A distinct Buddhist canon, claimed as the teachings of Buddha and derived from the *vedas* was authorized by a collegiate process of Councils. The core text is known as the Tipitaka[7] and is written in Suttas.[8] For short it is often referred to as the Pali Canon. The Canon also includes the *vinaya* texts, which are authoritative for the *sanga* or monastic orders.[9] Unlike Hinduism there is a clear originator of the tradition in the teachings of Buddha, which is what has led to a sense of a definitive Canon, evaluated as the sayings attributed directly or indirectly to Buddha, and considered to represent *dharma*. There seems to have been just one body of disciples and one canon in the first century after Buddha's death. Things began to schism at the Council of Vesali[10] and by the first century BCE 18 different communities could be discerned in India.

Thereafter further diversity developed through travel, with the development of regional canons like the Chinese *Taisho Tipitaka* publicized by Hsuan Hua,[11] lay-led Mahayana Buddhist Suttras and Tibetan Buddhism. The Tibetan *Kangyur* arose through adoption of Buddhism and reverence of the Pali Canon by King Songsten Gampo around 641CE, influenced by his Buddhist wives from India.[12] Although early

---

[6] Smith WC. *The Meaning and End of Religion*. SPCK, 1978 (Smith 1978), cited by Lipner J., op. cit., at p. 7 & p. 379.

[7] Or Tripitaka in Sanskrit.

[8] Suttras in Sanskrit.

[9] http://sacred-texts.com/bud/sbe13/sbe1302.htm. Accessed 11 June 2016.

[10] Second Buddhist Council; see e.g. *Buddhism*, p. 78 et seq in *A History of Indian Philosophy*. Ed. Surendranath Dusgupta Motillal Barnasidas Cambridge, 1922 at p. 112 (Dasgupta 1922).

[11] *Biography of Ven Hsuan Hua*. Buddhist Text Translation Society, 1981 (Ven Hsuan Hua 1981).

[12] Powers J. *Introduction to Tibetan Buddhism*. Snow Lion Publications, 2007, pp. 144–156 (Powers 2007).

Buddhism held Councils, diversification of the tradition left more local communal bodies called *sangas*; thus generally speaking like Hinduism there is no central authority making binding contemporary rulings on scriptural interpretation or ethical application. This means that, as in many other faiths, particular nuances, emphases and the additions or mediation of later teachers led to a significant diversity of texts, interpretation and ethical stances. Two major contemporary interpretations are the teachings of the Dalai Lama and Soka Gokkai International Buddhism, founded in 1975 by Daisaku Ikeda following the Nichiren tradition. The lack of personal deity and tendency to autonomous interpretation seems to have growing appeal in some parts of sceptical individualist western societies. Yet how many read the scriptures as opposed to books about Buddhism would be an interesting piece of research.

Judaism

Like the Hindu texts the original Jewish scriptures were composed through oral tradition over the course of more than a millennium before being written down. The *Tanakh* or Hebrew Biblical Canon, includes the Torah, the prophets and the writings, which include Psalms, chronicles and books of wisdom. Of these the Torah and Psalms are probably the most significant in terms of use within the community, through application of the law and in communal prayers at *schul*. The Torah, the first five books of the Bible, is often described as the law, although the books also include extensive narrative sections vital to Jewish history and self-understanding. The narratives ground the community's key events, the flood, exile, exodus and journey in the desert to the Promised Land. Whilst the definitive event for the law is the giving of the Ten Commandments to Moses on Mount Sinai the whole history shapes the more detailed laws and the community that Israel becomes. The Chronicles, histories and Prophets set further historical information in context of Jewish narrative. The books of Wisdom and the Psalms provide forms of narrative philosophy in Job and Ecclesiastes, celebration of life and love in the Song of Songs and good advice in Proverbs.

The first Biblical stories date from pre-history with suggestions that the patriarchal period, beginning with Abraham, dates from 2150BCE and the Exodus dated at 1550-1200BCE. The Deuteronomic history, can be dated more precisely between 1200 – 332BCE with much of the narrative being written down during the 2nd Temple period, from the Exile in 587BCE to destruction of the Temple in 70CE.[13]

The Canon and the law became established and fixed over the centuries, settling on 613 *mitzvot*. Yet any law needs interpreting and application, which gives rise to the *Mishnah* or writing down of the original oral law, the 'old Torah', *Midrash* or narrative interpretation of the Bible and the *Talmud* which are interpretations of the law. These secondary sources, along with the written Torah in the Biblical text, form the *halakah* the generic term for law, which equates to both religious law and ethics. Interpretation should be possible by all believers, although in some of the most conservative communities women only get to read those portions needed for their duties, the domestic law. However, the rabbis and jurists of the Beth Din carry most authoritative weight as teachers and lawyers.[14] Revered commentators and rabbis such as Hillel and Maimonides or the Rambam continue to be quoted but only as interpreters not developers of the law and tradition.

Christianity

As Buddhism grew from the Hindu *dharmic* traditions in which the Buddha was raised, Christianity came from the Jewish tradition as Jesus was Jewish. The Christian Bible therefore begins with Jesus' traditions of written Torah and the *Tanakh* in the Old Testament. To this is added the New Testament, which begins with Jesus' life and interpretation of the law as transmitted in the Gospels. Acts tells the history of the early Church, Paul's conversion and leads into his interpretation of the law

---

[13] Barton J & Bowden J. *The Original Story: God, Israel and the World*. Grand Rapids Michigan and Cambridge, UK: Eerdmans, 2005 (Barton and Bowden 2005).

[14] Hecht NS, Jackson BS & others (Eds.). *An Introduction to the History and Sources of Jewish Law*. Oxford University Press, 1996 (Hecht et al. 1996).

and the Gospels in his letters. The apocalyptic book of Revelations adopts another genre, reflecting a community under persecution and divided. Christians read the Old Testament through New Testament lenses of one sort or another. Some read backwards interpreting the Old Testament entirely as a foretelling of the coming of Christ, interpolating the Christian story back into the Hebrew Scriptures. Others read forward, viewing the New Testament in the light of Jesus' Jewishness, interpreting the New Testament as Jesus' interpretation of the Hebrew canon rather than Christianising the Old Testament. As a matter of historical accuracy it must be remembered that for both Jesus and Paul references to scripture are inevitably to the Hebrew Canon as the scriptures now known as the New Testament were not written until some decades after their deaths. Effectively the New Testament texts refer to events from 1–65CE, as written down from 50–150CE. By contrast with the *Tanakh* and Hindu scriptures the New Testament texts were written down comparatively soon after the events about which they speak, indicating a more literate society and possibly a more mobile and diverse one. The canonical corpus was determined around the time of the Council of Nicea in 325CE.

Christianity also refers to other religious texts, such as those of the early Church Fathers, the best known being Augustine and later theologians like Thomas Aquinas, Martin Luther and Calvin. However, they do not have the canonical status of the Bible and are mostly the works of the ongoing, living Church seeking to interpret and apply the Bible in their contemporary circumstances. Unlike the Jewish canon and its interpretation however these early theologians often speculated on the nature of God and more metaphysical questions than the Jewish interpreters of law and ethics. The comparative lack of Biblical content in such metaphysical theology led some of the more scripturally literalist, particularly after the Protestant Reformation, to reject such teachings.

Islam

The major Muslim scripts are the sayings and writings of Mohammed, known collectively as the *sunnah*. The main texts are the Qu'ran and the *hadith* or sayings of the prophet. The Qu'ran is the foundational text, which contains the revealed word of God as mediated through the teachings of Mohammed. It is a book of 114 chapters of variable lengths, each with a title for its subject matter. 93 of the chapters were revealed to the Prophet at Mecca and 21 at Medina after he fled Mecca. Much of the revelation was given in one sustained period of prayer known as the Night of Revelation. The text was memorized by followers during Mohammed's lifetime and written down by Zayd under Abu Bakr, the first Caliph. The content of the Qu'ran is predominantly by way of guidance although there are also some narratives, including some seen also in the Bible, like the story of Noah, the Queen of Sheba and references to Moses, Jesus and Mary.

Since the Caliphate of Uthman (the third Caliph, 644–656) the text has remained unchanged and there is no deviation from the Canon of 114 chapters. Again this is a relatively prompt capturing of the teachings in written scripture. The text also remains unchanged in its language as the traditional language for its reception, use in prayers and preaching is Arabic. However, the Muslim diaspora, the imperative of mission in a world dominated linguistically by English and the advent of the internet means that translations into English as well as other non-Arabic languages is now widespread.

Although the Canon of the Qu'ran has been set from its earliest days, as in Judaism there are interpretive methods to enable application to actual situations as life and society changes. These include *ijma*, which is the consensus of the *ummah* and *ijtihad*, which is the use of reasoning to interpret and develop the tradition in new conditions. Techniques of establishing authenticity are used in relation to the *hadith* but the Qu'ran is established as the authentic text and not amenable to processes of historical criticism that have been used in other traditions.[15]

---

[15] Abdel Haleem MAS. Qu'ran and Hadith. In *The Cambridge Companion to Classical Islamic Theology*. Cambridge University Press, 2008 at pp. 19–32 (Haleem 2008); Ramadan T. *Radical Reform: Islamic Ethics and Liberation*. Oxford University Press, 2009, pp. 11–80 (Ramadan 2009).

Sikhism

The Sikh scriptures, the *Guru Granth Sahib*, also known as the *Adi Granth*, are the latest in time as the Sikh religion is the most modern of all the major faiths. It draws on Hinduism and Islam with hymns from Hindu and Muslim holy men incorporated within the overall teachings of the ten gurus. The texts were written early in the life of the tradition and there is evidence that they were gathered in written form as part of the process of making clear that Sikhism was a new way and a distinct tradition with its own texts.[16] The key text is the Adi Granth which tradition generally states began to be written down under the second Guru, Guru Arjan with the final text completed by the tenth Guru, Guru Gobind Singh in 1707 or the 1680s. It is known as the Guru Granth Sahib and is regarded as the 11th Sikh Guru, to the extent of being given the status of a legal person in the Indian courts.

As in Islam the clear authority of a unified leadership has enabled greater clarity about the status and authority of the text. It is seen as a living authority in a way that is akin to the Christian understanding of the Bible rather than the more set written law of the Torah or Qu'ran. It is written in Gurumukhi script, a form developed for this text, based on Punjabi with traces of Hindi. Although written down very early in the history of the Sikh tradition it shares the Hindu sense of the word being heard, with the transcendent residing in sacred speech rather than writing.[17] This is also reflected in the poetic form of the writing and its regular use for chanting. The Guru Granth Sahib is the overarching authority covering all aspects of faith and life, metaphysical as well as applied and ethical and in some respects is a reaction against aspects of Hinduism like the caste structure. There is also a second text, the Dasam Granth, which is composed of the hymns of the tenth

---

[16] Singh Mann G. Canon Formation in the Sikh Tradition, pp. 10–25. In *Sikh Religion, Culture and Ethnicity,* Eds. Mandair As & Shackle C. London: Curzon Press2001 & London: Routledge, 2013 (Sing Mann 2001).

[17] Lipner J., op. cit., p. 63 and n. 16, p. 385.

(& final) Guru, Guru Gobind Singh. These however have less author-itative status than the Guru Granth Sahib.[18]

Interpreting Scripture

Revelation and Inspiration

As the review of religious text above indicates all forms of Scripture carry weight or force because of their status as forms of revelation about the divine or ultimate truth. The scriptures are mediated orally and in due course in written form by scribes as the revelatory teachings of prophets, leaders or *sants*. The canonical or recognized scriptures are then author-ized either through formal processes or by general acclaim and use in the communities from which they come. They are not simply ethical texts in the sense of ethics as rules for right conduct but they are ethical both in the sense of forming the customs of the community and the narrative context that gives them force. In addition, ethical norms or guidance as understood in post-Enlightenment societies, flow from the worldview, narratives, poetry, wisdom and in some cases laws, that scriptures con-tain. However, several factors affect the precise weight or priority given to such texts within a tradition with implications for interpretation and ethical authority. Some of the factors that lead to variable interpretation include:

• Understandings of the mechanism for revelation,
• The processes for determining the canon and ruling on its interpretation,
• The extent to which the canon has been agreed or remains contested
• The extent of scripture's normative role in the ethics of a tradition as compared with other sources of authority and revelation
• The ways in which texts are read

---

[18] Mann Gurinder Singh. *The Making of Sikh Scripture*. United States: Oxford University Press, 2001 (Mann 2001).

- The extent to which historical criticism, contextual analysis or developmental interpretation is permitted within a tradition
- The balance of personal versus communal interpretive authority

However, before going on to consider issues of interpretation, it is worth noting that besides being definitive sources of ethical authority and identity for the communities who guard, mediate and follow them, religious scriptures can also have meaning outside particular faith communities. Whether it is faiths recognising the overlap or parallel teachings of their tradition with others or those of no faith who nonetheless find things to admire in the scriptures of their cultural heritage, there is a significant role for scripture not only in private lives but also in the public sphere.

The Variety of Interpretations

As an example of how the factors outlined above can lead to widely different approaches to and interpretations of scripture, Christianity provides plenty of evidence, as well as some interesting reflections on the gap between theory and reality. Ever since the Reformation in Western Christianity the Protestant end of the Christian spectrum has insisted on the motto *sola scriptura* – scripture alone. This designates the Bible as the main authority in their understanding of Christian faith and ethics, which should be known, read and interpreted by all Christians in their own language. By contrast, the catholic end of the spectrum, most strongly emphasized by the Roman Catholic Church, sees the Bible as the product of the church as the living community of the body of Christ. This view is based on the fact that the Canon was not finally agreed until the Council of Nicea in the third century CE. Therefore the Church has an important interpretive role, taken to the extreme in the Roman Catholic Church which did not formally allow translations into the vernacular until the 1950s. Modern Catholicism does encourage members to read the Bible themselves but the Church still arrogates to itself a significant interpretive authority via Papal and Episcopal statements and priestly teaching.

In practice however, the distance of the hierarchy from most modern Catholics means that many simply follow their own consciences as regards their understanding and living out of Biblical and other imperatives. Apart from occasional messages about abortion and same-sex marriage that have been targeted at Catholic politicians most Catholics take or leave the Church's pronouncements, paying them some attention but not being bound by them. By contrast the smaller, more local, congregational operation of many Protestant churches, particularly Free Church and Pentecostal traditions, can lead to a closer guarding of Biblical interpretation by particular religious leaders. Within the Pentecostal tradition, its Protestant roots mean that the Bible is valued but more weight is placed on the spontaneous work of the Holy Spirit. This means that Biblical mediation is often through 'words of knowledge' from particularly charismatically gifted leaders, more than strict Biblical interpretation or scholarship.

There are also varied ways of understanding the content and process of Biblical revelation. At one end of the spectrum more literalist, conservative traditions view the Bible as the literal, infallible word of God, addressed directly in its totality to the faithful. At the other end of the spectrum it is an inspiring book with narratives and poems that have some interesting things to say. In between, the range of views includes ideas that it is:

- 'God breathed', ultimately from God but inspired by the Holy Spirit in its reception by the Christian community,
- An authoritative rule book that must be obeyed
- A source of basic principles and wisdom that must be taken into account
- A source of divine commands
- A direct or indirect vehicle for God to communicate with humanity
- A record of human encounters with God and divine revelation in whole or part, recognizing the human element of writing and ordering the text.
- Written by human beings, representing the indirect operation of God in the world via human agency and community.
- An inspirational book along with theological reflection and other sources
- Inspired as a whole book or in particular books or sayings
- A gateway where God can be found if faithful people seek Him there

- Historical examples and legends of interest to those that way inclined
- A book that funds the imagination

Broadly speaking more literalist interpretations will be found in evangelical churches and more liberal interpretations at the catholic or liberal protestant end of the tradition. It is however, interesting, given the different emphases on the importance of the Bible in the context of other faith sources that Roman Catholic clergy still spend 6 years studying theology, with significant proportions of time learning the original Biblical languages. By contrast the Protestant traditions, which place more reliance on *sola scriptura* are less likely to spend time learning the original languages but rely more predominantly on vernacular translations, the consequences of which are considered further below. A final difference between Catholic and Protestant churches lies in what is canonical; the Protestant tradition does not, unlike the Catholic, accept the books known as the Apocrypha, suspecting them of mere human not divine origin.

The Process of Revelation

Cantwell Smith in 'What is Scripture,' argues that, 'People – a given community – make a text into scripture, or keep it scripture, by treating it in a certain way.'[19] Thus 'scripture is a human activity' and ongoing process not a single event or document and the response of the community to revelation rather than direct revelation. The order, which allows for continuing scriptural development and interpretation, runs:
God – revelation – religious community/experience – scripture rather than:
God – revelation/scripture – given to religious community – applied to experience
By contrast with the diversity of revelation in Christianity and varied beliefs about how scripture is revealed, other traditions, particularly those with a more univocal source, have a less questioning or sceptical

---

[19] Cantwell Smith W. *What Is Scripture?: A Comparative Approach.* Fortress Press, 1993, p. 181 (Cantwell 1993).

understanding of revelation. It might be possible to see univocal sources of revelation as more obviously recounting a coherent divine inspiration and vision granted in prayer. Whilst belief in scripture as the direct inerrant word of God can produce more didactic, absolutist and often conservative, ethical prescriptions such interpretations are not necessarily tied to how scripture as revealed truth is understood. However, if viewed as an inerrant source of divine authority scripture may be taken and used as a God-given guide for life in the sense only of an authoritarian rule-book. A common voice in this sense may carry more weight in a society atuned to the simple message of sound bites but univocal interpretations often rule out more contextual interpretation and lead to misinterpretation of more metaphorical passages. Attempts to seek a univocal revelation, particularly in respect of scriptures like the Bible that are inherently varied, can also lead to distortion of texts in a search for a coherent whole and reconciliation of what appear to be inconsistencies.

There is an argument that more diverse sources of revelation and multivocal expressions of the divine are consistent with a divinity seeking mediation in as many ways as possible. Even in the most univocal and scripturally-based traditions there is also an understanding of God as revealed via other sources such as creation and experience. Karl Barth's advice to read with the Bible in one hand and a newspaper in the other is a good example. Whatever the understanding of scriptural revelation, questions of how that source is interpreted, used, applied and related to experience and other forms of revelation still need to be addressed. Reliance solely on literalist approaches to scripture as divine revelation also reduces the scope for Scriptural understandings to be shared with those outside the faith. There may be aspects of scriptural ethics that non-believers could share if they were not deterred by scriptural literalism.

Determining the Canon and Ruling on Its Interpretation

To the extent that no further text can be added to them each of the scriptures considered above is a closed canon, determined either by communal councils or the custom of the tradition. Yet the ways that the finality of the canon are treated varies. Thus the Christian understanding of the Bible and the Skih approach to the Guru Granth Sahib is that they are living texts in that they are living embodiments of the foundational leaders. For a Christian it is therefore a legitimate question to ask 'What would Jesus do?' and for the Church, at least in the Catholic side of the tradition, to develop theology as the living embodiment of Christ rather than just interpreting the existing text. Similarly it is appropriate for the Indian courts to determine that the Guru Granth Sahib, as the 11th Guru, is a juridical person. Such questions are less appropriate for other scriptures, which are to a greater degree seen as final; they can be interpreted in new contexts but their theology cannot strictly speaking be developed beyond the original text.

In practice, the variety of contexts and different Talmudic texts and schools of fiqh suggests that the scope for contextual application of the original scriptures can nonetheless be diverse. Such diversity over time and culture also means that even in the case of closed canons religious scriptures remain living documents to the extent of their applicability to contemporary life. The better they are understood the more appropriately or accurately they are likely to be applied. Principles of scriptural interpretation also have application outside their faith traditions in that many foundational ethical texts, whether Kant or Mills, Kirkegaard or Aristotle are also historical texts; they also require attention to context and foundational assumptions in order to apply and interpret them appropriately in contemporary debate.

How Texts Are Read

Literalism

The greater the degree of belief in direct revelation, as opposed to inspired words recorded by human agency, the more literal interpretation is likely to be. There is more scope for arguing that there is mistranslation or misunderstanding if it is a human being who has written something down. In terms of ethical analysis the more literalist interpretations effectively operate in a deontological framework. For those interpreting scripture as the direct word of God, according to monotheistic traditions with a personal apprehension of God, the deontology in question is a theonomic construct.

Those parts of Abrahamic scriptures that speak in terms of commandments or other imperative rules are most easily understood as deontological commands. For the *dharmic* faiths the deontological command comes from the understanding of what the *vedas* require by way of ritual and ethics to preserve the order of the universe.

The difficulty with literalism is that if parts of scripture conflict it can be difficult to reconcile them leading to forced and sometimes inhumane interpretations. Such approaches can reflect the sort of overly literal application of Kantian or utilitarian ethics so that impractical solutions are found as a result of taking things to logical though not common sense conclusions. Unhelpfully strained, distorted or reductionist interpretations can also occur when passages written as allegory or metaphor are taken literally, misunderstanding the type of truth engaged. A particularly unhelpful form of literalist reductionism is the selection of particular verses or texts as 'proof texts'. One illustration of this approach is the citing of the six Biblical verses[20] that are taken to condemn homosexuality as the final definitive word on the matter. Such texts have tended to be traded with those who take a different view in a form of knock-down contest, suggesting that those who take different interpretive approaches do not believe in Biblical authority. Similar approaches can be found in all traditions where, for example, as regards homosexuality, the *tanakh* and *Qu'ran* have similarly strong scriptural statements.[21] The greater diversity of the *dharmic* scriptures and comparative lack of univocal authoritative leadership, along with the narrative nature of much of the populist scriptures, tends to limit the tendency to reductionism. The fact that the *dharmic* texts are also revelations of aspiration to the transcendent rather than God downwards also gives them a different dynamic, less vulnerable to absolutist truth claims than the monotheistic traditions.

One problem with the proof text approach to scripture is that it is a selective approach to religious texts. Selection of proof texts ignores both texts and meta-narrative frameworks that might be inconsistent with

---

[20] Genesis 19 – Sodom & Gomorrah; Leviticus 18:22 & 20:13; Romans 1:26–27; 1 Cor 6:9–10; 1 Tim 1:10.

[21] Leviticus 18:23 – homosexuality is 'to evah', an abomination and Surah 7:80–84.

them, as well as differential contexts. Selection of texts to win an argument rather than explore the possibilities of creation is also a functional and utilitarian approach to scripture. There are several challenges to the approach. Firstly, there are comparatively few ethical issues in any scriptures with an unquestionably clear and literal mandate, without further consideration of the context. For example, 'thou shalt not kill' seems fairly clear and uncontested as an ethical stance. Yet, there are several situations in which 'thou shalt not kill' is qualified, by self-defence, defending a third party, just war theory and questions of when life actually begins or ends. In relation to another contested aspect of contemporary discourse around equalities, namely the role of women, the Bible includes texts that are inconsistent with each other. From Genesis' two different accounts of creation to opposing stances within Paul's letters it is hard to see one definitive Biblical view of women.[22] Similar contradictions are found in the Qu'ran.[23]

Secondly selecting the six 'proof' texts about homosexuality as a prime focus of ethical concern seems disproportionate in relation to the far stronger Biblical mandate of several hundred texts about the relief of poverty and oppression. One alternative reading, in the light of the general historical prejudice against those who are gay, is to see those who are homosexual as amongst the poor because oppressed and marginalized. This reading brings them into the fold of the church's welcome as amongst the poor and despised who Jesus particularly welcomed to his company. An alternative focus is to consider the Biblical meta-narrative of loving God and neighbour as self, which argues that excluding those who are same-sex attracted shows a lack of love that contradicts the overarching Christian commandment to love one another.

Thirdly, simply to take texts at face value, without recognising the context in which they were written and whether they deal with comparable situations, can also be seen as a reductionist or overly simplistic approach to historical texts. Many books have been written on the

---

[22] Compare e.g. Ephesians 5:25–31 with Galatians 3:28; 1 Tim 2:12 with Romans 16:1.

[23] Surah 2:228 and 33:35 can be read as promoting gender equality in some translations whereas 2:282 and 4:11 suggest otherwise as regards testimony and inheritance;

different interpretations of the Biblical texts, both Old and New Testament, about homosexuality. The story of Sodom and Gomorrah is fairly readily dealt with on the basis that it deals not with mutually consenting relationships but with male rape and breaches of hospitality. The fact that the means of preventing male rape is to allow the rape of Lot's daughters instead renders suspect any reading of the text as solely an argument against homosexuality.[24]

More difficult to interpret in an alternative way are texts like Leviticus 18:22 and 20:13, which do prima facie seem to prohibit same-sex practice. However, a contextual reading can distinguish Greek practices of men having sex with men in close friendship alongside heterosexual marriage and pederastic forms of same-sex relationships, from the mutual, consenting same-sex relationships seen in the twenty first century. The other dimension of contextual interpretation is epistemological; knowledge about human psychology, sexuality, physiology and a range of other disciplines is very different from that at the time any of the major religious texts was written. On one interpretation it could be argued that modern scientific and technological method has given very different perspectives on what is natural, calling for different understanding of those who are same-sex oriented than historical biological assumptions. An alternative post-modern interpretation is to recognize all knowledge and norms as socially constructed and therefore not limited to traditional interpretations or understandings of the natural order. There is further consideration of issues of context, culture and interpretation below.

The reductionism and non-negotiable premises of literalist interpretations of religious scriptures can cause problems in public debate, as notably criticized by the likes of Bentham and more recently Bishop Richard Holloway.[25] However, the criticism is unfair in many instances as not all religious traditions or theological approaches to ethics adopt either such a literalist approach or theonomic deontology. The alternatives to literalism

---

[24] Examples include Martin DB. *Sex and the Single Savior.* Westminster: John Knox Press, 2006 (Martin 2006); Vines M. *God and the Gay Christian.* Random House, 2014 (Vines 2014); Thatcher A. *God, Sex and Gender.* Wiley-Blackwell, 2011 (Thatcher 2011).

[25] Holloway R. *Godless Morality.*, op. cit.

outlined above are considered further below, along with other methodologies for scriptural interpretation. All of them show both processes of reasoning and searches for wider understanding along with features of theological ethics that can add more generally to ethical exploration.

Different Types of Books

Another challenge of religious texts when considering their implications for ethics is that they are neither all the same form of literary creation nor written in the forms, genres and intellectual styles of contemporary writing. For example, the 66 books of the Christian Bible includes laws, histories, prophets, Psalms and other poetry like the Song of Songs, philosophy in Job and words of advice in Proverbs, narratives of Creation and flood, lives of Joseph, Jesus and others and letters from Paul. The *vedic* texts add rituals and chants and most of the scriptures contain passages written as verses. Each of the styles of writing seen in religious scriptures contains different sorts of truth, with direct rules providing very different insights and guidance from narrative tales that illustrate ethical norms or principles. They are not, unlike most philosophical and ethical discourse, designed to be systematic. Even those portions of the Bible and Qu'ran that are read as the more systematic discipline of law are far less ordered then the sorts of laws found on modern statute books. Biblical Commandments jump from prohibition of homosexuality to eating shellfish and wearing clothes of mixed fibres; the Qu'ran moves from laws to problem solving and questions. Writings like the histories and lives are partial, written for the community rather than the objective histories or biography of modern academic study. Yet this partiality is a function not only of religion but of the times; other texts, histories and commentaries contemporaneous with religious scriptures, such as Josephus' history, illustrate the use of partial and rhetorical devices. Interpretation of such texts in any scientific or historically probative sense therefore misunderstands them.

Yet the diversity and lack of system reflects the realities of human experience. The enduring force of humanity in the Psalms, parable-style tales and the *dharmic* narratives touches on the truths of human existence, like enemies, hope, despair, forgiveness and love, which have eternally transcendent power. Such narratives also often highlight the paradoxes both of human experience and human behaviour. Any lack of system has not hindered the use and application of religious texts both by the millions of adherents of particular faiths and as ethical inspiration, guidance and example, in some cases outside particular faith communities. This inspiration can occur partly because of overlapping texts and influences but also because of the insights into human behaviour, dilemmas and failings that religious texts contain. The Golden Rule of loving neighbour as self, often identified with Christianity, was there before Christianity in the Old Testament and since in both religious and secular traditions.[26] The lack of system and breadth of ethic posed by these examples does not detract from the fact that the insights and concepts provided carry weight universally as well as in their own traditions of origin.

Arguably however it is the poetic and narrative style of many religious texts and their illustrative messages that particularly adds to the richness of ethical discourse. The popular Hindu scriptures encompassed by the *mahabarat* are notable examples of narrative and poetic rather than didactic or deontological ethical example and teaching. By contrast with the *vedic* purity codes, they are *dharma* concerned with 'living life to the full. . . . with the demands of love and hate, war and peace, wealth, ambition and power,' or *artha* and *kama*.[27] Elements of narrative and poetry can be found in all religious texts and in some cases texts overlap. For example, the Qu'ran shares stories like the Queen of Sheba's visit to Solomon[28] and Noah's flood[29] with the Hebrew[30] and Christian Biblical canons. An example of the power of narrative truth and guidance is seen in the Old Testament's Nathan's parable, at 2 Samuel 12:1–7. It is a tale of abuse of power, adultery, pregnancy and murderous cover-up, ending with a parable that shows

---

[26] http://www.thinkhumanism.com/the-golden-rule.html; http://www.religioustolerance.org/reci proc1.htm.

[27] gain and desire; see Lipner J., op. cit., pp. 148–149.

[28] In 'the Ant'.

[29] Surah 7:143–144 & S.11 and 71.

[30] 1 Kings 10; Genesis 7.

David he is not above God's law or in principle the law of the land. Although David gets away with adultery with Bathsheba and arranging Uriah's death in battle, he is held to account by the prophet Nathan. Fasching, Dechant and Lantigua in *Comparative Religious Ethics*[31] cite Nathan's parable as an example of the principle of loving neighbour as self; in turn the narrative can be extrapolated to illustrate Kant's universalizing of ethical maxims and Rawls' concept of the 'veil of ignorance'. The story has its own force, relevant to contemporary politics, yet pre-dates modern more systematic approaches to philosophical ethics.

The power of religious narrative adds much by way of emotional and experiential force to ethics, moving people, by the illustrations and sympathies evoked, from the rational and abstract maxims to action motivated by empathy. It is not intended to be rational, objective argument yet within the story and the emotions it evokes there are profound rational and equitable ethical principles and truths that can be understood and applied more widely than the Jewish tradition from which it comes. The same can be seen in the great Hindu narratives where it is irrelevant that the characters are not necessarily real historical figures. Another example used by Fasching et al is the Buddhist tale of the Doe, Hunter and Stag. The courage of a doe, in defending her trapped and injured stag, leads to a change of heart by the hunter who releases both deer. In return the stag (an early incarnation of Buddha) rewards the hunter by unearthing a gem so that he will never need to hunt or kill again.[32]

Some aspects of religious texts, such as the histories, play an ethical role intended to be more particular to their specific community. Histories and chronicles in the scriptural context are partial, partisan and aimed at building or sustaining community rather than objective and dispassionate accounts of events or movements. This presence of

---

[31] Fasching Darrell J, Dechant Dell & Lantigua David M. *Comparative Religious Ethics: A Narrative Approach to Global Ethics – Wiley Blackwell,* 2nd edition. 2011 at pp. 20–29.
[32] Fasching et al., op. cit., pp. 26–27.

narrative agenda and community history in the chronicles and poetry of the religious canon, along with the full diversity of the scriptures, must be borne in mind when interpreting scripture and its ethics. In the main, religious texts are not books from which rules can be taken in the abstract, or principles applied without interpretation, as context, historical perspective and narrative sympathies also make a difference. Yet as examples of how common narratives, histories and chronicles build norms and ethics of communal self-understanding such texts are important. They are intentionally normative and collective, providing an identity and ethic based around common historical experience. They are also an interesting contrast with attempts to create, for example, 'British values', by means of abstract principles but without a common purposive narrative, save that of 'othering' those seen as the enemy.

The understanding of scripture as narrative is also important in recognising the allegorical rather than literal nature of many passages. For example the accounts of creation in all religious texts are neither scientifically nor historically observed descriptions but attempts to describe and make meaning of the world. This has further implications for ethics and how the truths of scripture are lived. Ethics depends upon an epistemological framework and understanding of the world, which is profoundly affected by whether or not faith accepts science. For example belief in a creationist understanding of the Bible to the exclusion of scientific explanations like evolution often goes hand in hand with belief in the direct power of prayer to heal to the exclusion – or at least suspicion – of medical science.

Being able to recognize the compatibility of science and religion as different types of discourse and enquiry is an important lesson for both the atheists who reject religion as unscientific and those of faith who reject science as incompatible with religion. The risk to religion's reputation, as benighted superstition, because of rejecting natural science was noted by Al Gazali when he wrote: 'Just as it is not a condition of religion to reject medical science so likewise the rejection of natural science is not one of its conditions – nature is in subjection to God...An instrument in the hands of its creator...' He goes on to say that rejection of science makes believers look foolish; Islam cannot be defended by the rejection of other sciences.[33] The acceptance or otherwise of science is significant for theological ethics because science and technology are such major influences on human possibilities, control and understanding and the different contexts and questions raised by contemporary ethics. Religion also needs to be able to engage with science to assess scientific and archaeological challenges to its own texts and their very production.

Al Gazali also recognized the challenges of epistemology and what constitutes truth where texts bear literal and metaphorical interpretation and the multiple meanings that symbols or allusions generate. He developed interpretive rules, following a logic that words aim to convey truth and argued that signification 'by correspondence' (*dalalat al mutabaqa)* or 'inclusion' (*dalalat al tadamun*) brings analogies and metaphors within the scope of truth and the believer's assent to truth (*tasdiq*).[34] By recognizing all words, whether literal or metaphorical as bearing a sense and truth arising from their context he seeks to erase the epistemological division between 'literal and figural meaning.'[35] Such reasoning again shows the degree of philosophical analysis in theological thought long before the arrival of formal semiotics.

The power of story for communities, ethics and moving people beyond theory to action is enjoying a revival in a world dominated by various forms of highly accessible global media. Religious stories or morality tales are part of that picture which questions Alistair McIntyre's reading of religious texts and ethics as limited to the communities that produce them. Despite what particular communities wish to believe about their own scriptures the power of narrative texts is that they can reach beyond particular communities to a wider cultural hinterland.

---

[33] Al Gazali. *The faith and practice of Al Ghazali* – Trans. Montgomery Watt W. Oneworld Publications, 2000.

[34] Hardy Paul-A. Epistemology and Divine Discourse In *The Cambridge Companion to Classical Islamic Theology*, Ed. Winter T. Cambridge: Cambridge University Press, 2008, pp. 288–307 (Hardy 2008).

[35] Hardy Paul-A, op. cit., p. 295.

Religious Texts and Law

As discussed in the previous chapter, when considering authority, some traditions do see their religious texts as foundational sources for legal systems that are co-terminus with ethics and practice. The Qu'ran and the Torah of the Hebrew Bible are foundational for *Shari'a* and *halakhah* respectively. *Halakhah* derives from roots for the words 'to behave' or 'to walk in' which illustrates this ethical dimension of law. Similarly Shari'a is 'the way' as much as the law. Generally speaking the legal portions of religious texts have a greater degree of system than is obvious in the narratives and psalms but they still need to be read in the context of a theological sensibility and overarching narratives rather than isolated from their context. An example is the Old Testament texts from chapter 18 to 21 of Leviticus. All too often Leviticus 18:22 and 20:13 are taken out of context to say that 'men lying with men as with a woman' is an abomination. However, these texts also set out laws about not having sexual relations with close kin, not eating unclean animals or birds, the regulation of sleeping with slaves, not mixing crops, species or fibres, not shaving parts of the head or beard, not stealing or defrauding, ensuring that land is not gleaned to the edge so that there is food left for the poor. Chapter 21 also sets out rules especially for priests which, along with rules about ritual defilement by contact with blood or the dead, are particularly discriminatory towards those with disabilities.

To modern western sensibilities this mixture can seem strange. Provisions about degrees of kinship in marriage, not sleeping with mothers and daughters, sacrifice of children, not stealing and leaving food for the poor may still command support. They are rational in terms of preserving workable family relationships, avoiding the risks of genetic proximity, respect for life, property and for justice. Many of the other provisions about defilement, same-sex relations, mixing of fibres and unclean food, as well as the priestly rules all reflect purity codes. They may seem alien but in turn can be rationalized; eating unclean food or touching dead bodies are hygiene measures. The strictures on sexual relations and mingling of the species are both about sexual and racial purity and the need for healthy children to ensure survival. The priestly purity codes are about offering God the best.

The strange mixture of taboos has often led to the discounting of such rules as irrelevant and outdated. Certainly the rules on sexuality and purity in the sense of priests not being blemished would contravene modern anti-discrimination provisions. Yet the outlawing of such discrimination even in enlightened, secular Britain remains a very recent phenomenon and as campaigners point out, still in practice has some way to go. This is not to defend laws that are discriminatory but to set in context the attitudes underlying them. What is particularly interesting is that even where ethical codes are also laws there is scope for changes of interpretation. For example, both the Bible and Qu'ran condemn homosexuality and approve of slavery. The latter has been outlawed and no reader of either text would try to use the scriptural acceptance of slavery as a defence of the concept. By the same token there is scope for new understandings of the scriptural texts in other areas of applied ethics. How religious communities and theological ethics adapt or develop such laws, texts and norms to different ages will be considered further.

Translation or Interpretation?

Another challenge of the major religious texts is that none were written in English, Spanish or Chinese, which are now the nearest languages to a global *lingua franca*. In most cases the versions of the languages in which the scriptures were written does not reflect current usage. This means that for most faith communities, let alone the wider world, the language of the original texts requires some translation into contemporary and vernacular speech. There are significant issues in translating religious texts faithfully or authentically and faith communities have varied reactions to the question of whether their sacred texts should be translated at all. For example, there has been reluctance to translate the Qu'ran from the original Arabic because of the wish to preserve authenticity through the language of its original revelation. Yet there have been translations; the earliest being by Salman the Persian in the 7th CE.[36] Translations into Greek by Nicetas Byzantios and Latin, by Robert Ketenensis,[37] illustrate one problem with translations as both these versions, written by Christians, sought to disprove the Qu'ran. Similar concerns arise over the earliest translations into English by various clergy between 1647[38] and 1950.[39] More recent English translations by practicing Muslims are a response from publishers to the spread of the Muslim population across the English-speaking world.[40]

Missionary agendas from those outside the faith are just one problem with translation, although those within the tradition can also impose interpretations on texts from partisan theological stances that they do not naturally bear. An example is the NIV Bible translation of Ezekiel 43: 9 as 'prostitution' where other translations refer to 'idolatry.'[41] Yet even without such theological interpolations there is a balance to be struck between accuracy and fluency, verbal equivalence or verbal dynamism.[42] Fluency and how translations sound is particularly important for texts whose power derives from being spoken or chanted not just written and read. For both Hindus and Sikhs the sound of the word is holy, carrying the force of ritual and creative power.[43] For some Hindus the *vedas* are viewed as given, unmediated by a cognitive script; this means that translation, which necessitates cognitive engagement with the text, risks undermining its authority. Having said which there are

---

[36] Christian Høgel. An early anonymous Greek translation of the Qur'an. The fragments from Niketas Byzantios' Refutatio and the anonymous Abjuratio. *Collectanea Christiana Orientalia* 7 (2010), pp. 65–119 (Høgel 2010).

[37] Fatani Afnan. Translation and the Qur'an. In *The Qur'an: An Encyclopaedia*, Ed. Leaman Oliver. Great Britain: Routledge, 2006, pp. 657–669 (Fatani 2006).

[38] By Alexander Ross, chaplain to Charles I.

[39] The various translations by non-Muslims are assessed by Khaleel Mohammed. *Assessing English Translations of the Qur'an Middle East Quarterly.* Spring, 2005, pp. 58–71 (Mohammed 2005).

[40] Mohammed K., op. cit.

[41] NRSV.

[42] https://www.cokesbury.com/FreeDownloads/BibleTransGuide.pdf.

[43] Lipner J., op. cit., pp. 58–67.

translations of all Hindu texts into a variety of languages including English and relatively early use of the vernacular and mixed language poems, in Sanskrit and Bengali.[44]

The core issue when translating scriptures is to recognize that simple translation is insufficient, interpretation is also necessary, particularly when discerning ethical norms. Although interpretation and translation are related they operate differently. Translation seeks to provide an accurate mirror copy of the original text in a different language. This in itself is complex as not all words in one language have a precise equivalent in another. Even closely related languages use words differently; for example in American English and English it pays to be careful when using the words 'rubber' or 'pants'. Translating directly from language written in a pre-technological world also encounters problems of conceptual gaps and lack of words.

The limitations of translation give rise to interpretation and the search for concepts, mindsets and the deeper or more detailed meaning of words. The fact that religious texts are all historical, means that some interpretation is always necessary. For example, a 'household' in modern white western society generally means a nuclear family, couple or single person. In Biblical, Qu'ranic, Greek and Roman times it meant a far wider range of people, including the extended family, slaves and various other dependents and workers and (probably) the animals. Interpretation therefore requires not only a search for words but also an understanding of the context from which the passage is written or formed, the concepts used and a comparison of that context with contemporary understandings. The aim is to enable an authentic understanding and application of the principles with which the passage is concerned. An example is the translation of Jesus' injunction about travelling light at Luke 10:4 which most translations render as 'Carry no purse, no bag, no sandals...'[45] but which The Message, acknowledging it is paraphrase rather than translation, interprets 'Travel light. Comb and toothbrush and no extra luggage'.

---

[44] Lipner J. op. cit., pp. 62–65 & 78–80.
[45] NRSV.

As with the intentional agendas identified in the earliest Qu'ranic translations most translators will come to a text with particular assumptions about its characters and theology. Thus a Marian Catholic, who believes in virgin birth is more likely to translate the Greek *parthenon* as 'virgin' than 'young woman'. Views about gender politics will affect whether inclusive language is used. Understandings of the divine as a theist God or more diffuse *atman* affect translation of concepts of prayer and terms for meditation. Preference for particular religious characters over others also influence what gets translated and whose work is made known. Both translators and readers bring perceptions to the texts affected by their own backgrounds and wider religious sources, the popularity of the lower caste Nichiren over Buddha's privilege being an example. For Walter Wink, Jesus is a radical, resisting Roman rule,[46] but for Victorian hymn writers he is the perfect, quiet, obedient child.

Context – then *historical analysis and the discourse of the time*:

The essence of interpretation and application of religious texts is context, including history and circumstances at the time of writing, later treatment and the contemporary context in which it is applied. Issues to consider when interpreting scripture in its historical context include:

- Is the word or concept under consideration the same then as now? For example different understandings of 'household', as discussed above.
- How was society different then? For example, Athenian democracy was far more elitist than democracy in modern Europe.
- Are places the same? The Biblical *Tarshish* 'the ends of the earth' was Spain, the end of the Mediterranean, the known world; means and timescales for travel also differ from contemporary assumptions.
- Is the statement rhetoric within an argument? If so, what is the argument about and how objective, exaggerated or well-informed?
- Is the argument written from a partial and emotional point of view to encourage persecuted believers?

---

[46] Wink W. *Jesus and Nonviolence: A Third Way*. Augsburg Fortress, 2003 (Wink 2003).

- What literary forms are used? The Book of Revelation or *Apocolypsis* is meant to be exaggerated, stylized and poetic rather than an objective account.
- Are words literary short-hand? e.g., '3 days', '40 days' and '40 years' are Biblical devices for short, medium and long periods of time
- What are the assumptions of that time? If people believe in trial by ordeal as a means of resolving a dispute, or a world without God never crosses their mind such perceptions will affect their ethics

There is also the question of historical criticism such as archaeological evidence that contradicts the text or long held beliefs about the history of the scripture in question. Examples include casting doubt on records believed to establish that Jesus or Buddha existed or that the flood mentioned in the Abrahamic texts happened. Such methods also include literary criticism casting doubt on the authorship of writings such as Paul's letters. Some faiths are open to the challenge of such techniques, but others, for example Islam reject them as attempts to discredit the religion.[47] The issue is whether discrediting history as factual truth actually makes such a difference to the ethical maxims. Is it necessary to believe in Jesus to accept the moral force of his teaching and example in caring for the poor and looking after Samaritans as neighbours? Did Buddha need to exist in order to follow his teaching or the authorship of the Qu'ran be proved to come from Mohammed for the Qu'ran to be authoritative? The more liberal tendencies in most traditions are willing to accept the ethics and practices as good in themselves, without needing absolute proof that a particular figure existed.

And the Context Now – What Are the Changes and are They Material?

In many ways the context of contemporary society, in all parts of the world, will be different to a greater or lesser degree from the circumstances and times in which religious texts were written. There is almost

---

[47] Layman D. *The Qu'ran and historical criticism,* citing Sayedd Hossein Nasr. http://www.first things.com/blogs/firstthoughts/2010/09/quran-historical-criticism.

nowhere in the world that is unaffected by modern transport, science, trade and communications and that has not been affected by colonialism, shifting patterns of political supremacy and some degree of technological change. Yet the patterns and expectations of family life and relationships in European cities is a lot more different from scriptural times than are such institutions in much of Africa, South Asia and the Middle East. The following are just some of the contemporary questions to be negotiated in interpreting religious texts:

- If our understanding of particular practices has changed how does this affect our reading of practices that are now prohibited? e.g., slavery and caste are outlawed, yet they are accepted as standard features of Biblical, Qu'ranic and Hindu texts.
- Having moved from a society based on status to one, at least in theory, grounded in equality how should religious texts that discriminate against women, those who are disabled, gay and of different races be interpreted?
- In an age of nuclear technology how should just war, spiritual warfare and jihad be understood?
- How do we find ethical norms for things that do not appear in religious scripture e.g., IVF, nuclear weapons, social media?
- How do we deal with apparent contradictions either within the body of a set of scriptures or between those scriptures and modern practice?
- Is it inauthentic to religion to adopt modern standards or a failure of religious imagination not to?

Interpretation of scripture also raises questions about the source of ethics summed up by Euthyphro's dilemma. If scripture is interpreted as the definitive revelatory source then what the text says is right because it is divine revelation and therefore good. If scripture conflicts with contemporary societal ethics and other factors in ethical discernment such as reason, the reasoning dictated by the religious premises takes priority over the conflicting secular ethic. By contrast, for those whose interpretation of scripture draws on other sources of authority, reasoning external to the text can be brought to bear on its interpretation. In terms of Euthyphro's dilemma what is good is determined by an ethical reasoning to which scripture is also subject.

A stark illustration of the dilemma is the Old Testament and Qu'ranic story of Abraham[48] almost sacrificing his son Isaac, which represented the horrific near-sacrifice of his child but also the dreams of founding a nation that God had promised. For Kant, other Enlightenment thinkers and some modern, particularly feminist theologians, a God who could even ask someone to murder their son is a deeply unethical, despotic monster unworthy of worship. The despotism is not excused by God's last minute provision of a lamb for slaughter instead of Isaac. God's command is judged by ethics external to the text that life should be preserved, the weak and innocent protected and the life of one's innocent son doubly so. Yet for the believer who interprets the narrative from the perspective of the revealed text only, the moral of the story is entirely about obedience to God. God is the ultimate source of life, truth and ethical authority. Therefore in Euthyphro's terms God's command is ethically right because God defines ethics. This would hold even if Abraham had actually killed his son, had that been God's will.

The reality is that relatively few have such a completely black versus white view of ethical right and wrong and other interpretive factors come into play. The historical context, in which child sacrifice did happen, can temper the moral horror in its context. Other ethical principles drawn from the text include a more metaphorical story about ordering priorities, willingly putting the divine at the heart of life. If seen as a story about detachment from worldly ties the story begins to take on some of the ethical parameters of the *dharmic samsara* or detachment from worldly affections. It is a logic that makes sense in theological terms but may not carry much weight or ethical respect in wider society.

Both approaches to Euthyphro's dilemma are found in valid theological and scriptural interpretation in all traditions. The extent to which sources of reasoning and premises external to the revealed sources are countenanced affects approaches to epistemology and societal changes

---

[48] Genesis 22.

not envisaged at the time of the text's composition. In all cases the canonical scriptures are the last word on revelation. However traditions have methods of interpretive development that allow the application of scripture to new situations by analogy, extension and deemed understandings. Islam uses a method called *ijtihad*, Christianity contextual development. These methods can apply the story of Hagar, the slave girl bearing a son for Abraham at his wife, Sarah's suggestion,[49] to contemporary questions of surrogacy and IVF. The contours of how and which faith communities use ethical sources external to scriptural revelation and which do not are explored in more detail in the next chapter.

Historical and Literary Criticism

Most traditions engage in at least some of the interpretive techniques used above but some traditions have another layer of scriptural analysis known as historical literary criticism. This goes beyond considering historical context to questioning the scriptures that form the source of revelation. Archaeological analysis considers possible corroborative evidence of narrative facts and scientific methods date texts and other historical evidence. Literary criticism analyses texts in terms of linguistic style and consistency of authorship. In some instances this casts doubts upon the historical existence of key characters or aspects of the tradition, for example the sayings of Jesus, whether Paul really did write the letters attributed to him and the very existence of Jesus, Buddha or others. However, the analysis can bolster credibility by providing explanations for textual inconsistencies by recognizing multiple authorship or dubious attribution. The method does not present problems for those whose interpretation recognizes human agency in scriptural transmission and indirect mediation of God's word. However, for those with a more direct understanding of revelation historical critical research is rejected as hostile to faith. Islam, even in its most liberal iterations is reluctant to countenance such methods if, in the words of Tariq Ramadan, they challenge 'the belief that the Quran, the last Revelation, is the word of

---

[49] Genesis 16.

God (*kalam Allah*) revealed to mankind in clear Arabic language'. However, Ramadan distinguishes the rejected historico-critical approach that recognizes human agency in the writing of the New Testament, from the recognition of historical context in understanding the Quran.[50]

For other religions such historico-critical methods have less impact on the faith, truth, ethics and worldview of the tradition. For example, in Hinduism challenge to the founding texts is less critical as authorship is so diverse, there is less emphasis on proving the existence of God, saviour or prophet as key narrative figures are largely mythical and the vedic chants take their power from sound as much as cognition. For Christianity by contrast questions of whether Jesus actually lived, taught and was crucified have profound ethical implications because of Christian theology that God experienced humanity and ignoble death, thereby showing us how to live. However, for Christians who also accept the scientific critique of Biblical texts this does not necessarily undermine the essential Christian ethic and dynamic of Jesus' teaching about incarnation, self-giving and forgiveness at the heart of Christian belief.

Authority to Interpret Scripture

In practice questions about translating and interpreting scripture return to the question of authority, discussed in the previous chapter. A key dimension of the authority of scripture is its relationship to tradition. Tradition literally means 'handing on', from the Latin word '*tradere*'. It does not mean old-fashioned or set in stone, despite frequent misperceptions along such lines. Tradition refers to the practices of faith communities for developing scriptural and theological interpretation, negotiating ethics and relationships within the community and with wider society. Depending on the underlying theology, tradition can generate either conservative or modern interpretations of the original truths of a faith. Which interpretation is adopted varies with approaches to wider society, key authorities and the priorities given to scripture

---

[50] Ramadan T. *Radical Reform: Islamic Ethics and Liberation*. Oxford: Oxford University Press, 2009, pp. 14–17 (Ramadan 2009).

versus other sources of tradition and autonomy versus community. In turn this can give rise to relationships with wider culture that are either assimilative or counter-cultural and a range of perspectives in between.

As indicated earlier the position and experience of those with authority to interpret scripture, can significantly affect the interpretive tradition and how it develops. The preponderance of male leadership and interpretation in most religious traditions has tended to lead to conservative interpretations of scripture, at least at an official level, particularly around matters of gender and sexuality. Yet modern autonomy has affected faith communities, aided by the proliferation of religious sources, groups, charismatic leaders and the internet. These trends have led to more diverse interpretation and separatism at the same time, paradoxically, as heightened senses of global religious belonging.

This means that through the 'universal apostolic Catholic Church', evangelical, Pentecostal and Protestant alliances, the Muslim *umma*, Jewish allegiance to Israel and worldwide diasporas of Hindu, Sikh and Buddhist communities the use of religious texts remains alive and well. Yet to the extent that interpretation of religious texts and use of scripture has become more autonomous or local its role as a normative ethical authority, as opposed to inspirational source, has declined. This needs to be borne in mind when considering what faith communities believe, who speaks for those faith communities and how theological ethics relates to debates in wider society. This greater availability of scriptures may also have generated greater access across and outside particular faith traditions. Overlapping stories of some traditions, for example within the Abrahamic faiths and between *dharmic communities*, or the influence of theological texts on cultural history, can provide inspiration outside the traditions for whom a particular scripture is their revelatory source text. The next chapter considers the relationships of faith communities to wider society and the role of theological influences and ethics within wider public debate. This requires an engagement with the diversity of faith communities, authorities and scriptural interpretation, the paradoxes of local and global allegiance, the dynamics of conservative, liberal or contemporary interpretations and pro or counter-cultural stances and processes of faith development.

7

Religious Ethics as Cultural or Counter-Cultural

Having considered authority in faith communities, including the challenges posed by scriptural authority, this chapter explores the outworkings of those authorities for faith communities' lived theology. The impact of theological ethics appears more obvious in those communities who depart from society's dominant ethical paradigms. However, as Nigel Biggar[1] points out, faith does not necessarily have to be counter-culturally distinct in order to be authentic or have an impact.

RH Niebuhr's thesis in *Christ and Culture*[2] is used as the basis for an analytical model for this exploration. Although Niebuhr's paradigm was originally developed in relation to Christian communities it has been applied subsequently to other traditions by Keith Ward, amongst others.[3] Taking into account the nuances of different theological traditions, the analysis addresses the dilemmas for theological ethics and religious

---

[1] Biggar N. *Behaving in Public: How to do Christian Ethics*. Grand Rapids: Eerdmans Publishing, 2011, pp. 1–24 (Biggar 2011).
[2] Niebuhr HR. *Christ and Culture*. London: Harper Collins, 1951 – 2002 reprint (Niebuhr 1951–2002).
[3] Ward K. *Religion and Society*. Oxford University Press, 1999.

© The Author(s) 2017
C. Shelley, *Ethical Exploration in a Multifaith Society*,
DOI 10.1007/978-3-319-46711-5_7

communities of maintaining religious authenticity whilst living in a constantly changing world. Christians might use the Biblical concept of living 'in but not of the world' but for all religious communities there are challenges in discerning how to live out their faith in the realities of daily life and wider generally secular society.

It is diaspora communities that most obviously have to discern how to remain true to their faith whilst adapting to the practicalities of life and work in a differently motivated society and culture. For many diaspora faith communities the challenge may be presented as discovering what is strictly theological rather than what owes its origins to culture. Yet for all religious traditions the inter-twining of faith, theology and culture is often too complex simply to segregate out theological belief and practice from 'mere' cultural accretion. It must be remembered that all major UK faith communities are communities in diaspora. None of the major faiths originated in Britain; even the Judaeo-Christian heritage of Britain began in what is now the Middle East and developed for many centuries in the Middle East, North Africa and Southern Europe before reaching northern Europe some centuries later.

Throughout Biblical scripture there are examples of the dilemmas of remaining true to faith in an alien culture, often in exile or under imposed rule. Scripture also provides examples of differing resolutions to these dilemmas. For example, in Jeremiah 29:4–7 the exiles are encouraged simply to settle down and get on with family life for the foreseeable future, despite the conditions of exile. It is a focus that enjoins a degree of assimilation and respect for the Babylonian society in which the Jewish exiles find themselves. Yet Daniel, of lions' den fame, demonstrates the limitations of such an approach when alien societies impose laws that prohibit religious practices or require allegiances incompatible with faith. Such narratives reflect the dilemmas for many faith traditions in the UK of deciding which religious observances are essential where not easily accommodated by society's norms. This can be exacerbated by perceptions in the host community that the practice in question is 'merely' religious observance rather than a matter of significant ethical weight for the believer. An example is the courts' view that parental disagreement over children's circumcision is weighty enough for court decision but disputes about dietary rules are not.[4]

Faith communities have always had concerns about remaining true to theologically-grounded ethics, retaining religious identity, zeal, purity or salvation, against assimilation to broader social *mores*. Tensions over maintaining or identifying what constitutes the essentials of faith also arise as membership develops to include peoples' of different backgrounds. This is seen particularly acutely in the early days of Christianity as Ethiopian, Greek and Roman Gentiles joined a faith that began as a Jewish sect. Some of these new believers had attended synagogue but not become members because of the high bar to conversion in Judaism. Christian communities included different races and cultures within the first generation but difficult decisions had to be taken about which Jewish laws were required, alongside the development of Christianity's own distinct ethical practices of sharing goods in common and theologies around celibacy.

Besides the dilemmas of defining and protecting their own ethical stances and core practices most traditions also seek to live an ethical vision that one way or another has things to say to the wider society in which they are located. The fact that most faiths do not accept the conceptual distinctions of the Enlightenment between sacred and secular, public and private life, means that faith-based ethics automatically have implications for the public as well as private sphere and wider public debate. Historically in the UK it has been Christianity, generally through the established Church, that has commented not only on issues of conscience like marriage, sexuality and sanctity of life but also economics, war, housing, employment, refugees and other social affairs. On occasions this has drawn criticism for 'meddling' in politics if straying too far into the public sphere beyond 'appropriate' religious realms of personal morality. Examples include the infamous 'Faith in the City' report, which criticized Thatcherite economics and questioning of policies affecting destitute groups like refugees and those who are homeless or disabled.

---

[4] *Re U sub nom J [2000] 1 FLR 57.*

Non-Christian traditions have often focused initially on their survival as minorities in a Christian heritage land, with involvement in wider political issues developing later. However, the theology of Tariq Ramadan,[5] policy analysis of Tariq Modood[6] and theological and legal analysis of Abdullahi An Na'im,[7] have signalled a call to bring Muslim ethical reflection to bear on wider society. Similarly Rabbis Jonathan Sachs,[8] Jonathan Romain[9] and Professor David Novak,[10] amongst others, have made notable contributions to public ethics from a Jewish perspective. From the Sikh tradition Indarjit Singh has been a notable voice, along with the Hindu Council and various Buddhist groups. At international level the inspirations of Ghandi and the Dalai Lama have also contributed ethical vision from the *dharmic* traditions.

As with all things religious, there are no univocal or homogenous contributions and the ways in which theological ethical insights are brought to bear on public life are diverse. The remainder of the chapter considers how faith communities live out the ethical implications of their faith and examples of how such ethics contribute to wider society. Although the relationship of faith to wider society has tensions particular to the faith versus secular divide it is also worth remembering that there are tensions, even in theocracies and religiously homogenous societies, between the aspirations of faith and the realities of daily material life and human limitation. Although the aspirations and endpoints of ethics may

---

[5] See e.g. Ramadan T. *Western Muslims and the Future of Islam.* Oxford University Press, 2004 (Ramadan 2004); Ramadan T. *Radical Reform: Islamic Ethics and Liberation.* Oxford University Press, 2009 (Ramadan 2009).

[6] Modood T. *Multicultural Politics: Racism, Ethnicity and Muslims in Britain.* Edinburgh University Press, 2005 (Modood 2005), *Multiculturalism: A Civic Idea.* Polity Press, 2007/2013 (Modood 2007/2013); *Still Not Easy Being British: Struggles for a Multicultural Citizenship.* Trentham Books Ltd., 2010 (Modood 2010).

[7] An Na'im AA. *Islamic Family Law in a Changing world.* Zed Books, 2002 (An Na'im 2002).

[8] e.g. Sachs J. *Radical Now, Radical Then.* London: Harper Collins/Continuum, 2004 (Sachs 2004).

[9] Romain JA. *A Guide to Reformed Judaism.* Reform Synagogue of Great Britain, 1991 (Romain 1991); Romain JA. *Renewing the Vision: Rabbis Speak Out on Modern Jewish Issues.* SCM Press, 2011 (Romain 2011).

[10] Novak D. *Tradition in the Public Square: A Novak Reader.* Eds. Rashkova R & Kavka M. London: SCM Press, 2008 (Novak 2008).

be different as between theological and atheist worldviews, the tensions between aspiration and reality, authenticity and compromise, are common to all humanity.

Terminology

Language used about religion, faith communities and their relationship to wider society can carry connotations that are seen as pejorative from some perspectives. For the sake of clarity and in search of neutrality the following terminology is used to develop the theological analysis outlined. The terms are intended not as definitive groupings but to indicate positions on a spectrum, which in some cases may overlap. The term 'separatist' is used to denote a group or community that is counter-culturally withdrawn and self-consciously set apart. A separatist stance tends to be taken by radical or purist groups who seek to live in a self-contained way, apart from and uncorrupted by mainstream society. Dualist theologies recognize or accept greater involvement with wider society, for example in order to earn a living, but also regard the world as tainted and human institutions as suspect. The life of faith, salvation and afterlife are aspirations for the hereafter to some degree divorced from every day life. The theology of these two groups means that provided they are free to observe their own ethics they are less likely to seek to change wider society, arguing that such human efforts must fail because salvation can only come from God.

The idea of 'engagement' is opposed to separatism and denotes involvement in society and its institutions, for example through work, political office and school governance. Groups and individuals whose theology seeks engagement live faith through a vision for a better society according to theological values. Engagement is not about imposing a faith on society but sharing with wider society faith-based insights, values and ethics that proponents believe will be of benefit. This form of engagement and theology is for the benefit of the whole society, as another voice in the public square, rather than engagement which seeks accommodation for the practices of a particular religious group, for example over diet or clothing.

Engagement may arise, as in any other part of the public, from a variety of perspectives requiring further precision about terminology. The schema used in what follows includes 'conservative traditionalists', who interpret and practise traditions in ways that wish to preserve the status quo, resisting change in society and often in the religious community. 'Radical traditionalists', denotes those who seek 'purer' forms of faith and regard themselves as going back to their theological roots.[11] They may be separatist or engaged but if engaged tend to seek transformation of society in line with theologically-based values. Such values can lead to action across a wide spectrum of issues around social justice,[12] debt relief, liberation theology's option for the poor and peace campaigns[13] as well as 'moral majority' issues like sanctity of life, family and sexuality. Some faith-based campaigners are happy to make common cause with non-faith groups who share the same goals if not the same theological and ethical reasoning or motivation. Others prefer a more purist or exclusive approach based solely on the reasoning of their faith.

There may be less obvious religious or theological engagement in more 'liberal' sections of religious communities, where an open-ended theological stance is not only more tolerant of modern western society but has been marking by pro-cultural stances throughout history. Such theologies may adopt a more metaphorical interpretation of faith, less exclusively dependent on scriptural revelation as the only source of ethics. This enables greater recognition of ethical insights from other faiths and philosophies. Theologically such stances tend to draw on aspects of natural law and other theologies that recognize God at work in all creation, with reason not limited to belief in revelation. Assimilation to wider society means that faith may be more personal or private but may also motivate engagement with issues of social justice, equality and progressive politics, in both wider society and the religious

---

[11] Ramadan places the Muslim *salafi* movement in this category in Ramadan T. *Western Muslims and the Future of Islam*. Oxford University Press, 2004, pp. 25–29.

[12] e.g. Nishkam, a Sikh social justice charity; Christian Aid, CAFOD, Islamic Relief, World Jewish Relief.

[13] Ploughshares Campaign, Pax Christi, Muslims for Peace, the Brahmakumari Pledge for Peace.

community, often in opposition to more conservative co-religionists. Another assimilationist position goes further than theological liberalism seeking to identify teachings of faith as equating to the best of culture, marking faith through civic religion.

Theological Analysis

One of the best-known theological analyses of the ethical spectrum and communities' self-understanding encompassed by the descriptions above is HR Niebuhr's *Christ and Culture*.[14] Although it has been critiqued it retains sufficient cogency as a framework to analyse the variety of faith communities' theological responses to wider society. One shortcoming of the original Niebuhrian analysis in an interfaith context is its limitation to Christian communities, with some terminology and theology that is specifically Christian. Examples include the term 'two kingdoms' theology derived from the Christian concept of being in but not of 'the world',[15] and its consequent dualism. Yet similar analysis has been applied to other faith contexts, for example in Keith Ward's *Religion and Society*.[16] The exploration below outlines the five categories of Niebuhr's original analysis, develops the scheme to encompass a sixth group and considers theological paradigms arising from other faiths.

Niebuhr's *Christ and Culture*: The two poles of Niebuhr's spectrum are Christ against Culture and Christ of Culture, as follows:

Christ against culture[17] views history as a process in which Christianity is an exclusive faith, the only way and truth, which because it is God's way must ultimately succeed over other faiths and wider non-Christian society. It will succeed by the faithful being purist and preparing for the end-time. Niebuhr cites as examples Tertullian, Benedictine desert monasticism, the Mennonites and Leo Tolstoy. Contemporary examples include millenarianism and groups such as

---

[14] Niebuhr HR. *Christ and Culture,* op. cit.

[15] Exemplified for example in John 15–17 and 1 John 2: 16.

[16] Ward K. *Religion and Society.* Oxford University Press, 1999.

[17] Niebuhr RH., op. cit., pp. 45–82.

the Jehovah's Witnesses, Exclusive Brethren and similarly exclusive traditions. It reflects the conservative and radically separatist strands of faith communities.

Christ of culture[18] is the theology of liberal Christianity, which Niebuhr saw exemplified from Abelard to Albrecht Ritschl and through philosophers like Kant. Christianity is seen as embodied in the best values of society, enabling a broad, inclusive civic understanding of religion that embraces all. It is also consistent with understandings of natural law theology in which reason accessible to all citizens is baptized by faith. Its weakness is that when culture departs from the Gospel, critique proves difficult. This was markedly identified by Karl Barth and Dietrich Bonhoefffer's criticisms of Harnack, Schleiermacher and the established German churches which colluded with Nazism.

In between these two poles lie the further three categories of analysis:

Christ above culture[19] views the relationship as a synthesis of religion and culture, which are distinct but overlap as Christ is lord of both heaven and earth. It is also a view consistent with natural law theology in which history is a period of preparation under law, reason, gospel and the church for ultimate union with God in eternal life. Niebuhr's examples included Justin Martyr, Clement of Alexandria and Thomas Aquinas.

Christ and culture in paradox[20] is a dualist interpretation of the relationship between the two kingdoms of earth and heaven. History is seen as a time of struggle between faith and unbelief, between the giving of the promise of life and its fulfilment in the kingdom of God and Christ's second coming. The idea of the two kingdoms is classically associated with Martin Luther and the kingdom that matters is the one to come. Salvation is through belief in that kingdom as promised whilst enduring the earthly kingdom in the meantime. It is suspicious of surrounding culture seeing little point in trying to change society but is less antagonistic towards prevailing culture than Christ against culture.

---

[18] Niebuhr RH., op. cit., pp. 83–115.
[19] Niebuhr RH, op. cit., pp. 116–148.
[20] Niebuhr RH., pp. 149–189.

Christltransforming culture[21] also views Christian life as between the promise and its fulfilment. However, whereas two kingdoms theology awaits the kingdom of eternity disengaged from this world, those seeking to transform culture are actively involved with seeking to effect change in the world in response to God's call. The sense of seeking to transform the world is a call both on individuals to live out the ethics of their faith and on communities to be witnesses to Gospel values.

Each of these theologies seeks to live out Christian witness to God and the values of loving neighbour as self, loving enemies, seeking reconciliation and tackling oppression and poverty. This witness applies both to individuals and communities in each of the models but the type of witness displayed varies according to the theology.

Faith and Culture

In some respects the application of Niebuhr's analysis across other religious communities and their underlying theology and ethics is comparatively straightforward. The external outworking of the models through separatism to assimilation can be fairly readily compared. Yet fuller analysis and adaptation is required in considering other theological paradigms particularly in non-Abrahamic faiths. The underlying issues however are much the same, namely how faith communities retain theological and ethical authenticity in a predominantly secular society and how they participate in and contribute to that society.

Faith Against Culture

Niebuhr's concept of Christ against culture is a separatist, sometimes self-righteous even supremacist, withdrawal from wider society. Yet in extrapolating this paradigm to wider religious frameworks two alternative responses can be seen in some communities. At the core of this position is a view that surrounding culture is problematic, possibly corrupt and opposed to the values and practices of faith. The classic faith against

---

[21] Niebuhr RH., pp. 190–229.

culture pattern is to retreat from that corrupt society and seek to live in purist, separatist religious communities. This response, seen from the earliest days of Christian monasticism to modern communities like the Amish, is also found in many other faiths, particularly where compounded by issues of identity arising from minority status and disapora.

The withdrawn, separatist living out of faith within dedicated and comparatively enclosed communities is intended to be a safe, theologically pure place, focused on God. The marked countercultural differences of lifestyle provide a witness to faith-based ethics and dedication to God. However, that witness is incidental as the essence of such withdrawal is not missionary in the sense of converting others[22] or seeking to change society, save for any accommodation needed to enable the community to live its chosen life. Buddhist monks, Hindu *sants* withdrawing 'to the forest', as well as Christian monastic communities live countercultural lives foregoing family as well as worldly business. Separatist withdrawal is also possible for those with families who often run their own schools, do not take public jobs or engage in aspects of civic life like voting. Examples include Haredi or ultra-Orthodox Jews, Christian groups like the Exclusive Brethren, some salafi Muslims and de facto some migrant Muslim communities who have remained isolated by language and employment in comparatively self-enclosed societies.

The worldview underlying such separatism is varied. From a Christian perspective the argument is that the values of 'the world', ambition, power, money, pleasure and sexual licence are alien to faith; living separately is the only way to live ethically and avoid corruption. Variations on this theme are the *dharmic*, more specifically Brahminic and Buddhist, concepts that the world and its pleasures are illusory rather than corrupting. It is not so much that the world should be avoided but that life is best spent focussing on what really matters, *samsara* and the ultimate goal of *moksha*. The withdrawal of the ultra-Orthodox Jewish communities is more by way of indifference to the world rather than judging it corrupt; the focus is to preserve the religious traditions that the chosen people have lived for centuries.

---

[22] The Jewish *haredi* community has a mission to fellow Jews but not more widely.

For such separatist communities ethical authority is located entirely within the religious community, its revelation and practices. No valid ethics can be gleaned from the world outside the community. Engagement with wider society is oriented solely to ensuring that those aspects of faith that are counter to wider culture can be accommodated, for example through exceptions from educational curricula inconsistent with faith like IT and audio-visual technology, language, sex education, dress codes, holy days and dietary rules.

An alternative response prompted by the faith against culture paradigm maintains the sense of judgement or 'faith against the world' so that faith-based authority, ethics and practices are not compromised. This model may also have separatist schools, businesses and other institutions. However, rather than withdrawing entirely from the wider community, this alternative model engages with wider society. The aim is to convert those not yet under the authority of faith or saved. The model is seen in the more missionary-minded, exclusivist religious communities like Wahabi Muslims, particularly those seeking to re-establish a Caliphate or the more triumphalist and missionary Christian churches promoting countercultural personal morality, sometimes linked to a prosperity Gospel.

This paradigm could be termed counter-cultural engagement, seeking to live a life wholly inspired by religious vision but nonetheless engaged with societal structures and civic life. Countercultural but engaged communities are also suspicious of authority external to their faith and ultimately seek transformation of wider culture so that it conforms to their doctrine. This is distinct from the more gradual and piecemeal transformation envisaged in the next paradigm. Such groups may found charities in the name of faith that are exclusive in their employment practices to that faith and vision. They may provide services to the wider population but are less likely to work with those of different faith backgrounds.

Transforming Culture

By contrast with counter-cultural engagement, which seeks a wholly different society grounded in faith-based principles, the approach of transforming culture accepts some aspects of society, seeking only to transform practices that conflict particularly acutely with their faith and its vision. This requires an engagement with society not to achieve change to accommodate faith but to change particular laws or structures seen as unjust or unethical. The precise issues over which engagement is sought with civil society vary depending upon the theological priorities and ethical conceptions of particular communities. This category would include Quaker campaigns for peace and disarmament, campaigns for tax justice and poverty relief by groups that include Christian Aid, CAFOD and Islamic Relief. Here countercultural witness turns on issues of economic and social justice.

At the more conservative end of the spectrum are counter-cultural campaigns around sexual morality, challenging same-sex marriage or abortion, which can often be singled out as electoral issues. Another interesting example was the Hindu campaign during the 2015 UK election which endorsed the Conservative party's stance on regulations about caste. Although the issues are different the dynamic is similar to the extent that in each instance the engagement with society, and transformation sought, arises from the ethical priorities set by the community's theology. These groups are more open to working in coalition with those of other backgrounds, including within mainstream politics, even if they may not wholly share the same overall worldview.

Faith in Paradox

The dualist model of faith in paradox separates the religious or sacred realm from the mundane or secular sphere. Ethics and true faith are observed in the religious and sacred sphere, which will be realized fully at the end time or day of judgement. In the meantime the mundane and the secular are to be endured and struggled with, pending the realization of the kingdom, in Christian terms. This dualism is most associated with Christianity and was the template that enabled liberal secular accommodation of faith as a private matter in post-Enlightenment western society. It has tended to place more emphasis on orthodoxy and right belief, rather than the orthopraxy or right practice of other faiths.

Despite the association of the Faith in Paradox approach with a particularly Christian theology its impact on approaches to faith can be seen in some diaspora communities who conform to western norms during the working day and in the public sphere but celebrate their faith traditions in family and private life. This is not generally an indigenous feature of most world faiths but reflects the adaptations that many minority faith communities have made to liberal secular societies. Yet, although not so pronounced as in the western tradition, there is a sense of the paradoxes and tensions between the transcendent and immanent, the other-worldly and this-worldly in all faiths. The Hindu concepts of *prvritti* and *nvritti* represent the opposing poles of engagement with and enjoyment of the world versus detachment from the world[23] through *samsara*. For Buddhism the *nvritti* trend of *samsara* has tended to predominate. Yet there is recognition of the 'two worlds' paradox in the fact that monastic ethical and spiritual commitments are greater than those for lay Buddhists with families and employment.

To an extent Islam and Judaism practice an ethic that is more focused than other traditions on the daily practices and responsibilities of this world. Monastic withdrawal and celibacy have never formally been part of such traditions. Holiness in Judaism is found in domestic liturgies like the Shabbath meal as much as the Synagogue. This does not mean that they are less focused on God but prayer is built into the everyday. Mohamed was a businessman who withdrew for periods of intense prayer; Al Gazali, a teacher, took a couple of years off for contemplation but returned to his work and family. The tension of the Kingdom of this world and the realm of heaven is therefore present in all faiths but for the Jew or Muslim they are one life not two different lifestyles as in some parts of Christianity or Buddhism.

For some, faith in paradox tends to a social conservatism that does not challenge the status quo of society, as what matters is the sacred realm, not secular society. It was this conservatism that led to the reaction of Sikhism against Hindu and Buddhist trends to *dharmic* withdrawal and *nvritti*. The Sikh focus on religious observance as part of a lifestyle engaged with the world is a strong affirmation of a transformative relationship with culture. As other faith communities with more

---

[23] Lipner J. *Hindus: Their Religious Beliefs and Practices.* Routledge, 2010, pp. 208 & 246–250 (Lipner 2010);

countercultural or transformative theological identity become more prominent in British society, some of the Protestant traditions that historically adopted a two kingdoms approach are beginning to assert a more engaged counter-cultural identity. This is reflected in the return of evangelical Christians to politics and other social action.[24]

Faith Above Culture

Communities that see faith as 'above culture' regard God as the author of culture; thus culture is God-given and cultural changes are God's plan. The model synthesizes culture and faith and is the most assimilative accommodation of religion to society. Comfortable with the idea that faith develops with culture, it has a relative lack of capacity to critique or hold culture to account, tending to conservatism and the majority view, accepting and even endorsing whatever rule and systems operate in civic society. Natural law theology is a method that synthesizes faith and culture and Niebuhr cites Aquinas as an example for this category. Natural law theology in all traditions appeals to reason and equates rational observation of natural law and culture in wider society with divine law and vice versa. To that extent it represents the synthesis of faith and the world. However, to the extent that natural law theology defines *telos* by deontological principles external to culture, there are some objective standards to assess theological and cultural developments and discern God's will as distinct from culture.

In other models of faith above culture the assimilative trend is still more marked. The best of culture viewed as divinely-endowed provides a more voluntarist example of faith above culture, accepting cultural norms as God's will without any ethical challenge. Natural law theologians critique this voluntarist understanding for its lack of objective

---

[24] 19th CE activism included the Shaftsbury Society & Wilberforce's anti-slavery campaign; political Christianity, prominent in the US, is reflected in UK attempts to found a Christian Democrat party & the rise of e.g. Conservative Christian Fellowship & Christian Socialist Movement; Bretherton L. *Christianity and Contemporary Politics: The Conditions and Possibilities of Faithful Witness.* Oxford: Wiley Blackwell, 2010 (Bretherton 2010).

norms.[25] The voluntarist model relies on scripture as the norm external to culture but scripture can become a tool of culture or ideology rather than an independent witness and revelation. Such an approach uses scripture to endorse the existing models of civic culture, often led by the faith hierarchy in association with the government in power in such societies. Examples include the defence of the divine right of kings based on the scriptural mandate of Romans 13 and the book of Daniel. Other doubtful cultural norms accepted and defended on the basis of selective, culture-justifying readings of scripture have included slavery and South African apartheid and the racism that goes with both.

The criticism of Scriptural voluntarism in the light of the defence of apartheid is valid yet rationalist theology's capacity for complicity with unholy government is also forever marked by the compromises of the German Churches with Nazism. It was precisely the latter that led to Barth's rejection of natural law rationalism in favour of belief in the revelation of a radically voluntarist God. The reality is that whatever ethical or revelatory framework is applied can be used in a self-serving or culture-serving way. Acceptance of and accommodation with Nazism came from all parts of the theological spectrum in 1930s Germany. Hobbes, St Paul and Augustine, all advocated relatively uncritical obedience to the state illustrating that no form of ethics is immune from the risks of accepting serious ethical error by over-identification with civic life.

Illustrating the Paradigms: Education

Although helpful as an analysis the above scheme is neither definitive, exclusive nor exhaustive. However, it does provide a guide to some of the reasons why communities, in theory following the same faith, adopt very different ethical stances in relation to each other as well as the society around them. Education is a particularly sensitive area of ethical interface between religious communities and wider society, as it is the fulcrum for shaping the next generation. It provides a good illustration

---

[25] See e.g. Hauerwas S. *The Peaceable Kingdom: A Primer in Christian Ethics*. SCM Press, 2009 (Hauerwas 2009).

of the diversity of relationships and ethical stances. For most faith communities the key task and ethical commitment of parenting is to shape children in the ways, practices and beliefs of their faith tradition, as indicated by the following scriptures:

> Allah (SWT) will ask every caretaker about the people under his care, and the man will be asked about the people of his household (Nasa'i, Abu Da'ud).

> *O you who believe! Ward off yourselves and your families against a Fire (Hell) whose fuel is men and stones, over which are (appointed) angels stern (and) severe, who disobey not, (from executing) the commands they receive from Allah, but do that which they are commanded* (Tahrim 66:6) and

> Every one of your (people) is responsible, and everyone is responsible for whatever falls under his responsibility. A man is like a shepherd of his own family, and he is responsible for them. (Bukhari and Muslim)

> For learning about wisdom and instruction, for understanding words of insight, for gaining instruction in wise dealing, righteousness, justice, and equity; to teach shrewdness to the simple, knowledge and prudence to the young... Hear, my child, your father's instruction and do not reject your mother's teaching (Proverbs 1:2–8)

> The true congregation of the true Guru, is the school for the soul, where the glorious virtues of the Lord are studied. Guru Raam Daas, Raag Kaanraa, 1316

> Meeting with the Guru, be a sincere student of proper conduct, and suffering shall never touch you. *Guru Arjan in Siree Raag Fifth Mehl, 50*

Unlike many other states British law offers wide scope for confessional religious education and manifestation of belief, including within the state maintained sector. Academies and free schools, a diverse independent sector and home schooling in theory provide more choice for parents to educate their children in particular faiths than in most countries. This has generated opposition from the British Humanist

Society who oppose religion in schools.[26] Supporting parental rights to educate children in their beliefs protects rights of religious conscience under the European Convention on Human Rights. It is a right that is personal to individual parents but relies on communal exercise of the right to provide the schools. In practice, lack of resources and capacity mean that not all communities that would like to have faith schools have them. In practice too the number of communities who want wholly separatist education is relatively limited, for example many Muslim families are accept mainstream or church schools provided that ethics, values and God are recognized.

Faith-based education that provides relatively exclusively for students from a particular tradition is an example of education by way of religious accommodation within the wider framework of public life. Such schools often illustrate counter-cultural ethics and separatist stances to wider society. The independent sector offers wider scope for education and curricula that are particular to countercultural separatist religion for example teaching scriptural languages[27] and limited secular epistemology. Yet even in the maintained and mainstream sectors regulations allow those of particular faiths to exclude certain lessons or teaching methods that infringe belief. For example, on the grounds of faith, parents can withdraw children from IT and audio-visual teaching, music, RE, worship and, despite regular political discussion, sex education. As in other spheres of public life policy permits school dress codes that enable pupils to comply with their faith, although schools themselves determine the extent of such accommodation.

Some of the most counter-cultural and exclusive schools are run by Jewish *haredi* communities[28] and more recently several Muslim schools have been criticized as extremist.[29] Others that benefit from

---

[26] https://humanism.org.uk.

[27] Several *haredi* schools teach Hebrew and Aramaic – Bradney A. *Religion, Rights and Laws* Leicester. University Press, 1993 (Bradney 1993); *Faced by Faith* in *Faith in Law: Essays in Legal Theory*. Oxford: Hart Publishing, 2000, pp. 89–105 (Bradney 2000).

[28] *DfE v Talmud Torah Matzikei School (1984) Times LR*; OFSTED reports for Salford Jewish Boys High School 2008.

[29] Tarbiya School Dewsbury, Darum Uloom School, Birmingham, Rabia Schools https://www.rt.com/uk/347139-muslim-school-ofsted-racist/.

counter-cultural educational exclusions or tend to exercise the right to withdraw children from lessons include Exclusive Brethren schools and Jehovah's Witnesses. One allegation against religious, particularly Muslim, schools is opposition to gender segregation, which seems somewhat hypocritical given that single sex schools still exist in non-religious sectors. There are also non-faith schools, such as the Montessori tradition, which benefit from other exclusions and accommodations; counter-cultural educational ethics are not limited to religious schools. It must also be noted that the counter-culturally religious schools that have been criticized are a small minority and there are many Muslim and Jewish schools, along with others, that achieve outstanding OFSTED results.[30]

The majority of faith schools are however maintained sector Christian schools, mostly Church of England and Roman Catholic. Whilst they have permission to teach RE and worship according to their church traditions the rest of the curriculum is set according to the National Curriculum. Although significant numbers of church schools are becoming academies, which are exempt from the national curriculum, the academies framework requires a broad curriculum, with specific provisions to prevent the teaching of doctrines like creationism. Thus religious schools and academies in the maintained sector are obliged to teach a largely pro-cultural stance with epistemology and curricula assumptions that are liberal and western. Whilst such education might foster a stance attuned to the transformation of culture in line with the traditions or insights of the differential RE curricular, for the most part the approach is accepting of the prevailing secular culture.

The expansion of faith-based education following the School Standards and Framework Act 1998, linked with the Human Rights Act, saw a wider range of faiths running maintained faith schools. Yet the origins of faith-based education in England were not limited to the pupils of a particular faith community. The National Society was set up in 1812 with the aspiration, in conjunction with philanthropic donors

---

[30] http://ams-uk.org – Association of Muslim Schools; http://www.findajewishschool.co.uk/index.php.

of land, to provide education for the 'poor and labouring classes'. The original vision was oriented towards providing education for all, regardless of denomination although with an element of civic religion in the form of the established church. The fact that one third of schools, by the time that education was nationalized in 1944, were Church of England schools obliged by their foundational trusts to maintain Church of England education, led to the faith settlement that now exists. In the UK the Human Rights Act 1998 extended the option to schools of all faiths to seek maintained status. Other European states permit faith-based education, but schools of a particular confession are outside the state system. In this respect, paradoxically British religious schools promote a more tolerant, liberal education system than in some states because they are tied into national curricula. It is also an interesting reflection on the differences between Bentham's day and the 21st CE that in his diatribe against church schools and the National Society[31] Bentham criticized the Society's catechism and curriculum, arguing that schools should be teaching the Bible!

The diversity of the English education system illustrates an ethic of tolerant, liberal secular neutrality, not only respecting religious belief and conscience but promoting the right to exercise such conscience through education. The challenge of such a settlement is that respecting freedom of religious conscience to the extent permitted in English law might prejudice young people raised and educated entirely within religious communities that do not provide much instruction in the values or epistemology of wider society. It is one thing to assert a counter-cultural identity that is an informed decision; it is another for that counter-cultural stance to be a default position for lack of educational breadth.

Although independent schools are regulated by the independent schools inspectorate and in theory home-schooling is regulated by education authorities, taking action against a faith school is politically loaded. The backlash to an attempt to close a minority *Haredi* faith school led to a DfE compromise in 1984[32] that defined the purpose of education as being to fit

---

[31] Bentham J. 1818 – *Church of Englandism and its Catechism Examined.* Oxford University Press, 2011 (Bentham 2011).

[32] Talmud Torah Matzikei High School – op. cit.

children for their own communities, not necessarily wider society. Whilst there are not huge numbers of faith schools that are separatist to this degree the DfE concession is significant for children's futures, potentially limiting their worldview, the ethics it generates and the knowledge base, understanding of and capacity to function in wider society.

Whilst religious faiths are not the only groups creating the diversity of beliefs that operate in UK society they have until recently[33] been the only ones privileged with the opportunity by law to develop maintained sector schools. The ethical issues that arise are the rights of families and communities to keep alive particular forms of religious ethics and tradition, the merits of a diverse society and the values of tolerance. The challenge that arises is that these objectives are not always compatible particularly where views differ about the boundaries of what is tolerable, what constitutes harm and what is good, beneficial, pleasurable or right.

Managing Theological Ethics in the Public Square

Conflicts of ethics and conscience exist in various ways in all sections of the population, as identified in earlier chapters, but the ethics of religious groups or perceptions of them, have come into identifiable focus. Where there are concerns about harmful practices, notably in recent debate about forced marriage, Female Genital Mutilation, excessive fasting and corporal punishment, the child whose values, education and moral compass are entirely shaped by a separatist community and school is less able to protect themselves by challenging the practice of the community. In this respect better monitoring of education is needed along with a revision of the 1984 concession about what education should fit children for. The cases of Re K and Re AB illustrate the different ways that religious upbringing can affect capacity for autonomy. Both cases concerned teenage young women brought up in Muslim homes. Re AB[34] concerned an orphan from an

---

[33] Academies have enabled other perspectives to enter education e.g. the Co-op movement.
[34] *Re AB [2008] EWHC 1436.*

Indian Muslim family, although with extended family, including her brother, in Europe. AB found that she was to be married to an older man with a drink problem and some violence; fearing that she might be forced into marriage she sought help from the British embassy as her father had held a British passport. Through making her a ward of court she was able to join her brother in Glasgow.

In re K[35] an Afghani teenager from an asylum seeking family in Britain was entered into an arranged marriage aged 15 with an older man who was abusive. Social services intervened to rescue her from the marriage. Despite one bad experience and much support the young woman remained wedded (no pun intended) to her family and community's plans for a subsequent marriage arranged by her father. Unlike AB this young woman did not have the experience or enough education around autonomy to seek help before the first abusive under-age marriage. The question arises whether her choice to go along with the second arranged marriage was her own or whether, despite the support she had received she remained under the undue influence of her father. Both young women were from Muslim families suggesting that the difference is not so much theological as cultural.

Let's Talk About Sex

The privatizing of religion and the focusing of religious and secular differences around issues of personal morality, regardless of the actual diversity of views in faith communities, have led to a general sense of religion as counter-cultural over sexual ethics, regardless of their position on the cultural scale in other respects. The opposition of differences over sexuality as secular versus religious also feeds into a British cultural narrative arising from utilitarian arguments about pleasure. Yet such debates are influenced by culture as much as theology. The ethics of gender and same-sex relationships also exemplify the challenges of ethics where strong public communal statements combine with internalized

---

[35] *Re K sub nom LA v N & Others [2005] EWHC 2956.*

religious messages to limit capacity to exercise autonomy, conscience and ethical discernment. This can often mean that not only is there a clash between equalities legislation and some religious ethics but also between theory or doctrine and experience, particularly for those whose personal experience of sexuality is at odds with religious teachings.

The official line of most faith communities is that homosexuality is not accepted or is not equivalent to marriage engendering a counter-cultural stance for most faiths in respect of legal developments around same-sex relationships, such as adoption, civil partnership and same-sex marriage. The passages considered when discussing Scripture, for example Old Testament passages that condemn homosexuality as *to'evah or abomination* and the New Testament and Qu'ranic equivalents are bolstered by appeals to what is natural, particularly in those traditions that adopt natural law philosophy as part of their ethical tradition.

Yet in each case alternative, also authentic, interpretations are possible. The modern context of committed, faithful same-sex relationships is very different from the apparent promiscuity condemned by Paul in Romans and elsewhere. Recognizing those contextual differences provides a very different understanding of these passages than a literalist understanding. Those communities open to wider society either outside the religious community, in the case of separatist theologies or with whom they mix daily for the less separatist, are more likely to consider context in their interpretation than those who take a literalist view. Yet differences of understanding and interpretation of scripture are often also cultural as much as theological. The fact that perspectives on gender and sexuality have been so influenced by culture is particularly evident in relation to the *dharmic* faiths and Sikhism. There is no reference to homosexuality in the Gita, Pali Canon or the Guru Granth Sahib. Yet such traditions also tend to take a conservative view of sexual ethics, partly on the basis of natural law and partly because of other cultural factors, including concerns to hold on to some distinctive aspects of their faith, tradition and identity in the diaspora.[36]

---

[36] Lawton C & Morgan P. *Ethical Issues in Six Religious Traditions.* Edinburgh University Press, 2007, 2nd edition, pp. 10–15, 68–72 & 126–129 (Lawton and Morgan 2007).

These issues and the cases above illustrate the need for the protection of a commonly understood ethical baseline, protected if necessary by law and rights. This requires some boundaries and minimum epistemological and protective standards around religious diversity in education as well as the protection of minorities in religious communities. Yet this framework also needs to recognize that there is plenty of scope for difference and that in some instances arguments about religious ethics and practices are undoubtedly coloured by political agendas. The singling out of Islam for criticism over the veil and other religious clothing ignores the fact that Muslim communities are not the only ones in which women wear veils; similar dress codes can be found in Orthodox Judaism and some parts of Christianity; nuns have worn veils without comment for over a century. Whilst there are concerns about the lack of capacity to make an informed decision in the minority of separatist schools and communities, for the most part those in religious communities are engaged with wider society. This engagement is through education, work, neighbourhoods, politics, the media and most of the walks of life in which the population at large engages. Part of the challenge of assessing theological ethics is to hear the views of those who have made their own decisions and discernment about how to live their faith, discerning what is authentically religious as opposed to the additions of culture.

The challenges for faith communities and individuals of faith as to how they live vis a vis the ethics of wider society may for some of a counter-cultural stance be more acute than those without faith, simply because of the degree of difference. For members of religious communities there can also be personal dilemmas if caught in conscience between the official position of the faith community and the views of wider society, especially where their experience accords with the dominant cultural ethic rather than their faith. There are dilemmas for anyone faced with views that lead them to stand out against the crowd or wrestling with issues of conscience like whistle- blowing or turning off a life support machine.

Yet religious communities have as part of their DNA and identity a public profession that part of what they are about is reflection on the world, its priorities and the ethical demands that belief and religious practice entails. Even those theologies that are apparently more pro-cultural and assimilated reach those conclusions as a result of ethical reflection and discernment in the light of their faith. As Nigel Biggar notes theological integrity does not necessarily equate to theological distinctiveness.[37] The demands of religious faith will therefore always pose ethical dilemmas for believers as individuals and communities whether counter cultural or assimilated. Those dilemmas will also include how and when faith should be voiced in the public square.

Accommodation, Assimilation or Counter-Culture

Conversely, for wider secular or multicultural society, ethical dilemmas are raised by the degree to which the law and policy should enable religious communities to assimilate or maintain a counter-cultural stance, be involved in public debate or seek special accommodation. As noted earlier dilemmas are also posed in relation to conscientious decisions or dissent from societal norms based on secular premises, so issues of accommodation are not limited to religious perspectives and practices. The policies and processes developed in response to religious accommodation may have parallel application in other contexts. Essential to these ethical dilemmas and their resolution at societal level is an understanding and negotiation of the different premises involved as well as the conclusions reached.

When the law comes to accommodation case law shows that religious belief and practice is, at least in theory, comparatively well-protected where it is clearly religiously focused. Thus law and public policy recognized religious diet, clothing,[38] religious holidays and times for prayer as needing protection even before the enactment of the Human Rights Act 1998. Some might argue that religion has been better protected than matters of political conscience. For example, whilst pacifism[39] and environmentalism[40] are recognized as matters

---

[37] Biggar N. *Behaving in public,* op. cit., pp. 1–24.
[38] *R v (on the application of Miss Begum) v Denbigh High School [2006] UKHL 15.*
[39] *Arrowsmith v UK [1978] ECHR 7.*
[40] *Grainger plc v Nicholson [2010] IRLR 4 (EAT).*

of conscience, distributing leaflets urging soldiers not to fight in Northern Ireland was not an expression of pacifist conscience.[41] The reasons for this disparity of accommodation are complex but include the fact that the perceived grounding of religious conscience in transcendent or metaphysical premises is 'other', a clear exception to secular premises. In addition, the historical privatization of religion has meant religious communities' requests for accommodation have been less obviously political in terms of opposition than some movements of conscience like CND. By contrast expressions of conscience about secular matters are more easily dismissed as differences of opinion or politics and so more readily qualified by public policy. At a practical political level religious belief and ethics also have significant communal support with faith communities carrying some political weight, meaning that requests for accommodation may get more of a hearing than some other movements of conscience.

In some ways the issue of accommodating religious difference and particularly self-contained communities is more straightforward than what weight should be allowed to theological perspectives in public discussion. Accommodation of a private group in ways that do not affect others is entirely consistent with liberal society as it maintains the privatization of religion. Religious and theological engagement in wider public policy carries more scope for contention, yet this is the stance that is actually more common in practice than separatism.

The protection of religion can have a dual edge. On one side is the Enlightenment assumption that religion is a private matter, with some immaterial differences, practiced in private. Yet when religion becomes public, either because a theologically-based political stance is adopted, for example opposing war or when used on one side or another of an ideological argument, it can become politicized as seditious. This trend has been apparent in the British body politic long before Islamophobia and fears about radicalization. British politicization of religion has a particular history in relation to Catholicism most recently in relation

---

[41] Weller P, Purdam K, Ghanea N & Cheruvallili S. *Religion or Belief, Discrimination and Equality: Britain in Global Contexts*. Bloomsbury Publishing, p. 58.

to the IRA and Irish Catholicism but as far back as the reign of Elizabeth I, whose death sentences for religious dissent were not for heresy but for treason.

On the other hand the trend to assume that faith communities 'think like us' and that their ethics are largely mainstream save for additional religious quirks can mean that significant differences of worldview are overlooked. This becomes problematic where differences about what constitutes harm or welfare, the role of law or its authority differ fundamentally but either a material difference is not recognized or cannot be accommodated. At the heart of some religious counter-cultural stances lies the acceptance or otherwise of dominant epistemology as well as ethical premises.

One difference of epistemology is the classic suspicion of religion generated by Enlightenment scepticism about the metaphysical and anything that cannot be empirically proved. However, there are also differences of epistemology from the perspective of some religions, for example underlying some ethical differences are disagreements about the validity of western medicine, the appropriate basis for marriage or the purpose of education. Variation may be acceptable in a liberal pluralist democracy provided that it does not cross the normative boundary of being deemed harmful. The difficulty is that on both epistemological and ethical grounds communities differ over what is classed as harmful or how harm should be defined and evaluated. It is where worldviews and ethical stances clash over what is harmful that the challenges for both secular authority and religious, as opposed to cultural or ideological, authenticity are tested. The particular challenge for theological ethics is that much of what appears in the public square relates to this testing of the boundaries of religious difference and harm. Examples include FGM, forced marriage, corporal punishment and Jehovah's Witness refusals of blood transfusions. Yet theological ethics and religious communities also have positive insights to contribute to public debate.

The restriction of religion and ethics to matters of private life has often led to the ignoring or condemnation of more public or political aspects of religion and faith-based ethics. Whilst people assume that they know what the churches believe about homosexuality and marriage for example they are often ignorant of the fact that the Bible says significantly more about poverty and rejecting oppression. Yet all faiths have public dimensions and morality, with things to say about wider society. Indeed, as noted above, for people of most faiths and most of the world where such Enlightenment divisions are not so entrenched there is no distinction between public and private ethics, wider society and personal morality. Nor is such public manifestation of faith limited to the obvious issues of dress and dietary rules, the Sikh turban, the *hijab* or not eating pork that mark out particular faiths as publicly different. Many faiths have also made significant counter-cultural political and societal contributions as a result of their faith-based ethics.

A striking example is the Quakers, for whom all life is sacramental, necessitating a public living out of their beliefs. This has been most notable in their emphasis on peace as a key priority and ethical mandate lived out through civil disobedience. Such disobedience has included conscientious objection during both major European wars, more recent protests against military spending by withholding taxes and peace protests at military bases. Yet in the nineteenth century CE Quaker public action also took the form of ethical business. They invested in drinking chocolate and cocoa as an alternative to alcohol and through model villages like Bournville in Birmingham and Earswick in York also invested in their workforce, seeking to demonstrate humane and Christian employment practices. Other faiths have peace movements, notably Ghandi's opposition to Indian rule based on radical understandings of *ahimsa* or non-violence, mirrored in Buddhist *ahimsa*. Some also have significant ethical stances in business, an example of which is the Muslim approach to financial instruments and refusal to engage with usury.

Although less well-known and less clearly focused the Anglican Communion worldwide has taken as two of its five international priorities the call to social justice and care of the environment.[42]

---

[42] Anglican Five Marks of Mission. http://www.anglicancommunion.org/identity/marks-of-mission.aspx.

Similarly Roman Catholic encyclicals and social action cover key issues of public and social morality, like tackling poverty, war and environmental degradation.[43] In the UK it is no coincidence that six of the thirteen members of the Disasters Emergency Committee, NGOs working with the Department for International Development to respond to humanitarian crises across the world, are faith-based groups.[44] The presence of religiously-based aid agencies internationally is reflected in faith-based voluntary service domestically both through places of worship and in a multiplicity of charities across faiths.[45]

All these examples show faiths seeking not only accommodation of their own practices but striving to live out their ethical vision through responding to wider human need, challenging laws seen as unjust and changing practice through modelling alternatives. In addition to charities that retain their faith-based identity many modern secular charities began with a theological inspiration, amongst them the Samaritans founded by vicar Chad Varah and based on the Gospel parable, the hospice movement founded by Dame Cicely Saunders and Centrepoint housing charity for young people founded by a group of Christians in Soho. These sorts of campaigns recognize that theological ethics concerns the whole of society not just private religious life and practice, providing ethical authority from within faith traditions for political and public involvement.

Still so Contentious?

The contentious issues remain the degree to which society, in a secular, post-Enlightenment settlement, accepts or accommodates the contribution of theological ethics to national life and debate. Insofar as religious communities live out their ethics in ways that serve the

---

[43] http://www.papalencyclicals.net. e.g. Laudato Si on the environment; Laborem Exercens on Labour.

[44] Christian Aid, Islamic Relief, CAFOD, Tear Fund, Care, World Vision, Concern Worldwide.

[45] A search of the Charity Commission website lists 14008 charities under religious service – Accessed 21 June 2016.

wider community, through their extensive involvement in charitable and community activities, they are generally accepted. Providing international aid or responding domestically through foodbanks, homeless shelters and other projects of welcome and meeting need, gives them the authority of experience to contribute to public debate on such issues. Such obviously charitable and reasonable contributions to society are for the most part appreciated as what religions should be doing, helping people.

However, acceptance of religious ethics only if they adopt a particular form of reasonableness or serve a useful social role, important though that aspect of religious engagement is, reduces religious ethics and communities to utilitarian or functional rationales. Such an approach fails to take into account the full range of ways in which theological ethics can make a difference; focusing on service looks only at works rather than more contemplative, reflective aspects of theological ethics and positive contributions they can make to ideas. Such an approach also risks assuming assimilation in situations where it is unwarranted or alternatively demonizes communities that do not conform to mainstream parameters.

If it is true to itself a liberal society should be less concerned with whether theological ethics is within the mainstream of British values. In some ways theological ethics inevitably will not be mainstream as some of its premises and assumptions do not conform to western secular, materialist empiricism. It is also no concern of wider society whether the interpretation of religious scripture and tradition is conservative or liberal. The issue is whether there is an abuse of individual or collective power to impose interpretations rather than respecting the faith of community members to live the tradition in the way that they feel called. This goes for all traditions whether publicly identified as adopting countercultural practices like dress or the more hidden, because more assimilated, gendered divisions of conservative Christianity or coercion in any sector, religious or otherwise.

Some suspicion of religious ethics as divisive may be justified given the history. There are still divisions in and between religious communities and theological ethics is far from homogenous in any community. However, this division is no greater than many other parts of society and religious communities often differ is that there is also an ethic of seeking to remain together even despite the differences. This is dramatically illustrated by the Anglican Communion and the Jewish community, both renowned for wide diversity and disagreement, yet remaining together seeking to live difference well.

There may also be concerns to be checked but conservative religious communities are not the only place in British society where there are conservative ethics, politics and social attitudes or repressive exercises of power. Domestic violence, abuse, and limitations of role and aspiration are alive and well in non-faith communities too. The issue is to check abuse and enable genuine exercises of ethical discernment, not to condemn particular versions of scripture or tradition or external practices without understanding the underlying premises. Historically 'othering' and privatizing religious ethics has led to separatism without redress for those who were vulnerable. Greater transparency and involvement of religion in public life is in itself a protective factor enabling healthier and more democratic exploration of ethics.

Perhaps rather than being the butt of society's fears or the repository of society's anxiety about societal changes, for example over sex and gender, the positive aspects of theological ethics can also be brought into the public arena. Theological ethics has much to offer including the ethics of seeking to live well across divides of opinion, belief and interpretation, an ethic of living well with difference. This also provides a challenge to simplistic sound bites, enabling a greater recognition of complexity, paradoxes and shared journeys as humanity explores ethics together. Theological ethics can particularly address the ethics of paradox, of the reality of 'now' set against the aspiration of the 'not yet', in seeking to improve society and challenge injustices. Theological ethics also faces squarely issues of death, afterlife and the transcendent as well as the utilitarian functions of service and community building. This perspective of recognizing the finitude of life, the material and human knowledge, power and experience also leads to other important insights. Such insights, which come specifically from theological practices and recognition of human finitude, include observance of the sabbath as a limit on work, wealth as finite and not limited to the material and recognition of God as a limit on power, particularly the power of leaders and governments. The theological values of faith and commitment indicate a different sort of freedom; theological ethics of sexuality often seek to capture the sense of sex and relationship as sacred.

Conclusions

The account above provides, hopefully, some more understanding of the ways in which theological ethics vary and are lived out in wider western society. There are also a number of suggestions about ways in which theological ethics can add to and enrich wider ethical debate and action in society. Perhaps the overarching aspect of theological ethics that explains the strength of views often generated is that these issues engage hopes and fears for the eternal and the hope of the world as it could be in paradise, heaven or the kingdom of peace. The dilemma of the world as it is and the world as one might hope it could be is a reality for all, regardless of faith or worldview and even without the dimension of the transcendent. This division arises for everyone in relation to the personal stresses, upsets, pains and limitations of everyday life set against hopes for peace and happiness. On a wider world stage theology engages with realities of poverty, war, disaster and illness set against hopes for world peace, plenty and harmony. Perhaps theological ethics can above all focus the ethical perspective on the realities of the world as it is and the world as one might hope it could be, as the context for ethical exploration.

8

Theological Ethical Processes and Meta-Narratives

Having explored various stances that religious groups and faith communities adopt, consciously or incidentally, as they live out their faith in response to theological imperatives and authorities, this chapter explores in greater depth several processes of theological reflection and methodology by which faith-based ethical conclusions are reached. As noted in earlier chapters the dilemmas of weighing in conscience a multiplicity of ethical authorities and competing allegiances are not unique to faith communities; most of the paradoxes, tensions and problems of life with which faith grapples are common to all humanity. Besides analysing several theological methodologies by which faith-based ethics addresses these challenges the chapter considers further whether there are distinctive, positive contributions that theological ethics can bring to public ethical debate. The suspicion of theology and faith in parts of the modern public square and perception in others that it is irrelevant, means that the mode of theological contribution as well as the substance requires consideration.

'Western' suspicions of theology are based on perceived lack of rationality, misperceptions that theology concerns only heaven rather than earth, the metaphysical rather than experiential or empirical and

© The Author(s) 2017
C. Shelley, *Ethical Exploration in a Multifaith Society*,
DOI 10.1007/978-3-319-46711-5_8

unprovable deontological premises and commands. At least since the western Enlightenment theology has been viewed as antithetical to modern philosophical ethics and the realities of this life as opposed to the hopes or promises of an uncertain afterlife. Yet, as earlier chapters have sought to demonstrate, reason and a reasoned approach to revelation and other human faculties is a key feature of theological methodology and ethics. Likewise theological ethics are far from devoid of empirical experience and are developed from experience as a vital component of the methodology in all traditions. The factors that vary between methodologies are whose experience is taken as essential, normative or correct and the ordering of experience alongside other factors and authorities, particularly the theological, in the process. By contrast utilitarianism is also not as rational or objective as that classically secular approach to ethics likes to believe for both pleasure and pain are also subjective, sense-based and variable. Such experiences need to be included in the ethical equation but cannot stand as the only factors in a full reflection of what it means to be human and to discern how to live at one with humanity and the whole of creation.

Each of the methodologies considered below juggles, in varying ways, the elements that are summed up in what is sometimes known as the Wesleyan Quadrilateral or the Anglican trilogy. The Anglican trilogy relies on scripture, tradition and reason, the Wesleyan Quadrilateral adds experience, making explicit what is assumed, mostly under reason, in the Anglican tradition. Although these are specifically Christian classifications the reality is that all theological ethics engage with these factors in their methodology in one form or another. The issue in practice is what weight and ordering is given to each of these elements, which is in turn intertwined with approaches to authority and scriptural interpretation as examined in earlier chapters. The following exploration is not exhaustive but considers and critiques several theological methodologies. The aim is to illustrate further the ways in which authentic theological reasoning can give rise to very different ethical conclusions. The methods examined include another look at natural law theology, revelation based theologies, Hinduism putting experience before scripture, ethics of process, for example *samsara* and theology based on virtue ethics, Barthian Thomism, middle axioms, legal methodologies and casuistry, developmental theology for example through ijtihad, narrative theology and liberation theologies, with particular attention to other faiths and minorities. Some methods are more characteristic in some traditions than others, which will be noted in broad terms. However, the key aim of this analysis is to show how different theologies address the challenges and paradoxes of principle and practice and transcendent and immanent expressions of the divine.

Experience and Utility: Does Theology Make a Difference?

Although generally placed in an opposing category from natural law Utilitarianism can be seen as a philosophy based on and reacting to the experience of its times, including despair of wars over religious and metaphysical premises, rejection of hypocrisy around sexuality and mistrust of promises of eternal reward for earthly deprivation which preserved social injustices. It is at the opposite end of the spectrum to casuistical, detailed application of theological principle and revelation. The utilitarian move in some ways reflected Luther's rejection of Thomist natural law and the interpretive power of the Catholic Church a couple of centuries earlier. Luther's reformation included rejection of ethics that limited the purpose of sex to procreation and promoted celibacy, as a means to salvation, as superior to marriage. There was also a strand of social justice in Luther's rejection of Church abuses of power to fleece those who had little, again in the hope of eternal life. These goals of creating a better world and reining in abuses of power were neither limited to Luther nor to the utilitarians and in many cases are shared by theologies across the board. However the genesis of such theories in reaction against religious distortions has often obscured religious teachings on social justice and against oppression. All too often the institutional political dimension of debates has overlooked the actual ethical priorities and teachings of established religion. The critique may be summed up by Bernard Shaw's comment that Christianity has a great ethic but no-one has really tried it yet.

As discussed in Chapter 4 a few theological approaches have sought to adopt a theological utilitarianism, most notably Joseph Fletcher's Situation Ethics which is based on a calculus of love, as the Christian ethical paradigm, rather than pleasure. Whilst much-criticized as lacking both substantive and clear theological content, for example about what love means, Fletcher at least seeks to ground his ethics in the Christian theological value of love. He argues that love of neighbour as oneself, whilst Biblically grounded, has universal appeal in its wider application as the Golden Rule. Paul Ramsay amongst others critiques Fletcher as emptying the Christian commandment of its deeper understanding of love as self-sacrifice and forgiveness through the theology of redemption. Ramsay, who also appeals to love as the basis of Christian Ethics, grounds his ethic in the more specific deontological covenant of God with His people through Christ's pattern of all-encompassing self-sacrificial and forgiving love with the promise of salvific resurrection. He is amongst those who reject Christian or theological ethics that downplay God. Yet Fletcher's ethics do at least appeal to love as a Christian value grounded in God by contrast with those who follow the secular trend of seeking to find ethics with which Christians agree but that do not explicitly mention God.

It is notable that two such proponents of 'Godless ethics' have been members of public ethical committees. Thus former Episcopalean Bishop Richard Holloway's 'Godless Ethics' adopts utilitarianism wholesale, explicitly leaving God out of the equation on the basis that ultimately theological statements can only be deontological assertions with no place in public debate.[1] By contrast Svend Andersen, following Knud Logstrup, does not reject God from ethics but suggests that God makes no difference to ethics. Logstrup argues that Christian scripture gives no different rules or norms to decide ethical questions that are not available to anyone else. Andersen went so far as to state that at no point in his service on the ethics committee did his Christian belief and theological perspective make a difference.[2] Like Fletcher, Andersen and

[1] Holloway R. *Godless Morality: Keeping Religion Out of Ethics*. London: Canongate Press, 2004 (Holloway 2004).

[2] Andersen S. Die Rolle Theologischer Argumentation in Offentlichen Leben. In *Religion und Theologie in Offentlichen Diskurs,* Ed. Gotlind Ulshofer. Frankfurt Am Main Haag und Herchen

Logstrup rely to a significant extent on assumptions that the Golden Rule is universal, by means of natural reason without need for revelation following Luther's dictum 'Nature teaches how love should behave: that I should do as I would be done by.'

Biggar questions whether the Golden Rule is really as universal as assumed. He also critiques 'non-theological' Christian ethics on the basis that Christians cannot divorce the theological from their worldview and therefore are bound to make it known. This is despite his view that Christian ethics can be authentic even if not distinctive or different. For Biggar it is the intention and reasoning that are important whether or not the consequent conclusions are pro-cultural or distinctive.[3] The removal of God from ethics by theologians has been widely criticized by Biggar, Ramsey, Hays, Hauerwas and Millbank to name a few, as reductionist, timid, atheist, assimilationist and bringing liberal approaches to Christian theology into disrepute. The view that theologians, whose job is to speak of God, cannot exclude God from creation reflects the assumptions of early natural law theologians from all three Abrahamic faiths that, as God is creator and sustainer of all life, the theological is an inevitable part of seeking to understand His creation and its implications for life. It is particularly reminiscent of Al Gazali's criticism in *The incoherence of the Philosophers*.

To take God or the divine out of faith-based ethics is not only anathema to many Christians but incomprehensible to other faiths whose theology does not countenance the public versus private divide of two kingdoms theology. Yet to keep theology in discussions of ethics in a multicultural and multifaith public square carries significant challenges, whether the public square is defined as governmental, academic, business or the global media, whether traditional broadcast and print or social media. The rise in prominence of non-Christian faiths and some Christians unwilling politely to omit God from their reasoning in the public square has raised a variety of responses, from renewed calls to

---

Verlaag, 2005 (Andersen 2005); Logstrup K. *The Ethical Demand Notre.* Dame University Press, 1997 (Logstrup 1997) both discussed in Biggar N. *Behaving in Public: How to do Christian Ethics.* Grand Rapids: Eerdmans, 2011, pp. 30–34 (Biggar 2011).

[3] Biggar N., op. cit., pp. 30–37.

exclude religion to greater development of interfaith networks. In practice, however, faith has always continued to undergird many forms and spheres of public discourse and action, partly because of the UK's Judaeo-Christian heritage and the existence of established churches. In addition, theological ethics both motivates and arises from the faith of individuals, both those in key public roles for whom it may consciously or unconsciously affect decision-making and the approach to work and life of the average believing citizen, as earlier chapters have explored. There is also explicit theological comment by religious leaders asked to make public statements in the media. Additionally some faith communities produce research and reports intending to contribute to public debate and Academic theologians may contribute both through their research and via public ethics committees. The majority of these contributions tend to rely on natural law approaches that seek common ground with at least some dimensions of mainstream non-theological discussion.

Natural Law Theology

Reflection on nature, creation, the world around us, human experience and events of history, as well living well and governing well are at the root of ethical systems throughout the ages and across cultures. The more specific natural law theology seen classically in the Abrahamic traditions is one of the oldest systematic theological methods for reflecting on life, its meaning, operation, purpose and ends. Theological observation of natural phenomena and reflection on experience of the world and life, whether it tends to the systematically philosophical, the ritual or the celebratory, is seen in all theological traditions, in scripture, traditions, ritual practices and forms of atonement and celebration. Even in modern societies giving thanks for harvest and the gifts of the earth can be seen in the Jewish *sukkoth*, Christian harvest festivals and many other harvest celebrations. Similarly rituals for dealing with rites of passage at birth, coming of age, membership, marriage and around death are found as practices with ethical importance in most traditions. The development of specific ethical orders and rules has common elements as seen in rules governing the preservation of life, relationships, property, law and order and, in older systems, approaches to the divine. Engagement with issues of justice, public order and peace, in response to this natural order or its apparent breach, is also significant and in each case has its own reasoning from tradition as well as its own methodology. Thus natural law in the Aristotelian sense defines the 'good' from the *telos* or ends of things and actions, *nvritti* and *pvritti* make sense of the world through schemes of natural order and ritual and various forms of religious epic, from Gilgamesh to biblical Creation, Noah and other flood narratives all deduce or derive ethical meaning from observation and experience.

The contrast with more modern methodologies is not that earlier scriptural and theological methodologies failed to observe nature or take into account experience, it is that they took them into account in different ways. Thus in the absence of understanding about forces of nature such as gravity, tides, atmospheric pressure, bacteria, viruses and cancers alternative explanations were needed to make meaning of observations of the natural world. Some aspects of nature were understood, for example the relationship between drought and famine, sowing and harvesting and between certain meteorological signs and the weather that followed. This left many aspects of nature unexplained and open to theories with metaphysical, theistic or other divine premises in the absence of alternative explanations. Despite far greater knowledge of cause and effect thanks to empirical scientific method there are still major limitations to human knowledge even of such daily things as the weather, which remains predictable to a point but uncontrollable. Similarly for all the progress made in controlling symptoms of many diseases the knowledge of the cause of such commonplace illnesses as cancers, arthritis and Crohn's disease remains incomplete. Science has developed greater insight into risks and why some people develop these diseases whilst others do not, but there is no foolproof cancer or Crohn's prevention. Much modern epistemology is therefore an explanatory theory as much as the narratives of the ancients. Modern theology is called to engage with contemporary theory as Al-Gazali, Aquinas, Maimonides, Buddha, Manu and their contemporaries, forebears and successors engaged with the science and philosophy of their times.

Casuistry

Natural law theology and its interpretation in concrete situations were developed via a methodology known as casuistry, the application of principles to particular cases. It is identified primarily with the Roman Catholic Church under the auspices of whose priests and confessors it held sway for several centuries. It came into disrepute as a self-serving excuse for corrupt Catholic leaders, attracting significant vitriol from anti-Catholic writers, notably Pascal[4] whose critique of Jesuit confessors[5] was another plank in the coffin of religious involvement in public life.[6] Although it fell into disrepute casuistry at its best was a method of interpreting theological principle according to the specifics of particular cases, with the rigour of forensic analysis. It developed at its height in the wake of the Reformation and was spiritual direction not only for the monastic but for the secular faced with issues of conscience in business, politics and international affairs, so that morality was 'not confined to the private matters of personal conduct that so many moderns regard as the realm of conscience'.[7]

In its forensic, case-based application of natural law and scriptural principle casuistry is not dissimilar to the work of Muslim *alim* or Jewish Rabbis in the Beth Din, seeking to apply the law arising from their respective scriptures. They are examples not of rigid legal rules or speculative general principle but of discernment about what is the right thing to do in a particular difficult case or new circumstances, such as political or technological development. It is the recognition that whilst all creation is under God and therefore there is a unity in law and ethics, nonetheless some rules are universal whilst others are

---

[4] Pascal Blaise. *Provincial Letters*, particularly V-X. http://www.sacred-texts.com/phi/pascal/prov. txt.

[5] *On the confession of Princes* was issued by Aquaviva SJ in 1602 & confirmed by the Congregation in 1608. Toulmin S below p. 147.

[6] Toulmin S & Johnson A. *The Abuse of Casuistry: A History of Moral Reasoning*. University of California Press, 1988, pp. 146–151; 231–249 (Toulmin and Johnson 1988).

[7] Toulmin S., op. cit., p. 144.

more specific.[8] Just as *Talmudic* development in the interpretation of Jewish Torah arose from applying the law in situations of exile and diaspora, some of the first Catholic casuistry responded to questions about Catholics obeying newly-declared Protestant secular leaders or founding new communities in Latin-America. Casuistry, Rabbinic *midrash*[9] and Islamic *usul-al-fiqh* or jurisprudence all 'summon human intelligence to discern the difference between the categories, as well as the logic that underpins religious regulations...'[10] Rules for the interpretation of *fiqh* include distinctions between the equivocal and unequivocal, causative links (*illah*) and margins of interpretation. Religious practice (*al-ibadat*) is fixed as revealed in the text, with little margin for interpretation. By contrast in the wider realm of human and social affairs there are wider margins of interpretation, with scope for creativity through *ijtihad* (development by inference and probability), *al-maslaha* (the Common Good) and *qiyas* (analogy).[11] In the same way Hindu law or the codes of the *Manusmriti* and *Yajnavalkya smriti* continue to be relevant in modern Hindu communities using similar practical and contextual application in case-based interpretations.[12]

Barthian Thomism

Nigel Biggar's Barthian Thomism is conceived as a middle way designed to bring theology and faith into dialogue with practical realities and policy or pastoral detail, so as to forge a theological ethics that can hold its own in the 'real', material and fallen world. The middle way seeks to reconcile not only theological metaphysics and experience but also two generally opposed theological approaches. Barth is notoriously viewed,

---

[8] e.g. in Islam *al-ibadat* specifically religious practice is more absolutely revealed than rules for living in wider society – Ramadan T. *Western Muslims and the Future of Islam*. Oxford University Press, 2004. pp. 35 (Ramadan 2004).

[9] 'exposition'.

[10] Ramadan T., op. cit., pp. 35.

[11] Ramadan T., op. cit. pp. 37–51.

[12] Lipner J. *Hindus: Their Religious Beliefs and Practices*. Routledge, 2010, pp. 101–103 (Lipner 2010).

largely by his own self-declaration, as reliant solely on sources of Christian revelation. He rejected the liberalism of his tutor Harnack when confronted by the grim lives of his mining congregation in Safenwil and later the totalitarianism of Nazism. With Dietrich Bonhoeffer and others he rejected the compromise of the German national Church with Nazism grounding his opposition in the authority of scriptural revelation over any other form of authority. For Barth this involved standing firm to the prior authority of Christ, found in the Bible as against the fallibility of human reason. Barth opposed state suppression of the Church, academia and his neighbours in Jewish communities, in opposition not only to the state but also to other churches that accepted the Nazi regime.

By reputed contrast Thomism, the Roman Catholic natural law theology named after Thomas Aquinas, recognizes Greek philosophy as a source of authority and ethical reason. It is theology that sees God at work in and through the world, revealed in places other than scripture, which might suggest more flexible premises for theology than Barth's. Yet as Thomism developed it grew surprisingly rigid, with narrow understandings of nature and limited openness to the reason of experience, forming a very particular part of Catholic tradition and revelation. By contrast Barth's rejection of natural law did not in practice lead to completely ignoring natural inspiration for theology; Barth recognized God's hand in human affairs and reasoning, as demonstrated in some acute analysis of the natural science of his day. Accordingly the reputed opposition of Thomism as open to culture and Barth's scripture-based understanding of revelation as anti-culture is not the key difference between them. What is more strikingly different is the Thomist's conception of God and consequently the world as logically yet pragmatically ordered, with laws and ethics following suit, by contrast with Barth and other Protestant theologians' belief in a voluntarist, spontaneous God unfettered by human reasoning or affairs. For Thomism there are natural laws by which the cosmos is ordered some of which are revealed in scripture; for Barth God is the anti-nomian God revealed in the spirit that blows where it will, revealed supremely in the living word of scripture.

Biggar's interpretation of these traditionally opposed theologies leads to an understanding that unites the reason of natural law theology in

Thomism with its qualification by the specific understanding of Christological revelation according to Barthian theology. Thomist theology acknowledges ethics shared with wider society beyond the Christian community on the basis of naturally ordered reason open to all humanity. This view is justified not only on the basis of Christian natural law theology but also by the adoption of the same reasoning in Islam, Judaism and secular applications of what was originally Greek philosophy. Although ostensibly more exclusive Biggar argues that the Barthian Christological perspective is also open to ethical revelation from outside the Christian fold. The basis of that ethical revelation from 'outside' the Church is rendered 'Christian' through the doctrine of the 'virtual Christian', those who act unknowingly or implicitly in conformity with a Christian ethical understanding without adopting Christian belief or making a specific Christian commitment. Karl Rahner's 'anonymous Christianity' is a similar, model of implicit Christianity, by which non-believers act according to a Christian ethical pattern that underlies creation.

Some might argue that this argument for 'faithless reason' or ethics reached without explicit acknowledgement of faith, is not so different from the 'non-theological' ethics of Lopgrun or Andersen in which there is no difference between Christian ethics and ethical reasoning in secular society. Yet whilst the reason of Thomist natural law could be seen as more generic than Christian ethics, based as it is on an ethical philosophy that pre-dated the Christian event, it does also draw explicitly on Christian scripture and values. However, the addition of Barthian Christo-centric theology, adds an explicitly Christian reasoning process. Thomist ethical reasoning drawn from Greek observations of nature prioritizes preservation of life, procreation and natural flourishing. These priorities are replaced in the Barthian approach with a reasoning drawn from observation of life and experience that follows the Christian theology of life, death and resurrection. The latter is a more process-based ethical approach that reads events and patterns in life not just objects, species and behaviours. It also reflects but adds greater substance and ethical dynamic to Ramsey and others' basing of Christian ethics on the importance of love alone. Ethics are not shaped only by belief in an act of God's covenant love but by reflection on a pattern of life, death and resurrection that is implicit in creation and resonates with experience more than direct or explicit appeals to God's love.

From a Christo-centric and wider theological perspective the discernment of these common understandings is a search for ethical truth and the good under God. Whilst some in the non-theological world may suggest that this displays an arrogance on behalf of (particularly Christian) theology, it is not, as Biggar is at pains to note, the advancing of a theological domination or exclusivity. Rather it is a way for those of faith to live out their understanding of faith in public life, rather than an attempt at takeover. As Biggar puts it: "Since the good of [the world created by God] is not only individual but common, Christians should care to shape public life. . . . sometimes by way of prophetic critique and alternative politics' but also in the case of the 'morally ambiguous . . . where public deliberation is properly secular, liberal and polyglot, Christians should take the opportunity to say it as they see it, so loving the world as to orient it towards moral reality and not care a fig about how distinctive their own identity appears.'[13]

Middle Axioms

There is a truism that has acquired the status of a kind joke that the Church of England is a religion of moderation and 'the Middle Way.' The reality is of course more mixed, however the development of Middle Axioms as a theological analysis of complex social realities might be thought to be emblematic of this Anglican middle of the road approach. Yet Middle Axioms are not about finding a moderate position or a middle of the road consensus so much as a way to combine principle and practice in analysing ethical issues and problems. It is a methodology most closely associated for its origins with Archbishop William Temple[14] whose involvement with the Beveridge

---

[13] Biggar N. *Behaving in Public: How to do Christian Ethics.* Grand Rapids & Cambridge, UK: Eerdmans, 2011, pp. 107–109.

[14] Temple W. *Christianity and Social Order.* Shepeard-Walwyn Publishers, 1984 (Temple 1984).

Report supported development of the welfare state and with Ronald Preston[15] whose principle areas of theology focused on economic and social issues such as employment and housing. The starting point is to take the data, analysis and reports of experts in a particular field, such as unemployment and the economy, immigration, poverty or medical ethics. Relevant meta-ethical principles from scriptural and other theological sources are then assessed in relation to the empirical research data. Thus for example the parable of labourers in the vineyard can be considered as authority for awarding a minimum wage and the parable of the talents for the right to work. The morals of the parables are brought into dialogue with the data and opinions from the experts so as to ascertain axioms or ways of proceeding that apply the Gospel imperatives to practical and workable situations.

The pragmatic dimension of applying Gospel principles may also take into account other aspects of philosophical reasoning such as utilitarian analysis of resource questions but not to such an extent as to override scriptural principle. The method of developing middle axioms may draw also on natural law theology, particularly when considering issues of human flourishing and beginnings and ends of life. However, as the raw material of experience and observation is drawn from a wider range of sources and expert analysis, one of the advantages this method holds over natural law theology is the capacity to engage with epistemological and technological change without being bound by limits to natural law experience and purpose arising from the difference of historical context. The dynamic of bringing facts and detailed expertise into dialogue with meta-ethical scriptural principles also avoids the restrictions of scriptural literalism. This theological methodology was developed for a technical and bureaucratic age; its high point was Temple's involvement in the welfare state in tune with the postwar zeitgeist. However, subsequent use of the approach has tended to provoke criticism that it is too political, bureaucratic or secular.

---

[15] Preston Ronald H. *Explorations in Theology 9*. SCM Press, 1981 (Preston 1981).

Theologies of Ethical Process

The methodologies considered above all focus to a significant degree on the aspects of ethics that require discernment and decision-making. By contrast virtue ethics, derived from and effectively the counterpart to natural law theology, offers an ethical process that is about character formation rather than decision-making. Both are processes but whereas the decision-making process focuses on the situation, virtue ethics focuses on the character of the agent. The theory is that if agents grow in holiness and virtue then their actions will follow suit. For those focused on the decisions alone – and in particular on their consequences – the character, motivation, intention and other interior aspects of the agent are irrelevant. Iris Murdoch provides a concise analysis of this removal of interiority from ethics in '*The sovereignty of Good.*'[16]

Underlying the process of growing in virtue and judgement is methodical analysis of what is virtuous. The science of virtue considers the spectrum of character, value and emotion by which human beings are motivated. For example there is a spectrum when responding to the emotion of fear and situations of danger that ranges from cowardice to fearless ignorance of the danger; the median point is courage. When dealing with disappointment and failure there is a spectrum from despair to ignoring the bad news, with a median point of resilience. Virtue is the median between the extremes. The same analysis is applied across the spectrum of all aspects of human character and applied to other values like justice. The process of virtue ethics is growing in wisdom and discernment as to where the median lies which will inform the whole of life and its decisions, as well as character, as the two processes are inter-related. Whilst virtue ethics is a process of seeking holiness through the mean, which inevitably entails some level of restraint and growing in maturity, it is nonetheless a process that is fully life-affirming. Another process of growing in virtue that is clearly focused in the Christian tradition rather than simply Aristotelian, is the Ignatian Spiritual Exercises. This seeks detachment from particular choices or immediate

---

[16] Routledge, 1970 at pp. 10–26.

superficial preferences so that decisions, both short and longer-term, are discerned by reference to sources of revelation and the rationalizing or schooling of feelings and intuition. Whilst Ignatian Spirituality teaches detachment its purpose is to enable better processes of decision-making and discernment tending towards the holiness sought by virtue ethics but within a context of worldly engagement and affirmation of material reality.

By contrast with the process of Christian virtue ethics, the *dharmic theology of nvritti* and process of growing in holiness, towards *moksha* and the stages of *samsara*, requires a virtue of detachment that is sceptical about the world. The virtue and wisdom of *dharma* is recognizing that this world and material things are not bad but illusory; therefore the process of growing in virtue is a growth of detachment from all that might limit someone to the illusory world and affect progress towards *moksha*. This differs from the detachment of Christian virtue ethics, whether the Thomist growth in holiness through virtue or the process of Ignatian detachment; in those cases detachment seeks to make better characters and more rational, less self-interested decisions but affirms the material in line with the Christian theology of incarnation. The fact that the theology of *nvritti* tends to be identified with Hindu holiness means that the more usual daily practices of virtue in the *pavritti* strands of the tradition are overlooked. Yet there is also much in both Hinduism and Buddhist spirituality that affirms and accommodates processes of virtue in daily life as well as the super-virtuous detachment of the *sants* or *sangha*.

The process of virtue ethics is often cited as opposed to the decision-making aspects of ethics but both are necessary to any ethical process. Virtue ethics is the longer, lifelong process of growing in holiness, virtue and judgement, a process that also matures with the wisdom of experience in making decisions, which still need to be made for particular and new situations. This means that virtue ethics and those methods focused on making decisions are complementary rather than opposed. However, the focus of virtue ethics and other forms of process centred on the individual character and holiness of the agent tends to limit their effectiveness in addressing the ethics of political process and social justice.

Liberation Theologies

By contrast with the individual, agent-oriented focus of virtue ethics the process of Liberation Theology, one of the most recent theological developments, is at core a call to ethical change at the communal and societal level. Individual ethical responsibility also matters but is set in the context of wider social realities and structures. Liberation Theology originated in the 1980s in Roman Catholic Latin America as a reaction against the absolute poverty and divisions of wealth and power in the Latin American Catholic Church. The theological methodology begins, like the method of Middle Axioms, with experience and particularly the experience of those suffering from enforced – as opposed to elective – material poverty and marginalization. However, rather than the professional experts' reports predominantly relied on for Middle axioms, liberation theology starts from empirical data and observation gleaned from personal and collective narratives of those experiencing the particular forms of poverty or marginalization under discussion. This is not to say that professional reports are ignored but it is those with the direct experience of what causes, perpetuates and maintains poverty who are considered the real experts. It is an ethics that empowers those who are suffering as both ethical and political agents and its original terminology and theological inspiration is inevitably Christian.

Liberation theology was a reaction not only against poverty and societal and ecclesial structures that perpetuate inequality but also against the conservative, patriarchal authoritarianism of Roman Catholic Thomism. Whilst analysis of poverty was romanticized as blessed in the beatitudes' promise that the poor would see the Kingdom of God, the better-off were reassured that it only means 'blessed are the poor in spirit', sanctifying middle class comfort at the expense of addressing the poverty of the worst off. Although some were moved to charity this left the 'poor' as objects of the 'kind', salvific, self-interested acts of the better off, who were praised for their philanthropy. Liberation Theology recognized that charity could be patronizing, disabling those in poverty and undermining their humanity, agency and capacity. Charity preserved the status quo of class and wealth, spiritualizing equality before God rather than equal treatment for all made in the image of God.

By contrast liberation theology begins with the option for the poor, listening to the experiences and realities of those in poverty of various descriptions. This enables greater appreciation of the challenges of poverty and barriers to improving the situation including the associated stigma and prejudice. The agency and dignity of those in poverty and the claims of justice due to that dignity and equality in God's image are also recognized. Truth is at stake too, contradicting perceptions that the poor are idle authors of their own poverty with a counter-narrative of those who work long hours, often at anti social times, for low pay and with limited job security. This highlights often significant resilience and courage in the face of considerable insecurity and crisis. Such personal realities have historically been ignored in the professional expert reports. However, some engagement with expert analysis is also necessary to foster common dialogue and to test the truth or reality of the professional opinions against the experience on the ground.

The second, hermeneutic stage of the methodology is to bring the narratives grounded in experience of poverty into dialogue with scripture, particularly stories of liberation like Exodus and the Gospels. This recognizes that there is a lot more about liberation from poverty, captivity and oppression in the Bible than teaching about sex and personal morality with which the church – and religion generally – is often more publicly associated. The meta-narrative lens through which scripture is considered is that of the poor or marginalized rather than rulers' dilemmas, an emphasis that reflects the extensive Biblical and Gospel concern for those marginalized through poverty, illness, bereavement, as aliens and other reviled groups outside the law. It also reflects the tilt of scripture against those who use power or law hypocritically. All sources of theological revelation can be applied at this stage of the analysis and Ellacuria[17] has assessed Liberation Theology against catholic systematic theology. However, in practice scripture has provided the bedrock of liberation theology's revelatory authority in a move to recover authentic Christian roots and encourage marginalized or oppressed peoples, much as the rhetoric of New Testament writing was aimed at survival in the face of

---

[17] Ellacuria I & Sobrino J. *Liberation Theology and Systematic Theology.* SCM Press, 2012 (Ellacuria and Sobrino 2012).

persecution. The third stage of the process applies the reflection on sources of revelation to the original analysis, critiquing both power and structures that maintain poverty, with a view to change. The final stage is to implement the changes agreed and review the effect, always returning to the start of the cycle in recognition that this side of the kingdom of God, heaven, paradise or nirvana there will always be injustices and inequalities to address.

The original vision for liberation theology was to develop a church oriented towards praxis, through base communities (*communidades de base*) seeking to recapture the church communities portrayed in Acts as sharing all goods and meals, alongside their prayers. The bias of liberation theology to the marginalized and against power, alongside the focus on socio-economic concerns and practical political change, has attracted charges of Marxism, atheism and divisiveness. Paradoxically the emphasis on analysis and policy has also attracted criticisms that liberation theology is a creature of academia and church leaders of a particular socialist stripe, rather than genuinely of the people. Those who level the latter challenge point to the rise of prosperity Gospel Pentecostalism at the expense of Roman Catholicism in Latin America although there is an argument that the Pentecostalist rise is simply proof of the power of government and external funding. Prosperity Gospel theology is also suspect in many theological ethical circles as a simplistic reward system. Although there is some evidence that part of its success is attributable to changes in lifestyle that assist in escaping poverty it remains confined to personal morality rather than addressing the broader political realities underlying poverty.[18]

Wider than Poverty

Liberation theology as a method addresses far wider situations and understandings than the common identification with its origins in Latin American Catholicism, politics and economics. Writers from several traditions have applied the method in their own situations,

---

[18] Wolffe J. *Evangelicals and Pentecostals: Indigenizing a Global Gospel*, pp. 13–108 (Wolffe 2002a); Martin D. *The Explosion of Protestantism in Latin America*, pp. 247–266. In *Global Religious Movements in Regional Context*, Ed. Wolffe J. The Open University, 2002 (Martin 2002).

theologies and sources of revelation. For example, Marc Ellis[19] writes about the 'prophetic social critique' and 'the paradigm of liberation that forms the heart of the Jewish experience' and points to the ways in which that Jewish experience has informed other movements for liberation such as 'the songs of African slaves' and 'the Exodus tradition ... within the struggle of Latin Americans for justice'. Yet the primary focus of his liberation theology is the recovery of an empowered and renewed post-Holocaust Judaism rather than victimhood. He also assesses the dilemmas of empowerment that eclipse ethical and social critique and the scope for solidarity with other liberation movements, including paradoxically Christianity, despite that tradition's implication in anti-Semitic persecution. Tariq Ramadan's 'Radical Reform: Islamic Ethics and Liberation' progresses from his earlier work seeking reform or *Islah* through *ijtihad* to a more radical critique of Islamic *fiqh* in the light of ethical social challenges of life in the west. The call to liberation is for the Muslim community to emerge from protectionist isolation and become involved in the socio-political challenges of the wider societies in which they live.[20] A practical outworking of this critique is the development of Islamic finance as an alternative to the dominant model of capitalism. Several other Muslim writers have also considered a liberationist analysis; Hamid Dabashi reflects the Latin American experience with a searching socio-economic analysis through Islamic sources,[21] as also does Shabbir Akhtar.[22] Ahmed Alehossein[23] appropriates Islamic theology for feminist analysis.

Interpreting the teachings of *Advaita Vedanta* and the *Gita as* theology from revealed sources, rather than simply philosophical experimentation,

---

[19] Ellis Marc H. *Towards a Jewish Theology of Liberation Orbis Books*. New York: Maryknoll, 1987 (Ellis Marc 1987).

[20] Ramadan T. *Radical Reform: Islamic Ethics and Liberation*. Oxford University Press, 2009 (Ramadan 2009).

[21] Dabashi H. *Islamic Liberation Theology: Resisting the Empire*. Routledge, UK, 2008 (Dabashi 2008).

[22] Akhtar S. *The Final Imperative: An Islamic Theology of Liberation*. Bellew Publishing, 1991 (Akhtar 1991).

[23] Alehossain A. *Islamic Liberation: Theology for Women*. Grin Verlag GmbH, 2014 (Alehossain 2014).

Anantand Rambacham's *A Hindu theology of liberation: Not two is not one*[24] applies liberationist critique to Hindu teachings. Liberation is grounded in normative Hindu theology of freedom through 'informed detachment' from 'the fickle nature of pleasures' and fears of inadequacy at the heart of suffering, which are so subjective. This then informs a critique in Part Two of patriarchy, homophobia and the concept of the third sex, anthropocentrism, violence against children (particularly female children) and liberation from caste. His critique keeps to the fore the priority for the poor and social justice and notes the systems of power, including upper caste male leadership of the tradition, that perpetuates inequality and discrimination particularly against untouchables or *Dalits*. Within Buddhism the liberationist tradition has come to be known by the title 'Engaged Buddhism', by contrast with the detachment advocated in seeking nirvana. In practice engaged Buddhism also practices detachment from self but with the greater purpose of seeking freedom for all. A striking example of 'engaged Buddhism' is the campaign for liberation led by Ang Sang Sui Kyi in Burma but the tradition stretches across wider social and human rights concerns.

The focus on experience, prophetic vision and change for social justice means that liberation theology is not just prayerful theological theory but a process focused on praxis. Much theology and particularly theological ethics shares this applied dynamic. However, liberation theology differs in that it seeks radical engagement for practical change in all dimensions of society. Whereas the scope of more traditional theological praxis has been limited to living out and following existing patterns of religious practice and ethical codes, liberation theology seeks ongoing renewal, both within and more widely than the religious community. Within various communities across the world, particularly in the UK and U.S., Broad Based Organising, which gathers groups around particular political and social issues, has galvanized support from faith communities operating out of liberation theology models. The Broad Based Organising movement locates its origins in the work of Saul

---

[24] Rambachan A. *A Hindu Theology of Liberation: Not Two Is Not One*. Albany: State of New York Press, 2015 (Rambachan 2015).

Alinsky an early 20th CE organiser whose 'Rules for Radicals'[25] was a conscious antidote to Machiavelli's 'Rules for Princes'. The movement is not limited to those from faith groups but its philosophy of solidarity brings together organizers of all faiths and none calling for specific commitments to change from those in power. Liberation theology underpins many religious groups' involvement in Broadbased Organising, providing a focus for political engagement, living out faith commitments of freedom and speaking truth to power.

Besides criticism of Liberation Theology as political, even Marxist, the starting point of experience may be perceived as a subjective and inappropriately variable foundation for ethical truths. Yet all ethical methods are shaped by particular experience, whether utilitarianism's subjective understandings of pleasure and pain or the construction of nominally objective natural law precepts from the experience of the particular classes in positions of theological authority. Like several sociological movements[26] liberation theology is conscious of and explicit about its experiential starting point in contrast to traditional ethical methods where experience is assumed to be universal. By starting from alternative experiential standpoints liberation theology acts as a corrective to traditional, often patriarchal, perspectives. It is for this reason that, besides addressing socio-economic poverty, liberation theology addresses other forms of marginalization. Liberation theologies from stances other than Christianity inevitably challenge dominant ethical, theological and cultural perspectives in western society. Liberation Theology has also grounded challenges to prejudice, particularly at institutional level, on grounds of race and ethnicity. Whilst in some cases race and ethnicity overlap with prejudice against religious difference the two should not be confused.

Liberation Theology also challenges various forms of prejudice and discrimination outside and within faith communities, with marginalized groups drawing hope from scriptural and revelatory sources that speak of freedom and equality. Sikh writers highlight the essence of theological

---

[25] Alinsky S. *Rules for Radicals*. London: Vintage Press, 2013 (Alinsky 2013).

[26] e.g. social constructionism, standpoint theory and critical theory as well as Marxism.

ethics as grounded in social justice and lying at the heart of faith, alongside and inextricably bound up with the holy.[27] One of the initial inspirations of Sikhism was the reaction against Hindu caste and an alternative vision of equality before the divine. The centrality of social justice is reflected in Sikh perspective by the fact that the Akal Takht, the highest seat of Khalsa or temporal justice in Sikhism is located at Amritsar, the holiest of Sikh sites.

Distinctive approaches have developed within liberation theology including feminist and womanist theology,[28] reflecting successive waves of feminism, Queer theology,[29] black theology,[30] perspectives from those with disabilities particularly the deaf community,[31] and both child theology[32] and theology from survivors of child abuse.[33]

---

[27] http://shaheed-khalsa.com/theology.html.

[28] Feminist theology is effectively first wave feminism; womanist theology is the second wave, with greater diversity of experience; examples include Rosemary Radford Reuther. *Sexism and God-talk*. Beacon Press, 1993 (Radford Reuther R 1993); hooks, bell. *Talking Back: Thinking Feminist, Thinking Black*. Boston: South End Press, 1988 (Hooks 1988). Haviva Ner David. *Life on the Fringes: A Feminist Journey Towards Traditional Rabbinic Ordination*. Ben Yehuda Press, 2000 (Ner David 2000); Rabbi Elli Tikvah Sarah. *Women Rabbis in the Pulpit*. Kulmus, 2016 (Sarah 2016); Fatima Mernissi, 1975: *Beyond the Veil: Male-Female Dynamics in a Muslim Society*. revised ed. 1985, 1987, reprinted London: Saqi Books (Mernissi 1975); Mir-Hossaini Ziba. *Islam and Gender: The Religious Debate in Contemporary Iran*. Princeton University Press, 1999 (Mir-Hossaini 1999); Kamini Roy. *The Fruit of the Tree of Knowledge* published in *Talking of Power – Early Writings of Bengali Women from the Mid-Nineteenth Century to the Beginning of the Twentieth Century* edited by Malini Bhattacharya and Abhijit Sen. Kolkata: Stree: Distributed by Popular Prakashan, c2003 (Kamini 2003); Namita Malhotra. *The World Wide Web of Desire – Pornography and Technology*. http://cscs.res.in/events_folder/abevents.2007-03-17.5334271271/abevent.2007-12-20. 5420095926 and the Pink Chaddi Campaign http://timesofindia.indiatimes.com/india/Pink-chaddi-campaign-a-hit-draws-over-34000-members/articleshow/4126529.cms.

[29] Marcella Altheus Reid. *Indecent Theology*. Routledge, 2000 (Altheus Reid 2000); Loughlin G. *Queer Theology: Re-Thinking the Western Body*. Wiley Blackwell, 2007 (Loughlin 2007).

[30] Cone J. *A Black Theology of Liberation*. Orbis Books, 1970 (Cone 1970); Carter Anthony J. *On Being Black and Reformed*. P&R Publishing, 2003 (Carter 2003).

[31] Lewis H. *Deaf Liberation Theology*. Routledge, 2007 (Lewis 2007); Hull John. *Touching the Rock: An Experience of Blindness*. SPCK, 1990 (Hull 1990); *On Sight and Insight: A Journey into the World of Blindness*. One World Books, 1997/2001 (Hull 1997/2001); *In the Beginning there was Darkness: A Blind Person's Conversations with the Bible*. SCM Press, 2002 (Hull 2002).

[32] Couture P. *Child Poverty, Love Justice and Social Responsibility*. Chalice Press, 2007 (Couture 2007).

[33] Pais J. *Suffer the Children: A Theology of Liberation by a Survivor of Child Abuse*. Paulist Press, 2001 (Pais 2001).

The variety of experience challenges patriarchal assumptions about women's complementarity or subordination to men, ideas of what is natural or sinful and assumptions of inferiority or lack of capacity that have been perpetuated as theological norms over the centuries by those with privileged theological leadership. The experience of those on the margins and suffering from the aftermath of abuse, can challenge the presumptions and stigma of poverty and marginalization, providing those in positions of power with evidence about the barriers and structures that actually cause poverty rather than the personalized attribution of blame that often arises. The experience of those with disabilities is a particularly clear and powerful challenge to the prejudices, assumptions and blanket disabling treatment and restrictions of wider society. Many of these areas of liberation theology draw for their analysis on both personal experiential accounts of barriers to full engagement in society and sociological theory, such as constructionist theories of sexuality and socially rather than medically modelled understandings of disability. The following comparative worked examples illustrate the difference that liberation theology makes to theological ethical analysis.

Classical Thomist Natural law theology, such as defended by Germain Grisez[34] and John Finnis,[35] argues that:

- Sex is designed with procreation as its *telos* or end
- Therefore sex must be heterosexual and open to conception
- Consequently same-sex relationships and use of contraception are unethical as being against nature
- Additional ethical requirements are added in relation to marriage being the appropriate context for heterosexual sex and raising children on the basis of reasoned order in society
- This is reflected in the fact that all human societies include some ethical rules for the regulation of sexual relations, procreation and family.

---

[34] Grisez G. *Christian Moral Principles*, Vol 2, *Living a Christian Life.* Franciscan Press, 1993 (Grisez 1993).

[35] Finnis J. *Moral Absolutes: Tradition, Revision and Truth.* Catholic University Press of America, 1991. pp. 9 & 85 (Finnis 1991).

These arguments are bolstered by reference to scripture, for example Genesis 1 and 2 illustrating that heterosexual relationships represent the complementarity of divine order and other passages demonstrating the enduring, and therefore divinely ordained, institution of marriage.[36] In this analysis scriptural revelation is an addition to the reason, observations and precepts of natural law, which provide an over-arching interpretive framework. Natural lawyers argue that the diversity of ethical teachings about sexuality, relationships and family in scripture illustrates the need for such an overarching framework or external objective paradigm, such as natural law.

Appeals to Revelation

The defining issue for a revelation-based ethics is reliance on scripture. Much scriptural interpretation by religious leaders has tended to be conservative and patriarchally oriented, fuelled by the historic nature of scripture and contemporary position, experience and issues of communal identity, in a multicultural world. Whilst the general trend of scriptural teaching on family and sexuality in most religious traditions is what would be styled conservative understandings of heterosexual, patriarchal family, what scripture actually teaches is not necessarily so straightforward. Procreation is a divinely ordained good[37] but not the only end of sexuality or marriage[38]; marriage is the prime place for the containing of sexual desire.[39] Texts about the equality of sexes can be found in all the major scriptures[40] but there are others that are less positive.[41] Homosexuality – or at least men sleeping with men – is not generally accepted[42] but the Gita includes a concept of the third sex.

---

[36] e.g. The wedding at Cana John 2.

[37] Genesis 1, 9:1 & 7, 35:11; Jeremiah 23.3; Qu'ran 4:1; Gita Ch.7:11.

[38] Guru Granth Sahib Ji, 773–774 & 963; Anand Sahib, Song of Bliss; Song of Songs.

[39] Guru Granth Sahib Ji, 152; Sura 70:29–31 Sale, p. 552; Qu'ran Sura 2:197, 2:222, 24:2; Exodus 20:14; Matthew 19:6&9.

[40] Guru Granth Sahib Ji, 473; Sura 4:124, Sura 53:45, 92:3 and 75:39; Genesis 1; Galatians 8.

[41] Sura 16:97, 40:40; Sura 4: 34, 30:20, 38:52, 37:44, 52:20, 56:10–25; Genesis 2, 1 Timothy.

[42] Qur'an 7:80–81; Qur'an 26:165 Lut; Leviticus 18:21–23 and 20:13; Genesis 19:5; Romans 1: 26–27.

There is also evidence of polygamy and keeping of concubines as an acceptable practice in most scriptures.[43] Endorsement of marriage is not always paramount and Christianity, Buddhism and Hinduism all have texts encouraging celibacy,[44] although the Hindu tale of *samkara* includes a paradoxical fable about a spiritual sexual experience designed to overcome the experiential limitations of an ethical celibacy.[45]

Whilst this is a traditional picture, nonetheless to say that the only form of sexuality and family endorsed by scripture is monogamous, nuclear heterosexual families misrepresents scripture for a cultural agenda. Those who rely on revelation alone inevitably bring their own interpretive understandings to the exercise with just as much of a meta-narrative as those relying on other theological methods. Karl Barth is an interesting example; often cited as an exclusivist, conservative, literalist, his weddedness to radical reliance on scriptural revelation and a literal reading of Genesis 2, leads most people either to adopt him victoriously or reject him as ultra-conservative on issues of gender and sexuality. However, as Katharine Sonderegger[46] points out, there is a more sophisticated engagement with experience and other sources around gender and sexuality than might be supposed from Barth's conclusions about Genesis. By contrast with natural law theology and based on Genesis Barth not only advocated companionship alongside procreation as the purpose for marriage but argued that in some cases Christians could, in good conscience, decide not to have children. He recognized varied patterns of relations between the sexes, was open to single as well as married life and his demolition of patriarchal 'science' about female inferiority suggests that had he lived in a different age, he might have placed Genesis 1 and Galatians 3 before Genesis 2.

---

[43] Abraham David & Solomon had more than one wife; Mohammed was polygamous and polygamy features in Hindu scripture.

[44] Jesus own example, plus Paul 1 Corinthians 7–9; the *vinaya pittaka* sadàrasantuññho, A. III,348; the Saüyutta Nikàya includes advice about guarding the senses *indriya saüvara*; http://www.buddhisma2z.com/content.php?id=71#sthash.caNevWPr.dpuf; màtucitta, bhaginàcitta, dhàtucitta – http://www.buddhisma2z.com/content.php?id=71#sthash.caNevWPr.dpuf.

[45] Lipner J., op. cit., pp. 198–199.

[46] Sonderegger K. *Barth & Feminism: Cambridge Companion to Karl Barth.* Ed. Webster J. Cambridge University Press, 2000. pp. 258–273 (Sonderegger 2000).

Ghandi provides a contrast to Barth's views on gender; although Ghandi took a liberal view about the equality of women in the struggle for Indian freedom, he nonetheless accepted conservative *Advaitic* texts and underlying essentialist assumptions about the complementarity of gender.[47] Whereas Barth's epistemology was relatively progressive, possibly influenced by his relationship with Charlotte von Kirschbaum his live-in amanuensis, his Biblical interpretation was not; Ghandi's perspective was almost precisely the reverse. Barth is open to radical cultural contingency around sexuality, amounting in fact if not by name, to a social constructionist understanding of gender and sex. By contrast Ghandi is essentialist in his understanding and interpretation of sex, sexual orientation and gender, seeing both as fixed and therefore determining the choices someone has to make and the ethical options open to them.

Liberation Theology: The Process

By contrast with natural law theology, including the contemporary theology of Grisez and Finnis, or the revelation-based analyses developed above, liberation theology starts with experience and recognizes a wider range of sexuality and relationships than married heterosexual sex. The analysis is as follows:

(i) sex is not just procreative but also beneficial physically and emotionally; some people are infertile and psycho-sexual attraction varies across the Kinsey scale; personal stories highlight the realities

(ii) scripture and other sources of revelation have important things to say about sex and relationships, but the texts are varied as are their comparative contexts, meta-narratives and interpretive frameworks. In addition the experience, discernment and prayer of believers affected by prohibitions in restrictive interpretations are also a source of revelation to be considered.[48]

---

[47] Ananchand A., op. cit., pp. 103–106, pp. 91–114.

[48] There is a range of good examples from LGBT, feminist and womanist, black and disabled standpoints, one of which is Gene Robinson, Bishop of New Hampshire's. *In the eye of the storm.* Canterbury Press, 2008 (Robinson 2008).

(iii) Whether what theology says applies to contemporary experience and if so, how?

(iv) Whose interests are served by the status quo and current teaching, remembering that liberation theology has an option for the poor or marginalized.

(v) The implications of this analysis for ethics, decision-making and action

This methodology is more able to take into account the development of scientific and psychological understanding about sexuality, in the same way that attitudes to race and slavery changed with experience of slaves' stories, their actual abilities and recognition of humanity beyond cod science and prejudice. Analysis develops from the reality of experience to acceptance of various non-traditional or theologically normative understandings of sexuality such as divorce, childlessness and LGBTI realities, within scripture and theological tradition.

The core features of liberation theologies are that they proceed from the experience of those who are marginalized and theological reflection follows, unlike other theological methods that begin with theological or philosophical presumptions and fit them to the facts. More than any other method liberation theology is primarily a process that leads to a variety of liberation theologies and ethical paradigms. Attention is paid to the individuals affected by moral dilemmas but another key distinction of liberation theology is its capacity for reflecting on structures, discerned collectively in the face of injustice and praxis for change.

Narrative Theology

A significant stage in liberation theology's process is the telling of stories, relating the experiences of marginalised peoples and seeking to make sense of them and their ethical implications. Yet story telling and narrative are not unique to liberation theology but a notable feature in theological process and scripture generally. Delchant, Fasching and Lantigua[49] focus particularly on

---

[49] Fasching Darrel J, Dechant D & Lantigua David M. *Comparative Religious Ethics: A Narrative Approach to Global Ethics.* Wiley Blackwell, 2011. (Fasching et al. 2011).

this dimension of experience in their exploration of interfaith dialogue and ethics. What traditional and ancient forms of theological and philosophical explanation add to systematic analysis is truth telling through story. In an age dominated by media, social media and the subjective in the form of valuing both empirical, often transitory, experience and personal autonomy (at least in theory) the power of narrative and human story is acknowledged to be once more to the fore, if it ever went away. At a cynical level narrative and the human story are powerful because of their capacity to move and persuade people, often acting at an intuitive and emotional rather than a rational level. However, as many religious leaders and the narratives of their traditions have recognized, story and poetry are not only important motivators but more importantly from the perspective of ethics can convey important truths at a more holistic level, encompassing not only the rational.

Whether in novels,[50] folk tales,[51] sermons[52] or scripture the capturing of emotion and intuition, the generating of passion leading to action are all factors that create change and the larger perspective for ethical reflection. Reason remains important by way of evaluation but reason does not encapsulate or generate the initial material for reflection, it is the second stage in the process after experience in all its facets. Reason in the narrative process is inductive, a process of recognition rather than logical deduction and it is this process of recognition that gives narrative and theology its power, not only to grasp complex and sometimes paradoxical truths but also to see hope beyond the immediate and the power to change. The scope of narrative as part of theological process is widely varied. It includes immediate personal experience, the reflective experience of story that has been processed, the exemplary story to illustrate a moral point or message, the overarching meta-narrative against which other ethical understandings are formed and inspirational stories of outstanding exemplars of the faith.

---

[50] The power of novels to re-tell age old myths and themes is powerful; Jeanette Winterson provides an interesting example of a writer who re-casts Biblical and other ancient themes in her novels e.g. *Boating for Beginners*. Vintage, 1990 (Winterson 1990) based on Noah and *Weight*. Canongate, 2006 (Winterson 2006) based on Greek myth.

[51] Folk tales are found in all traditions but India has particularly rich folk traditions, both in its religious scriptures but also in more general folk tales such as the Hitopadesha and Jataka tales.

[52] Many good preachers use narrative in their sermons; a good example is Barbara Brown Taylor. *The Preaching Life: Living Out Your Vocation*. Canterbury Press, 2013 (Brown 2013).

Narrative also forms the mythos and identity of a people, community and tradition, which may be grounded in what believers hold to be provable historical facts or in stories acknowledged to be imaginary, yet powerfully illustrative. For virtue ethicists in the footsteps of Alasdair MacIntyre it is this communal religious story that shapes the ethics of particular societies.

The power of narrative, whether the imaginary story or the construction of reality in the stories told about experience, is to capture the paradoxes not only of the non-rational such as emotion and intuition but also the paradoxes of competing rationalities and limits of reason. For reason and pure systematic ethical theory, whether theological or philosophical, falls short when faced with the diversity of reality and human experience. Human Systems based on reason without compassion or objective critique fail to deliver perfect human societies as Stalinism, Maoism and Nazism demonstrated. Reason alone also fails to deliver for humanity precisely because it does not encompass other dimensions of human experience such as physical, emotional and intuitive reality and factors such as mortality, finite knowledge and other aspects of human finitude. Narrative and particularly narrative theology that embraces the transcendent and immaterial aspects of experience alongside the materially empirical has the capacity to encompass all these dimensions and paradoxes not only of human experience but also more broadly of creation. Narrative broadens perspectives on the world, provides more sophisticated pictures of reality and is often more accessible and illustrative than academic or systematic approaches to ethics.

Narrative is by no means limited to the theological but by building on the richness of its narrative heritage in scripture and community the narratives of theological ethics can add richness and realism to debates that may have been lost in the more abstract reaches of ethical speculation. By way of example, the classic criticism of Kantian adherence to truth that betrays, to a Gestapo officer, the hiding place of a Jewish fugitive at risk of being killed,[53] is not a common situation in modern Britain.

---

[53] e.g. Varden H. Kant and Lying to the Murderer at the Door . . . One More Time: Kant's Legal Philosophy and Lies to Murderers and Nazis. *Journal of Social Philosophy* 41, 4 (Winter 2010), pp. 403–421. © Wiley Periodicals, Inc., 2010 (Varden 2010).

The employee aware of the bullying behaviour of senior management towards junior staff, faced with the dilemma of telling the truth or keeping a career, is a more recognizable and realistic scenario. Similarly the majority of women faced with decisions about whether to have an abortion are considering it in complex and nuanced circumstances. Theoretical arguments from male ethicists[54] claiming that the foetus should be dispensed with as a trespasser in the woman's body fail to take into account the impact of hormones, emotional and relational factors and the physical issues that women actually have to face.

Narrative theology also functions at a rational as well as an intuitive and emotional level. Stories are effective through rational extrapolation by analogy and alternative or broader application. Nathan's parable, told to King David in 2 Samuel 12 provides a moral tale about the rich and powerful abusing their position to take the little that is precious to those who are poorer. The wider story highlights injustice and hypocrisy amongst leaders using their power to cover their tracks and the concept that whilst kings may manipulate the law of the land they are not above the moral law. Nor can leaders control either their subjects, as shown by Uriah's refusal to break the law by going home to his wife whilst at war, or illness and death for all the praying, fasting and bargaining in which David engages. There is also a significant ethic of greed and gratitude as David, whom God has blessed so much, abuses his power to take still more. From the feminist perspective there is the abuse of power over Bathsheba whose consent seems irrelevant either to the adultery or pregnancy and who mourns her husband's death and that of her son.

Other stories that illustrate the power and diversity of narrative as a source of ethics include the tale of Gilgamesh, which is the oldest surviving tale (3000BC) of quest and the search for meaning. The paradox of fighting for justice and peace and dilemma of the common good in tension with family ties, are illustrated by the story of Arjuna.

---

[54] Evictionism advanced by Murray Rothbard. *Personal Liberty for a New Liberty.* MacMillan, 1973, pp. 131–132 (Rothbard 1973); Walter Block & Roy Whitehead. Compromising the Uncompromisable: A Private Property Approach to Resolving the Abortion Controversy. *Appalachian Journal of Law* 4, 1 (2005), pp. 1–45 (Block and Whitehead 2005).

Other great religious tales speak of more mundane, ambiguous and confused aspects of life, like Jonah running away from duty only to find it follows him in the whale,[55] the power of addiction undermining reason as seen in the Mahabarat's second epic of *Sabha Parvan*[56] and the power of forgiveness in the parable of the Prodigal Son.[57] Stories of foundational figures such as Buddha's worldly renunciation for other-worldly happiness, Mohammed combining business and public life with extraordinary prayer and the diverse ordinariness of Jesus' disciples also provide inspiration for lives that seek more than the ordinary. These are a small sample of theological stories that yield various and complex ethics, with recognizable context and reality, example and encouragement.

The diversity of theological narratives engage, as ethics must, with the hard stories and the bigger, more complex picture of human endeavour arising both from experiences of living communally and with emphasis on individual guidance, pastoral care, listening and discernment. As Nigel Biggar points out the reality of pastoral experience is a powerful moderator to claims of ethical supremacy or hard and fast rules, which is not to embrace an 'anything goes' relativism but to recognize the claims of real lives. In debates about euthanasia much religious opposition to the legalization of 'mercy-killing' or voluntary euthanasia is not, as Richard Holloway pejoratively suggests a simplistic theist deontology or absolutism. Rather it is a recognition that many frail and unwell people are subject to both external and internal pressure not to be a burden and hate feeling dependent, thus making them vulnerable to pressures that vitiate any genuine consent to euthanasia. There is recognition of the power of relationships for good and ill, the limitations on autonomy now also flagged in secular ethics like Bordieu's concept of *habitus* that constrain and shape ethical parameters and understandings.

---

[55] The Old Testament Book of Jonah.
[56] Lipner J., op. cit., pp. 229–252.
[57] Luke 15: 11–32 – NRSV.

Conclusions

It is engagement with the diversity of experience through and in faith communities that shapes theological ethics as a practical discipline concerned with this life as much as the next. Theological ethics also engages with the complex paradox of human capacity, the realities and limitations of human existence, as well as aspirations to the best of humanity. This contrasts with Hobbes' despair of humanity and reductionist ethic of minimal protection to survive or with Rousseau's over-optimistic naively naturalistic view or Bentham, Mills and Kant's over-optimism about human rationalism. Whether through Christianity's understanding of God engaging in human existence as the incarnate Christ, Hindu embracing of *parvritti and nvritti* or Jewish focus on this-worldly duties and religious patterns that keep the transcendent at the heart of the mundane, theological ethics seeks the fullness of life in its complexity rather than reductionist maxims that fail to recognize life as lived. The fostering of virtues, through engagement with life's harder sides, sickness, death, conflict, cruelty, poverty and injustice also recognizes the fullness of ethical challenges. It is recognized that some aspects of these limitations are addressed in secular theories but the enlightenment optimism in the capacity of human self-rule seems to have been confounded in practice whether in the dramatic totalitarianism of Nazism or Stalinism or in the downside of global capitalism. It is recognized that religion has failed at times through totalitarian visions but such failures have also been due to over-simplification and absolutist abuse of theological resources for this-worldly power at the expense of the humility necessitated by engagement in this-worldly community, under the presence of the divine.

Religious failures and divisions have rightly been highlighted and criticized but also to a degree used as a scapegoat that can disguise or distract from other divisions, conflicts and failures in secular theory, the incomplete aspiration to equality being an interesting example. What is less well-examined is the positive contributions of religious ethics and action. The list of charities that could be cited as examples of theological ethics put into action for the public benefit is wide, from education, healthcare, the hospice movement, initiatives to tackle homelessness, international aid, employment, credit unions, ethical investment and so the list continues. Specific counter-cultural innovations are also seen as a result of particular theological stances. One example, interest free Islamic investments that challenge many assumptions of the capital markets, was hailed as a possible solution to the failures of the banking sector in 2008. In a wholly different sector the development of a new form of parental care, the Special Guardianship Order as an alternative to adoptions that wholly sever birth family identity, has been derived in part from understandings of adoption as long-term care for another's child in Jewish and Muslim law. Theological ethics therefore has a practical, action and solution-focused direction, as well as its more meta-ethical and philosophical tendencies. Above all theological ethics uses process, analysis of context and engagement in the fullness of life and experience to resolve the dilemmas and paradoxes of life's challenges and injustices. It also has global reach through worldwide communities of faith. Accordingly the next chapter will consider the role that theological ethics has played and may continue to play in the development of global ethics.

9

Global Ethics and Theological Ethics

Earlier chapters set out the claim of theological ethics to a place in public discourse based on experience in and representation of a wide variety of communities and approaches to the fullness, complexity and paradoxes of life. Contrary to the caricature of religious involvement in public ethical debate as based on non-negotiable, irrational deontological command theological ethics brings to the table a variety of philosophical and theological methodologies along with a range of resources from tradition and scripture. Through engagement in social action around poverty, sickness and death, in education and pastoral support, faith groups' theology also engages fully with the experience, sources and realities of life that constitute the material of ethics. Theological ethics is also international; the structure of all the major faiths, accompanied by various forms of diaspora, mean that theological ethics has a place on the global as well as the domestic stage.

Globalization as the process by which the world has become a village, through interconnected media,[1] capital, trade deregulation and growing migration began to attract comment from academic ethicists only in the

---

[1] Possibly the greatest spur to contemporary democratic globalization was the foundation of the Worldwide Web in the 1990s by Tim Berners Lee.

© The Author(s) 2017

C. Shelley, *Ethical Exploration in a Multifaith Society*,
DOI 10.1007/978-3-319-46711-5_9

past few decades.[2] This ethical turn was a response to ethical dilemmas and issues that can only adequately be addressed on a worldwide basis. Such issues include some of the most serious facing the human race and the planet such as global poverty, environmental degradation, population size, war and violence from international to domestic, migration and access to resources, equality and human rights.

In practice, as seen earlier,[3] theological ethics and the exploration of ethical thought has always had a global reach through academic and religious diasporas whether prompted by trade, war or persecution. Nor are multicultural societies a new or modern phenomenon. The world of the Middle East, Southern Europe and Northern Africa at the turn of the millennium BC to AD was a highly sophisticated multicultural society with Alexandria and Babylon as cosmopolitan as any modern capital city. Until Christian rulers expelled Jews and Muslims in the 15th CE much of Europe contained vibrant multicultural communities. Much of the Ottoman Empire was not Muslim but permitted subjects to live by their existing faiths and customs, albeit limited by some discrimination. British rule in India, whilst also discriminatory and imperialistic, left faith and personal law and law courts untouched.

From the perspective of faith communities themselves there has also in many ways been a sense of globalism. Christianity has been global from its earliest days, signalled by the visit of the Magi to the manger and Paul's mission to the Gentiles, from Jerusalem to Rome and Ephesus. The major contemporary Christian traditions also operate as worldwide churches, with varying degrees of coherence. The Roman Catholic Church has an international hierarchical structure, the Anglican Communion is effectively a worldwide federation as are Methodist, Baptist and Quaker networks. Orthodox and Coptic communities spread from Russia across Eastern Europe and down to Ethiopia and India. Within Tibetan Buddhism the Dalai Lama provides an international figurehead not only for Tibetan Buddhists but also for many others both within and outside the

---

[2] Widdows H. *Global Ethics: An Introduction.* Routledge, 2011. p. 1 (Widdows 2011); Hutchings K. *Global Ethics: An Introduction.* Polity Press, 2010 (Hutchings 2010).

[3] Chapters 2 & 3.

Buddhist fold. Islam has always had a transnational self-understanding; although no part of the Muslim community has a leader like the Pope Muslim theology speaks of a worldwide Muslim community or *umma*. Jewish communities have had a sense of solidarity across national boundaries through diaspora communities from at least the exile to Babylon and wide dispersal across the ancient world at the turn of the millennium BC to AD. The diaspora of *dharmic* communities, in the wake of colonialism, is more recent although the evidence suggests some dispersal even by the 8–9th CE with the appearance of Hindu research on the cosmos and maths in the work of Muslim natural law theorists.[4]

Theological enquiry, often on an interfaith basis, has also played a part in the ethical development of diaspora communities and multi-cultural societies seeking ways to respect, accommodate and live alongside each other. Historically much global development of common ethical enquiry was and remains academic. For example, at the height of natural law exploration from 9th to 12th CE religious institutions were academia and exploring knowledge across the range of sciences came from a world-view that was both international and theological. The association of education and faith as vital human values, not just functional formation for the workforce, also remains within theological ethics. What is new is the search not only to live alongside but for solutions to common ethical problems. Although logistics means that it is the occupation of a minority, events like the World Parliament of religions[5] are tangible products of theological aspiration to work together towards a global ethical framework.

It is not simply that theology has insights and ideas to contribute to the common ethical debate but also that faith underlies the belief systems of the majority of the world's population.[6] Current statistics suggest that around 90% of the US population continues to profess belief in God, the vast

---

[4] Al Biruni and Avicenna both seem to have had knowledge of Sanskrit and exposure to Indian philosophies in Persia see e.g. Mauro Zonta's. *Possible Hebrew Quotations of Avicenna's Oriental Philosophy.* In *The Arabic Hebrew and Latin Reception of Avicenna's Metaphysics,* Eds. Dag Nikolas Hasse & Amos Bertolacci. Walter d Gruter & Co, 2010, pp. 177–196 (Zonta 2010).

[5] Discussed by Alan Race in *Interfaith Encounter: The Twin Tracks of Theology and Dialogue.* SCM Press, 2010.

[6] Davie G. *The Sociology of Religion.* Sage Publications, 2007. pp. 1–11; 135–180 (Davie 2007);

majority are Christian and although numbers unaffiliated with religion are growing that group is not necessarily anti-religion, with the growth of the label 'spiritual but not religious'.[7] UK statistics show some of the lowest levels of belief across the world but according to the 2011 census 59% of UK citizens still claim Christianity as their faith, 4.8% are Muslims and 25–30% claim no faith.[8] To achieve a consensus and find common ethical frameworks that will be owned and make sense across varying faith perspectives it is therefore essential to take theology into account. Whilst there are inevitably differences of view both within and across faith communities religion is not, as so often painted, uniquely divisive. Gut intuition and deontological mandates occur in many other aspects of society at local, national and international levels, particularly around issues of race, nationalism and identity. As noted earlier it is when theology gets hijacked by such nationalist and identity based politics that it tends to be at its worse.

Difference per se is not to be feared; after all the expression of different views is of the essence of the democracy to which most of the world, and particularly its international institutions, subscribes. It is in seeking to understand the causes for difference and engaging with them that democracy is truly lived out, not imposing hegemonic assumptions about democratic values. The fact that some of the concerns about human rights, for example concerning gender equality, have their roots, at least in part, in what purport to be religious worldviews also means that engaging with those who hold such views is essential to achieve change. Such engagement is required at international level, particularly given that the Vatican and several Muslim states have seats at UN international rights conventions. Engagement is also needed at local level so that concerns can be addressed in grassroots practice not just legal or international instruments.

Removing religious parties from such fora can only add to alienation, opposition and disengagement from processes of developing human rights. It also ignores or silences the strengths and insights that faith communities can

---

[7] http://www.pewforum.org/2015/11/03/u-s-public-becoming-less-religious/.

[8] http://www.ons.gov.uk/peoplepopulationandcommunity/culturalidentity/religion/articles/religioninenglandandwales2011/2012-12-11.

contribute to global ethics. Such communities bring insights about global problems based not on their theological heritage alone but on the experiences that they have undergone which forged that theology. Many diaspora faith communities have been forced to migrate, living as minorities not only in foreign lands but also under oppression in countries of origin dominated by colonialism. In some instances they have moved to the west bought in as cheap labour or slaves, experiencing formational struggles of injustice, rejection, resentment, harassment and de-humanizing treatment. In other cases religio-political expansion brought mixed blessings through faith, whether the Catholic Holy Roman Empire, the Muslim Ottoman Empire or colonialism by Christian heritage countries from the 16th to 19th CE. In South Africa and India for example Mission Schools provided education that, whilst in some instances imposing alien values, nevertheless also provided knowledge that eventually enabled revolution against colonial government. Ghandi, whilst loyal to the *Dharmic* traditions of his heritage was also inspired by Tolstoy's radical Christian pacifism. In some instances Christians who sought to colonize found themselves learning different understandings of their faith and not a little humility from the tribes amongst whom they came to live.[9] In some respects it was the 15th CE encounter between missionaries to Latin-America and indigenous peoples that began to forge modern understandings of rights based on conscience and absolute human dignity through protecting indigenous peoples against the predations of slave traders.[10]

The experiences of those oppressed, the resilience fostered, the challenges posed in terms of holding onto humanity and the essentials of faithful ethics in an alien land, all have important lessons for societies and a global village seeking to resolve global ethical challenges.[11] On the other side of the equation the experiences of those learning humility by

---

[9] Donovan Vincent J. *Christianity Rediscovered.* SCM Press, 2001 (Donovan 2001).

[10] Ruston Roger. *Human Rights and the Image of God.* SCM Press, 2004 (Ruston 2004).

[11] Fiddian-Qasmiyeh, Dr E & Ager Professor. A *Local Faith Communities and the Promotion of Resilience in Humanitarian Situations.* Refugee Studies Centre, Oxford & Columbia University. https://www.rsc.ox.ac.uk/files/publications/working-paper-series/wp90-local-faith-communities-resilience-2013.pdf; Heist D & Cnaan Ram. *A Faith-Based International Development Work: A Review.* School of Social Policy, University of Pennsylvania. *Religions* 2016, 7, 19; doi: 10.3390/rel7030019. www.mdpi.com/journal/religions (Heist and Cnaan 2016).

discovering the limits of conversion and imposition of empire are also salutary experiences to recall in an age of continued rapid globalization. The power of global capital, employment, advertising, materialism and secularization is perceived in many parts of the world as another form of imperial colonialism. The call to democracy can be a smoke-screen for far from democratic contract and employment practices and recent spotlights on taxation have revealed the limitations of democracy to hold capital to account. The fact that so much of the world's population continues to adhere to forms of religious faith despite the power of secularization means that faith-based worldviews will continue to be a factor in global ethics. In addition that faith could be, as it has been in many cases historically, a force to counter the worst impact of de-humanizing capital. In another approach to narrative theology Rodriguez and Fortier consider the power of narrative memory and faith as resistance in the lives of minority communities.[12]

The fact that many religious communities are global, both via community structures and individual families, affords a diversity of experience and access to the reality of what is happening on the ground in particular communities. This means that in considering global ethics the realities and obstacles to particular policy and courses of action can be assessed from experience. One of the strengths of faith-based development agencies is that they work through partnerships between western and southern communities, drawing on the knowledge and experience of local experts,[13] avoiding repetition of such disasters as growing crops unsuited to the climate.[14] There is also redistribution of wealth, experience and building of relationships across

---

[12] Rodriquez J & Fortier T. *Cultural Memory, Resistance, Faith and Identity*. University of Texas Press, 2009 (Rodriquez and Fortier 2009).

[13] Kessler E & Arkush M. *Keeping Faith in Development: The Significance of Interfaith Relations in the Work of Humanitarian Aid and International Development Organisations*. Woolf Institute of Abrahamic Faiths. http://www.woolf.cam.ac.uk/uploads/KeepingFaithinDevelopment.pdf; https://www.rsc.ox.ac.uk/files/publications/working-paper-series/wp90-local-faith-communities-resilience-2013.pdf.

[14] Wood Alan. *The Groundnut Affair*. London: Bodley Head, 1950 (Wood 1950); Williamson C. *Exploring the Failure of Foreign Aid: The Role of Incentives and Information*. The review of Austrian economics, Springer Publishing, March 2010, Vol 23:1, pp. 17–33 (Williamson 2010).

continental divides via family, community twinning and partnerships in fair trade. These relationships build communities acutely aware of the poverty, differences of lifestyle and expectations generated by global capital. Faith communities are faced with such issues not as distant strangers but as near neighbours, co-religionists and members of the same community. The ethical challenge is therefore closer to home and informed more strongly by the personal narratives that lie beneath the statistics and de-personalization of international politics and capital.

The sense of international community that comes with the global village includes the experience of having to negotiate radically different perspectives from within the diverse parts of the one international body. This poses the challenge of how to live together with difference, either seeking a common mind about ethical issues that face the global community or learning how to negotiate and respect difference. Again religious communities and faith-based agencies have been developing an international voice based on their international relationships for centuries. The models for that negotiation vary significantly but unlike the hierarchies of command in international companies, most faith communities[15] operate on the basis of voluntary co-operation, solidarity and local autonomy. This requires mutual commitment to conversations, relationship and partnership based on a common vision of faith and universal divinity. Such relationships enable challenging conversations not only about difference but also about failings, whether over economic corruption, differing views on capitalism and freedom and the headline grabbing rows about sex. Faith communities and the theologies they develop in seeking to live ethics and faith authentically, in diverse contexts, are inevitably faced with addressing the paradoxes of thinking globally but acting locally.[16]

Above all however, as considered throughout this exploration, theological and religious perspectives on ethics can bring alternative insights to bear on ethical dilemmas facing the whole of humanity and indeed

---

[15] The Roman Catholic Church being an exception.

[16] Although the origins of the phrase are contested one candidate for coining it is Jacques Ellul, radical Barthian Christian, sociologist and lawyer whose Christian Universalism questioned state power and borders. Ellul J. *On Freedom, Love and Power*. University of Toronto Press, 2010 (Ellul 2010).

creation. These alternatives may provide additional ethical resources,[17] a brake on a particular course of action,[18] a forum to address hard to reach groups for the implementation of action and so on. The latter is particularly important because whilst the exercise of seeking to reach global agreement through international conventions or Parliaments is commendable it is pointless if those agreements remain no more than words on a page. This is where all of civil society and faith communities as some of the major forces within civil society across the globe, have a major role to play.

The advance of the global village means that all decisions have ethical implications and global reach, from the food on our plates to the clothes on our backs and much more. Additionally the global village or rather the global market means that many of these issues are interlinked. Thus the food on our plates and clothes on our backs are linked to issues of employment, labour and production costs, markets for raw materials and global financing, transport and communications systems. The issues that stand out most from this picture as requiring a global response include:

(a) Worldwide access to resources and the basic necessities of life
(b) The impact of consumption on the environment, animate, plant and other life
(c) Worldwide trade and labour, its conditions and what can or should be traded including human bodies or body parts
(d) Migration, war and violence
(e) Global media, politics and power

Resources and Necessities

A foundational principle in all religious ethics is the preservation of life, whether based on natural law ethics about flourishing and procreation, scriptural mandate and respect for God's image or the *dharmic* principle

---

[17] For example the generosity of *Sikh langar*, Islamic financial instruments.

[18] Richard Holloway concedes that the religious ethics he rejects might provide helpful brakes on technological progress – Holloway R. *Godless Morality*. Canongate, 2004, pp. 131–149 (Holloway 2004).

of respect for the divinity of life in all creation. Generally speaking the preservation of human life in most ethical systems, theological or otherwise, is a paramount value. The only exceptions to this general principle of preserving human life are found in utilitarian or consequentialist analysis of the value of a particular life in the context of a larger collective good. Examples of such exceptional circumstances include 'just war' theory, which justifies sacrifice of life to save more lives longer-term through winning the war and establishing peace. Calculation of more life, longer life and quality of life for some at the expense of others is also needed in distributing limited resources, like food or healthcare. Whether dealing with war or resources, decisions are made by those in positions of power over and on behalf of others. The majority of religious ethical codes recognize some element of consequentialist thinking in these difficult scenarios of collective decision-making.

By contrast with this collective consequentialist qualification to the sanctity of life, the second exception is the argument of personal autonomy over one's own life. This qualification is generally less accepted by the majority of religious ethical codes on the basis that, deontologically, life is a gift, not a personal possession to be given or taken away. The ethical construction of this exception is complex although religious reservations reflect the Kantian duty not to commit suicide. It is utilitarian to the extent that it vests in the individual authority to decide where the balance of the hedonic calculus lies i.e. does the pain or limited quality of my life outweigh the usual principle of preserving life as a good? However, to the extent that it places the decision of one individual above the greater good of maintaining life generally, individual autonomy is prioritized over the collective.

Yet from another possibly more sinister perspective, the decision to take one's life may be construed as for the greater good; the calculus that creeps in is not only that someone finds life insupportable for themselves but may argue that ending their 'useless' life, saves resources for the greater good. It is to protect against the latter that theological perspectives of life as divinely ordained and not amenable to financial calculus, most strongly strive. This links with theological ethical duties to protect the vulnerable and those destitute through widowhood, orphans, poverty and exclusion, which is clearly anti-utilitarian.

The principle of valuing each life as gift beyond the economic, applies in the pastoral care of those facing terminal illness but also to many global ethical dilemmas. An example is quota systems for refugees, which put economic value on an international asylum system that should be unquantified as the value of life is paramount if someone is forced to seek asylum. Countries closest to war have no option but to take whoever comes over the border seeking refuge.[19] There is a generosity in many countries' response based on a theological ethic of welcoming the refugee or stranger, often recalling one's own oppression, for example Exodus 22:21 'do not oppress a stranger for you were once foreigners in the land of Egypt'.[20] This theology is also based on recognition of the divine in each person giving rise to duties to recognize the equality of all people, for example as the image of God in Judaeo-Christian tradition, equal before God in Islam and foundationally challenging caste in Sikhism.

Another ethical imperative is to share the goods we have as good fortune is ultimately from the creator, rather than holding onto wealth for oneself alone.[21] Although aspects of Christianity and Buddhism are ambivalent about wealth, with renunciation in both Jesus' and Buddha's lives, for other faiths, particularly Islam, Hinduism and Judaism, wealth per se is not a problem. Yet wealth engenders a sense of gratitude; it should be shared and used charitably to support those in need through alms-giving in Judaism and the *dharmic* traditions, charity as the expression of neighbour love in Christianity and *waqf* or *salat* in Islam. The Sikh tradition of *Langar*, providing food for whoever turns up at the gurdwara door epitomizes the extent of generosity expected. Seasons such as Lent and Ramadan also emphasize giving as part of penitential preparation but tithing and regular giving are expected all year round. It is this essential principle of giving within religious traditions that lies behind the

---

[19] In 2015, 65.3 million people globally were displaced by war; 40.8 million were internally displaced. Of the 21.3 million seeking refuge only 2.3 million were refugees in industrial countries; 86% were in low/middle income countries, 2.5 million in Turkey. http://www.unhcr.org/uk/news/latest/2016/6/5763b65a4/global-forced-displacement-hits-record-high.html.

[20] Also Deuteronomy 10:19, Leviticus 19:34.

[21] 'All beings and creatures are His; He belongs to all' Guru Granth Sahib Ji 425 & 349 & 1426.

significant numbers of faith-based charities noted above. Some still bear religious names for example Christian Aid, Church Urban Fund, Islamic Relief, Khalsa Aid and Sikh Relief, the Jewish Toremet. Others have begun from the engagement of faith groups with issues in wider society and developed their own life and identity beyond the faith community, examples, as noted earlier, include Centrepoint for homeless youngsters and the Samaritans.

Yet theological ethics around poverty and resources are not limited to charity and alms. Concepts of justice include social justice and redistribution both through the natural law tradition and scriptural revelation. The Judaeo-Christian tradition of Jubilee sets regular periods of time for forgiving debts, re-distributing burdens and freeing those enslaved by debt at 'the year of the Lord's favour' effectively preventing too great a disparity of wealth arising and limiting the scope for exploitation.[22] This is the theology that grounded campaigns for debt forgiveness that began at the millennium.[23] The command not to retain a debtor's pawned cloak beyond nightfall sets another floor to imbalances of power and exploitation of those in penury.[24] Whilst many faiths require care for the destitute including orphans the Qu'ran requires justice through a careful accounting of any property an orphan may inherit, ensuring that caring for others' offspring is not an opportunity for profit and orphans do not remain indebted to their carers. Sikhism requires not only equality but also willingness to take action and intervene to protect the oppressed and correct injustice.[25] Ghandi's commitment to peaceful protest combined *ahimsa* with concepts of justice, again combatting caste and calling equally to freedom.

Judaeo-Christian duties to liberate the oppressed and free the captive are also seen in the Jubilee concept.[26] Duties to visit those in need, even in prison, provide not just a material but a humanitarian and pastoral

---

[22] Isaiah 61:2.

[23] http://jubileedebt.org.uk.

[24] Exodus 22:26; Deuteronomy 24:12–13.

[25] 'The Merciful Master has now ordained that no one annoys, oppresses or inflicts pain on, another. All shall abide in peace in a benign regime.' GGS 74.

[26] Isaiah 61.

response that can maintain the humanity of those otherwise isolated or stigmatized by poverty and exclusion. This too is not just charity but a call to genuine engagement rather than an 'othering' of those who have been battered by life. There is also a call not only to challenge the stigmatizing of those who are poor but to resist calls to status or class and to recognize an equality of humanity before God, whilst wrestling with what that means in real societies. For all religious traditions commitment to equality is an equality of humanity, encompassing but going beyond economic access or mere equality of opportunity to equality of respect and treatment.

Environmental Justice

In addition to positive duties of intervention theological ethics includes significant traditions of renouncing wealth, embracing poverty and not seeking status. It may seem paradoxical that tackling poverty requires giving up wealth and this sort of renunciation was strongly critiqued by Bentham's utilitarianism. Yet if poverty is a relative measure that involves not being able to maintain adequate living standards in society and the stigma attached, then renouncing greed and divisions of wealth can assist in reducing poverty. In the light of the now stark evidence of links between poverty and environmental degradation causing the drought, flood and famine that often lies at the roots of poverty, the links between tackling poverty along with climate change and environmental damage are well-established. It is in this context that theological ethics about wealth, success, material renunciation and detachment are significant.

Although contested at the fringes there seems to be fairly compelling scientific evidence that population growth, consumerism, oil and carbon consumption and de-forestation are causing major environmental damage. CO_2 emissions are producing 2 degrees centigrade increases in global temperatures[27] causing drought in much of Africa and the Middle East, with related impact on food production, health and mortality. Other severe

---

[27] http://climate.nasa.gov/evidence/; http://news.nationalgeographic.com/news/2004/12/1206_041206_global_warming_2.html.

weather developments such as floods and hurricanes are also linked to these changes, which the evidence strongly suggests are caused by human behaviour and consumption patterns. Added to disasters that have an impact on human lives, the encroaching of human cities on forest areas and Eco-systems, is reducing the tree coverage that assists in regulating CO_2 and is devastating both plant and animal bio-diversity. 80% of US corn and over 90% of oats are fed to beef cattle; producing beef also uses 2,500 gallons of water per pound of meat, against 25 gallons for a pound of wheat.[28] It is this factual matrix that theological and environmental ethics seeks to address.

Environmental ethics distinguishes androcentric from ecocentric ethics; the former considers the environment and its protection from the perspective of humankind, the latter from the viewpoint of the whole planet. Broadly speaking the Abrahamic faiths have tended to an androcentric view; whilst all creation is the work of God, humanity made in God's image is its pinnacle and acts as co-creator with God. This construction is based on scripture[29] but is also matched by Greek philosophy, which saw humanity as pre-eminent in creation on account of the capacity for reason. At its worst, some Christians have interpreted Genesis' words that 'man shall have dominion' over the earth in ways that support patriarchal exploitation, condemned by eco-feminists as the rape of the earth.[30] Understandings of heaven as limited to those of human reason and soul, excluding animals and other parts of creation, have done nothing to redeem Christianity in particular from charges of species-ism. Such limited understandings are almost certainly a misreading of heaven.[31]

---

[28] http://www.peta.org/about-peta/faq/how-does-eating-meat-harm-the-environment; http://science.time.com/2013/12/16/the-triple-whopper-environmental-impact-of-global-meat-production/.

[29] Genesis 1: 26 – 'let them have dominion over the earth . . .' Qu'ran 2:31 *Allah taught Adam the names of all things . . . & 30:2–21* injunction to dwell on earth in peace.

[30] Hamer MD. *The Rape of the Earth and the Human Ego.* Countercurrents, 14 May 2010; Gunarsdottir S. Rapes of Earth and Grapes of Wrath. *Feminist Theology* 18:2, January 2010, pp. 206–222 (Gunarsdottir 2010); Wilson SR. *Rape of the Land: Twenty-first Century Ecofeminism and Rape Culture Comment,* 24 February 2016; Dr Hans Adam. *The Rape of Mother Earth.* Salzburg, 16 January 2002; Vacks GJ. *The Rape of the Earth: A World Survey of Soil Erosion.* Faber & Faber, 1939 (Vacks 1939); Collard A & Contrucci J. *Man's Rape of the Wild: Man's Violence Against Animals and the Earth.* Indiana University Press, 1998 (Collard and Contrucci 1998).

[31] See e.g. Paula Gooder's. *Heaven.* SPCK, 2011.

By contrast the *dharmic* faiths have a more holistic view of creation. Within Hinduism the *Vedic* rites and codes are grounded in awareness that any part of creation out of its natural order will have an impact on other parts of creation. The chain of being or *pratiya-samutpada* in Buddhism, is inter-connected leading to higher incidences of vegetarianism within Hindu, Jain and Buddhist culture as all life and creation are respected as hallowed. Sages of the Jain tradition take this to great lengths, pictured in Kipling's 'Kim' sweeping ants away lest they step on them and wearing masks to avoid swallowing flies. The *dharmic* approach to salvation and judgement realized through reincarnation throughout the continuum of animate creation, adds to respect for the divine in the whole of creation. The horror of Victorian Christians when confronted with Darwin's evolutionary theory connecting them to apes would have been less of an issue for *dharmic* sensibility.

Yet opposing *dharmic* and Abrahamic faiths might over-simplify the contrast. For example, whilst viewing creation as responding to *kharmic forces* in a continuous cycle of *samsara* or reincarnation, it is clear that humanity is the apex of the created cycle and the nearest to *nirvana* or *moksha*. Those who draw from natural law theology appreciate humanity as part of the whole creation, which shows forth the glory of God. Both Aquinas and Al Gazali explore natural sciences as part of a spectrum of enquiry with theology and many key Muslim natural law thinkers were also natural scientists and physicians. Those whose theology draws predominantly on scripture can also find plenty to inspire holistic love of the natural world. Passages of scripture, notably Genesis' account of creation[32] and many of the Psalms celebrate creation. St Francis, whose commitment to itinerant poverty is notable, spoke of a unified creation with brother sun and sister moon.

The appreciation of nature as divinely created and ordered, along with recognition of the limits of humanly generated wealth, affords respect for earth's integrity. In turn this imposes duties of environmental care, whether through *dharmic* rites and *Kharma* or Abrahamic concepts of

---

[32] Genesis 1 & 2; notably Psalm 148–151; the Song of Songs.

stewardship.[33] Such duties ground a theological environmental ethic that is supported by other sources. In the life-affirming Vedic Samkhya tradition the five elements[34] of earth,[35] water,[36] fire,[37] air,[38] and space[39] are the material invoked in daily worship or puja as objects of reverence. The world denying Advaita Vedanta tradition promotes environmentalism in an opposite mode, living lightly on the earth through renunciation, which is also the basis of Buddhist environmentalism as expounded by the Dalai Lama.[40]

Western responses to environmental concern began in the 1960s as environmental activism grew more generally. From a contemplative Catholic perspective Thomas Merton[41] joined forces with the Dalai Lama and Protestant writer Matthew Fox to put environmental ethics on the map with theories of *Gaia*, drawing on the holism of *dharmic* thinking as the basis for a Christian theology of the environment.[42] Western Buddhist Joanna Macy's Ecofeminism, expounded in *World as lover, world as self*[43] speaks of the move from ego to eco-self, recognizing the interdependence of humanity with wider creation and the need to live relationally rather than autonomously. Some of the earliest Christian environmentalism was also feminist in origin. For example, Rosemary Radford Reuther's *Gaia and God: An ecofeminist theology of earth healing*[44]

---

[33] The Hebrew word for Dominion over the earth *radah* is a world for kingly rule; but the wise Israeli king is a steward and a servant.

[34] *mahabhuta.*

[35] *prthivi.*

[36] *jal.*

[37] *tejas.*

[38] *vayu.*

[39] *akasa.*

[40] http://www.dalailama.com/messages/environment/buddhist-concept-of-nature.

[41] Fox Matthew. *A Way to God: Thomas Merton's Creation Spirituality Journey.* New World Publishing, 2016 (Fox 2016).

[42] Matthew Fox. *Creation Spirituality: Liberating Gifts for the Peoples of the Earth.* Harper Publishing, 1991 (Fox 1991).

[43] First published 1991, updated by Parallax Press, 2007; more mainstream Buddhist writing includes Akuppa. *Touching the Earth: A Buddhist Guide to Saving the Plant.* Windhorse Publications, 2002 (Akuppa 2002).

[44] Harper Collins, London, 1994.

critiqued the implications of patriarchal understandings of God for the order of society and creation. Eco-theology employed liberation theology to analyse the reality of the world, seeking to rectify patriarchal misreadings of scripture for the good of the planet as well as in the cause of gender equality. Leonardo Boff's *The cry of the earth, the cry of the poor*[45] also developed liberation theology's responses to ecological concern and links with poverty.

The range of theological responses to environmental ethics has grown with Andrew Lindsay's exploration of animal rights[46] and Pope Francis' encyclical *Laudato Si*[47] amongst other publications.[48] In Islam *Green Deen: what Islam teaches about protecting the plant*[49] sets out a Muslim manifesto for environmentalism covering over-consumption, energy, water, jobs and Mosques. A similarly practical guide is *Simple Actions for Jews to Help Green the Planet: Jews, Judaism and the Environment.*[50] In addition to new work there is also re-evaluation of older theologians' work in the light of environmentalism, including for example Kathryn Tanner on *Creation and Providence* in Barth's work.[51]

Yet environmental theology, particularly arising from a liberationist stance, cannot remain a theoretical interest. As a worldwide Communion the Anglican Church adopted the goals of social justice and environmental stewardship as two of their collective 'five marks of

---

[45] 1997 Orbis Books.

[46] Linzey A. *Animal Theology.* SCM Press, 2000 (Linzey 2000).

[47] Pope Francis. *Laudato Si or Praise Be to You: On Care for Our Common Home.* Ignatian Press, 2015 (Pope Francis 2015).

[48] Blanchard KD & O Brien K. *An Introduction to Christian Environmentalism: Ecology, Virtue & Ethics.* Baylor University Press, 2014 (Blanchard and O Brien 2014); Butler M & Morris AP. *Creation and the Heart of Man: An Orthodox Study of Environmentalism.* Acton Institute for Study of Religion and Liberty, 2013 (Butler and Morris 2013);

[49] Ibrahim Abdul Matin. *Green Deen: What Islam Teaches About Protecting the Plant.* Kube Publishing, 2012 (Abdul Matin 2012); see also Akhtaruddin A & Clarke A. Ed. *Islam and the Environmental Crisis.* Ta-Ha Publishers, 1997 (Akhtaruddin and Clarke 1997) and Haleem HA. *Islam and the Environment.* Ta-Ha Publishing, 1999 (Haleem 1999).

[50] Rabbi D Peretz Elkins. *Simple Actions for Jews to Help Green the Planet: Jews, Judaism and the Environment.* Create Space Publishing, 2011 (Peretz Elkins 2011); see too by Hava Tirosh-samuelso. *Judaism and Ecology: Created World and Revealed Word.* Harvard University Press, 2003 (Tirosh-Samuelso 2003).

[51] Tanner K. *Creation and Providence,* p. 111–126 of *The Cambridge Companion to Karl Barth.* Cambridge University Press, 2000 (Tanner 2000).

mission' in 1984. The Papal encyclical *Laudato Si*, focuses on the theological imperative to protect creation and the causative link between poverty and climate change. These themes are also explored, through action and practical change, by campaigning organizations such as Christian Aid, Caritas, Tear Fund and Islamic Relief amongst others. The challenge of environmental ethics is not only to campaign for greater political commitment to change by governments as measured by statistics for carbon use and recycling, but also to effect change in consumer behaviour and lifestyle. The essence of all theological analysis is that human beings, indeed all created life, is more than the material and that there are forces and factors that are larger and more mysterious than human reason. This does not discount human reason but necessitates humility before the glory, wonder and complexity of creation.

The traditions of renunciation found in theological ethics and world-views all present an alternative ethic to the materialistic utilitarianism promoted by economies dependent on capitalist consumerism. The latter is promoted the world over, whether in the growing economies of the BRIC nations, the oil dependent states of the Middle East or the consumer-driven production of South East Asia, the US and Europe. The focus on religion as personal morality means that the counter-cultural dimensions of religion in relation to wealth and capitalism have often been overlooked. Whilst the Weberian capitalism of the Protestant work ethic has tended to predominate in modern times Christianity has an ambivalent relationship with wealth as does Buddhism. Siddharta gave up both wealth and position to devote himself to meditation in the search for wisdom and ultimately *nirvana*. The tradition of Buddhist monasticism affirms that principle of complete renunciation. Whilst many Buddhists do not follow a monastic path, the observance of Buddhism remains framed by the context of renunciation and suspicion of the material in favour of transcendent wisdom and reality. In the light of a global ethic that affirms the material and worldly as real this Buddhist and more broadly *dharmic* tradition of renunciation is a significant countercultural antidote.

Christian renunciation operates slightly differently. The theology of incarnation by which God became human in Jesus affirms the material and incarnate world. There is no sense of seeking release from the material, despite early dualist tendencies from Platonic philosophy. In Jesus' teachings there are several points at which he calls followers to renounce the attachments of home, family and wealth to follow him. Several disciples took this literally for example leaving the family fishing business, at least for a while, although later in the Gospels they return for a while to their livelihoods, Peter's mother-in-law and presumably wife and family. Jesus himself also lived a quite ordinary life in Nazareth, probably following in the family business of carpentry, for the first thirty of his 33 years. Yet there is no getting around Jesus' fairly radical giving up of that life, his injunctions to followers, particularly rich ones to give up their wealth and the radical sharing of property in the early church. Over the years many Christians have followed this example, relinquishing much in material terms to be missionaries or members of religious orders. As the immediate return of Jesus grew less apparently imminent the call to evangelical poverty moderated but that call remains and there is a clear duty on Christians, as in other traditions, to avoid attachment to wealth or material achievement and to share wealth with 'the poor.' This recognition of values other than wealth, material possessions or their accompanying status, grounded in scripture and traditions of renunciation, simplicity and sharing, adds a significant theological ethic that counters the dominance of market capitalism.

It is not that all theological ethics are necessarily against capitalism and markets. Liberation theology has been critical of consumerism and the impact of capitalism but many theologies are not and liberation theology does recognize that such is the complexity of society we are all bound up in capitalism to some degree. After all, Mohamed was a businessman, Judaism and most of Christianity has affirmed capitalism and the *dharmic* faiths recognize that most of the faithful need to engage in the world and earning a living. Yet even those theologies and scriptural examples that affirm the material, trade and worldly affairs have strong accountability to a God-centred view of life which relativizes all human endeavour, including running businesses. Theology cannot view the capital markets as ethics-free zones, which has led to ethics promoting fair trade and ethics around what commodities are traded. A further constraint that relativizes all work is the principle, still adhered to by most Jews and many Christians, of taking a Sabbath day for rest. It is a day when business is not done, partly at a human level to allow rest and time for family and personal relationships but also to recognize God at the heart of all endeavour and life. It is a day to give thanks to God for life itself and so to put the rest of life, with its successes, failures and everything in between, into a much larger and longer-term perspective. It is a day that should highlight the limitations of material success, placing other values and timescales centre-stage.

The discipline of Sabbath is reflected in all religious traditions' times of the day or week, when time is set aside to put the material and immediate world in perspective of the bigger picture of life and creation. Whether it is Shabbath, Sunday mass, morning prayer, salat or Jummah prayers, daily meditation or offering puja at the Temple this time set aside to focus on God, life and creation is fostered and celebrated in religious and communal ritual. As noted above *puja* celebrates the earth in prayers, the recitation of Psalms praises creation, and acts of contrition and thanksgiving enable reflection on how God, including creation and neighbor have been served. The Sabbath and other times for prayer are to foster what is healthy for humanity. As Jesus puts it 'the Sabbath is made for man'; God or the divine does not need it but humanity does need the opportunities and reminders to put the daily and material into this larger, transcendent perspective, which means that even if wealth is affirmed it is not made absolute.

Just as 'the Sabbath is made for man' so wealth is to serve the goals of flourishing rather than becoming the overarching benchmark for assessing human value and success. If that larger perspective is allowed to relativize the material and androcentric concerns so prevalent in western traditions it can also enable the wider perspective of living in harmony with creation so much more valued in the *dharmic* world. Additionally whilst wealth is to be enjoyed true wealth is not necessarily evaluated in material terms and other forms of wealth, such as beauty, health and the values of love in relationships can be counted. Judaism, Islam and Sikhism are the most life-affirming traditions in the sense that none has much tradition of monasticism, withdrawal from the world or celibacy. Yet in each case the there are limits to seeking wealth and a focus on regular disciplines that put the divine at the heart of life mean that whilst this world is enjoyed it is never enjoyed in isolation from the eternity of God's creation.

Other dimensions to theology that provide correctives to the absolutizing of the material or the pursuit of wealth include regular prayers for those in need, fostering an awareness of human mortality and frailty in illness. Recognizing suffering and mortality as inevitable and part of the human condition, rather than to be avoided and evaded in the pursuit of eternal happiness, is a reminder that wealth is no protection against illness and death. It is a strong antidote to consumerism to recognize that no amount of retail therapy will cure the anxieties of modern competitiveness. This is particularly pronounced in the Hindu tradition of withdrawal from the world after contribution to its continuity through engagement with life and family. There is a sense of the *samsara* of the later part of life as preparing for the eternal and focusing on the core values of life, prayer and eternal happiness through release from the world in *moksha*. This does not deny the world in the sense of rejecting it but puts it into the different perspective of recognizing that it is not the only dimension of life.[52]

Trade and Labour

Another dimension of global capital is the radical division of the 'haves' from the 'have nots'. Deregulated world trade and markets have left some with less than a dollar per day for living costs and 62 others owning 50% of the world's wealth.[53] This has also led to a dramatic contrast not only between lifestyles in terms of what people can afford but also in terms of what is trade-able. In the same way that environmental degradation exploits the earth a major concern about global capital markets is the exploitation of people through global labour markets and the depression of wages at the less skilled end of the market. Here again theological ethics that affirms the integrity of each human person, as made uniquely yet in the image of God or according to the

---

[52] Lipner J. *Hindus: Their Religious Beliefs and Practices*. Routledge, 2010, pp. 268–269 (Lipner 2010); Menski W. in *Ethical Issues in Six Religious Traditions*. Edinburgh University Press, 2007. p. 27 (Menski 2007).

[53] Oxfam.

pattern of the divine in creation, may have a different perspective on some more utilitarian aspects of the markets. This is particularly the case in relation to the sex industry and sale of bodies. Whilst even the most utilitarian would object to trafficking people for sex and arrangements that lack consent as offending against autonomy, many accept a consensual sale of sex as a legitimate means of earning money.

By contrast most religious ethical views on sex and the integrity of sexual expression within a marriage or at least a committed relationship, would view the sex industry as immoral and exploitative. This view is based partly on the argument that genuinely free consent to sale of sex is not possible, as there will always be an element of exploitation. Additionally sex is sacred and not therefore a commodity that can be sold.[54] Such arguments about the sex industry are as old as religion and human civilization itself although the scale of the industry in contemporary global markets and its manifestation through electronic and virtual media have added whole new dimensions to the nature and extent of the exploitation involved.

A newer argument around trade in humanity is the market that has arisen in human body parts. A few theological perspectives, for example Jehovah's Witnesses and some branches of Judaism[55] or Islam[56] argue that any donation of human organs or blood offends against the integrity of the human person and is therefore contrary to creation. However most faiths accept voluntary consensual organ donation to alleviate suffering and save life. Yet the sale of organs and creation of a market for the sale of organs removes this act from a relational act of love and altruism to a commercial transaction, open to exploitation not only by those in need of a transplant and rich enough to buy one but also to the

[54] Morgan P & Lawton C. *Ethical Issues in Six Religious Traditions.* Edinburgh University Press, 2007. pp. 13–15, 70–71, 128–129, 174, 226–227, 297–298 (Lawton 2007).

[55] Generally speaking Judaism qualifies theology about the integrity of the body by the principle that if donating organs saves a life that is a higher commandment; however, removal of organs after death is often removed as use for research is not the same – or ethically valid – as donation for the immediate saving of life.

[56] Like Judaism the principles of bodily integrity and preserving life apply in Islam but opinion is divided; many Muslims will apply the principle that preserving another's life takes precedence following Surah 5; others regard bodily integrity as paramount.

middle men who broker the trade. The argument for autonomy is that if someone wishes to sell body parts they should be entitled to do so, on the basis that it is their body. The objection is that if someone is so hard up they are prepared to undergo the risks of selling internal organs the genuineness of their consent is undermined by economic duress and the purported contract is inevitably exploitative.

Other markets that potentially involve the trade of human beings are the international adoption and surrogacy markets. British law prohibits the payment of money, other than expenses, for either adoption or surrogacy principally to prevent the risks of duress and exploitation, keeping the arrangement as one of voluntary, charitable gift. Yet others would argue that favours those able to afford such generosity as against those who could do with the money for providing a service that is ethically the same if offered for expenses only. The difference between the market in adoption or surrogacy and that in body parts or sex is that third party interests, namely children, are involved in the transaction and in even greater need of protection than potentially exploited adults.

When dealing with the interface between autonomy and exploitation the Biblical tradition includes multiple references to guarding against oppression and exploitation. Even though there is reference to slavery as an acceptable practice at the time it was written, as is the case in other religious scriptures, even slaves had to be treated humanely and were members of the owner's household. The concept of Jubilee by which slaves were freed and return of the pledged cloak are strong reminders of the humanity even of those enslaved. This is not to justify slavery but to emphasize the need for basic minimum standards of treatment for employees and human beings even in the direst poverty. The fact that internationally slavery and caste are now prohibited and freedom is an absolute human right, qualified only by judicial punishment, provides even stronger arguments for humane conditions, such as a floor to wages, working conditions and safety at work, to prevent slavery in all but name.

The universal prohibition of slavery is also a strong challenge to all parts of global society to address any practices that continue to enslave human beings, whether extreme libertarian employment practices, markets that exploit peoples' poverty or conservative interpretations of religious tradition. The fact that changes occurred in all parts of society's thinking over slavery, including the interpretation of religious texts, shows that where human rights are concerned there is scope for a universal morality, based on the essential dignity and freedom of all human beings, that can challenge ethical conservatism in all sections of society. To ground that universal morality not only in a framework of rights but a framework of rights that protects the most vulnerable and least able to protect themselves, is essential to challenge the imbalances inherent in human societies. That protective framework and restraint on the power to exploit has been an important part of faith traditions throughout time. As noted above Biblical scriptures consistently prophecy against exploitation and urge welcome and care of the poor.[57] The *dharmic* re-working of caste, from the development of Buddhism and the Sikh tradition also shows that even where scripture or tradition includes temporally-based cultural practices of discrimination these can be challenged by sources and meta-narratives within as well as external to the tradition.

Peace and War

Whilst the role of the capital markets and environmental depletion in creating worldwide inequality and poverty is significant, another major cause of poverty and environmental destruction is war. The role of religion as a purported cause for war cannot be avoided although it can be qualified by the argument that most such uses of religion are more political and nationalist than religious. Whilst all major faiths include strong mandates for peace and in the *dharmic* faiths, for *ahimsa* or non-violence, each tradition, as noted when discussing utilitarianism, also makes provision for war by way of self-defence and in a just cause. However, even in the worst case scenario of going to war there are constraints around how war can be fought both within just war theory

---

[57] See e.g. Wolterstorff N. *Justice Right and Wrong.* Princeton University Press, 2010 (Wolterstorff 2010).

and scripture. For example, the Hebrew Torah includes in the under-standing of Just War, a requirement that trees should not be destroyed in laying siege to the city.[58]

The difficulty is that this injunction, along with other facets of just war theory, is ineffective in the face of modern weaponry. It is parti-cularly in opposing modern warfare that faith communities have played a role in seeking peace and in movements against the most destructive of wars particularly nuclear weapons. Fasching, Dechant et al explore the work of faith leaders and activists in the quest of peace considering the joint work of Ghandi, Thomas Merton, Martin Luther King and eventually Malcolm X in challenging the use of nuclear arms.[59] Stanley Hauerwas has argued that the essence of Christianity is a countercultural stance on war particularly the use of nuclear arms. He argues that the destruction involved in modern warfare and post-war legacies like landmines, means that war can never be proportionate or therefore just. Groups like the Quakers, Ploughshares and CND[60] argue that the threat to peace is so significant that civil disobedience at nuclear bases and through withholding taxes is ethically justified. Campaigns against war draw people from across the spectrum but again faith and interfaith organizations have a significant role in such movements.[61]

States and Injustice

Another aspect of Just War theory that fits uneasily with contem-porary politics is state-hood. From the earliest days of just war theory in Athenian states to Hobbesian and other Enlightenment thinkers, the state was unquestioned. Faith communities have often found themselves suspect by the state because of transnational allegiances to

---

[58] Lawton C. *Judaism* in *Ethical Issues in Six Religious Traditions.* op. cit., p. 170.

[59] Fasching Dechant & Lantigua. *Comparative Religious Ethics.* Wiley Blackwell, 2011, pp. 1–84 (Fasching et al. 2011).

[60] Founded by Catholic priest Bruce Kent.

[61] see e.g. http://pluralism.org/research-report/interfaith-and-faith-based-peace-organizations/.

co-religionists, through the *umma*, church or diaspora. In some cases allegiance to international leaders like the Pope or Caliph has led to suspicion of treachery.[62] The ethic in many faiths of defending people from oppression has also led to faith involvement in questioning unjust rule. The issue for theological ethics is whether such uprisings should involve violence or be limited to peaceful resistance. Several movements for peaceful resistance have come from faith leaders, for example the Anglican Archbishop Desmond Tutu in apartheid South Africa, Martin Luther King in the American South and Ghandi in India. Yet the Christian pacifist Bonhoeffer concluded that assassination of Hitler was the only way to end World War Two. Just cause for rebellion based on armed self-defence and scriptural precedent was grounded in Judaism by the uprising at Massada or the Sikh defence of Amritsa against the British empire. Once again no single principle can be deduced from any particular faith but the role of faith communities, spurred by theological vision, has been to the fore in peace movements and peaceful resistance.

Refuge

Migration in search of refuge is another side effect of war. As noted earlier, faith groups have long been involved in welcoming refugees, both welcoming co-religionists and based on scriptural injunctions welcoming the stranger. In the Abrahamic faiths this was not only hospitality to the individual traveller but quite clearly to the 'alien in the land'. Within Hinduism the stranger is the *atithi*, one who can arrive at any time and to whom hospitality is due by way of welcome. The Sikh tradition of *langar*, open to anyone is also the welcoming of the stranger by hospitality in terms of offering food that knows no bounds. The principle applied to the individual coming to one's home is extended to a similar welcome for refugees on a national level.

---

[62] Particularly notable in Catholic persecution in Elizabethan England and justifiably suspect in some modern extremist Islamist movements seeking restoration of the Caliph.

Media

A final aspect of the ever-increasing pace of globalization is to consider how technological changes in both traditional and new or social media, have affected theological ethics and faith-based movements. As in most parts of society the picture is mixed. Global capital has enabled greater concentration of power and ownership of traditional broadcast and newspaper media in the hands of a limited number of proprietors. This has led to a homogenization of discourse and what constitutes news, including a growth in nationalism and the 'othering' of non-nationals and non-western causes, marked by references to 'migrants' and 'bogus' asylum seekers. This contrasts with faith communities' injunctions to welcome strangers. The othering of Muslims through Islamophobia, partly but disproportionately in response to terrorism, mirrors anti-Catholic prejudice in the UK at the height of IRA terrorism. Some religion, in its interfaith civic form, is being slightly rehabilitated and used for 'community cohesion' but much religion is portrayed as extremist, by association with phenomena like terrorism, FGM, forced marriage or anti-abortionist activity, adopted by only a small minority in any community. Maintaining, and finding airtime for countercultural narratives and ethics in the face of these developments is not easy.

By contrast the development of social media has given some groups an alternative platform and audience for ethics of international solidarity against authoritarianism, the uprising against authoritarian Muslim states seen in the Arab Spring being an example. The scope for greater autonomy, exchange of information and more democratic responses to faith and its interpretation provided by social media can be seen as a positive development. It has a similar dynamic to the revolution of access to scripture via the printing press during the European Reformation. Yet such access has also led to greater fracturing of communities, less common voice and in some quarters has allowed scope for, if not led to, extremist reactions seeking to preserve traditional purity of belief.[63]

---

[63] Discussed for example in Ilesanmi S, Lee WC & Parker WJ (Ed.). *The Rule of Law and the Rule of God*. Palgrave MacMillan US, 2014 particularly, pp. 15–52 & 145–188 (Ilesanmi et al. 2014).

It is unclear whether these developments have simply exposed the reality of faith communities' diversity or whether it has generated greater diversity. The result however is religious communities in which education and empowerment are needed so that members can exercise their responsibility for ethical discernment amongst the competing narratives, in the same way as is necessary in the wider public square.

The greater awareness of the international, whether international religious community or wider society and transnational causes, refugees and wars all have both positive and negative sides. There is greater scope for positive responses, from which organizations like the Aid agencies have benefited, supported by their religious communities. However, the risks of fear and compassion fatigue through overwhelming levels of need are also significant. The faith-based imperative to respond to need, to care for neighbour and care for creation all offer some resilience and hope in the face of disengagement. Issues of truth, accuracy and properly informed narrative so as to make good ethical decisions, set against the risks of propaganda, also loom large in the contemporary public square, locally and globally. Paradoxically these trends arise from the over-concentration of media and power in the hands of a few traditional media owners and the lack of accountability and objective checking in the new media. Issues of truth and accuracy must be of importance to those seeking ethical integrity through their faith. Liberal democracy now surrounds and pervades faith communities who are inevitably part of and formed by their culture. The capacity to participate in democracy is about personal freedom but also personal power to discern and hold to account both in the wider public sphere and the forum of faith.

Conclusions

The accounts of the ethical issues identified in this chapter inevitably barely scrape the surface of any of them but they highlight the variety of ethical challenges in the global village to which theological ethics both responds and is a part. It is not suggested that theological ethics has all the answers to the challenges of the global village and the ethical dilemmas that these pose. However, there are significant ethical approaches and teachings, along with an ethos of action not just theory and people power amongst believers, that can make a difference in local and international communities. The involvement of faith communities in responses to homelessness, refugees, environmental and debt campaigns and movements such as Citizen or Broad Based organizing around poverty and political change, illustrates this ethics in action around issues of global concern. It is not that faith communities are the only groups involved in these movements but a quick look on the Citizens website[64] reveals strong faith representation, both in the UK and across the globe. The minority problematic faces of religion tend to eclipse the more positive role of many faith communities but the need to engage with both facets, to maximize the contribution of the positive and understand so as to challenge the negative, means that ethics globally cannot ignore the role of theologically based ethics.

---

[64] http://www.citizensuk.org.

10

Concluding Thoughts, Looking Forward

By way of concluding this exploration a review of theological and philosophical paradigms and arguments to identify where Rawls' vision of 'overlapping consensus' is possible, seems appropriate. In practice it was not a concept invented by Rawls but has been pursued for centuries. Overlapping consensus may apply both to conclusions over particular issues or to the processes of ethical discernment and reasoning. The purpose of this overview is not only to conclude the book but also to consider ways forward for further and deeper exploration.

Overlapping Consensus

Contrary to the perception of those who reject theology as having any place in ethical debate some of the earliest overlapping consensus was found in theology derived from Aristotelian natural law philosophy. This consensus also confounds the rejection of theology on the basis of irrationality as a basic premise of natural law theology is an appeal to universal reason, inherent in humanity regardless of faith. Whether the premises of universal reason are as universal as assumed is another issue

© The Author(s) 2017

C. Shelley, *Ethical Exploration in a Multifaith Society,*
DOI 10.1007/978-3-319-46711-5_10

but the fact that natural law theology endorses reason as the key faculty in ethical discernment refutes the narrative of unreason.

The appeal to nature in observation of the natural order, natural science and discernment of natural and scientific laws refutes the argument that theology is opposed to science. It is an appeal that is found not only in natural law theology but also scriptural narratives, *Vedic* practices and the human capacity to reflect on experiences of life. Other areas of near-universal ethical consensus that arise from aspects of natural law include respect for the dignity and flourishing of human life, extended to respect for all life under the *Dharmic* principles of *ahimsa*.

The challenge of ethics based on principles attributed to nature is that whilst reason and observation of nature are at one level universal, the deductions and ethics derived from nature differ. Experience, perspective, beliefs about human nature and society, from Hobbesian pessimism to Rousseau or Bentham's naive optimism, as well as theological beliefs about the nature and role of God, salvation or *nirvana* all affect the conclusions drawn from natural observation. It is at this point that the consensus breaks down and the implications of different beliefs and practices need to be discussed. Such conversations may enable either consensus at a deeper or more comprehensive level or a consensus about accommodation and living with difference. This is in fact the process that goes on in all societies as different peoples, wherever their differences lie, seek to live together. What varies is the extent of difference that is firstly acknowledged and if acknowledged is then tolerated.

In considering aspects of ethics arising from natural law or observation of nature, in which a fair degree of consensus still pertains, the importance of life and its dignity, just war theory and binary understandings of gender remain. This means that criminal trafficking groups apart there is international consensus that slavery is wrong, that consent is needed for sex and marriage and that discrimination on the basis of race or class are wrong. Where further discussion is needed lies in what constitutes equality, particularly around issues of sex and gender and equal treatment as opposed to equal opportunity. These questions come back to meta-ethical concepts of justice and what that looks like in the particular rather than general principle. In all these instances the degrees of difference across faith communities are not significantly different from the rest of society. There may be more articulated conservatism in some faith communities around sexuality and equality, often framing equality as complementary rather than equivalent. Yet statistics on pay, representation at senior levels and the incidence of domestic violence suggest that the implementation of equality in wider society is variable and often adrift from the rhetoric, whilst feminists in many faith groups are part of challenging the status quo.

Just war and the natural law analysis of war as a last resort, with conditions about aims, protection of civilians and fair conduct, also achieves significant consensus at international and domestic level. Whether based on natural law theory, utilitarian consequentialism or *ahimsa*, principles of self-defence and protection of the oppressed, the concept of just war as a last resort finds some support in all theological traditions. The exceptions are comparative minorities, like peace movements that seek non-violent resistance based on Christian principles of turning the other cheek and beating swords into ploughshares or on strict *Dharmic ahimsa.* At the other end of the spectrum are extreme minorities such as *Daesh* who apparently reject standards of just war *in bello* by executing civilian relief workers and journalists. Barbaric and indefensible as it is, their argument that in a democracy there are no civilians as all are responsible for war, is a consistent if warped application of just war theory.[1] The rhetoric of 'war on terrorism' simply plays into the *Daesh* narrative rather than countering it with alternative narratives that remove glory or justification of war and recognize it as barbaric criminality.

Whilst natural law and appeals to nature are the most obviously shared bases for ethical methodology and perception of the world, some other theological methods also overlap with or draw from secular sociological methods. These include middle axioms and more technical methodologies that contribute to the process and the use of critical theory and social constructionism in liberation theology. Whilst these

---

[1] Richardson L. *What Terrorists Want.* Random House Trade, 2007 (Richardson 2007); Kelsay J. *The Just War Argument in Islam: Who's Up, Who's Down?* Ilesanmi SO, Lee W-C & Parker WJ (Ed.). *The Rule of Law and the Rule of God.* Palgrave MacMillan, 2014. pp. 173–188 (Kelsay 2014).

methods are brought into dialogue with theological sources the methods provide a similar critique to secular dialogue and begin with empirical experience rather than imposing a theological analysis on that experience.

Differences

Perhaps the most significant meta-ethical differences between views based on faith and those based on this worldly empiricism lie in questions of purpose of life and accountability, not so much to religious authority but the ultimate sense of how life has been lived in the light of the divine. This is not just a question of mortality and what happens after death such as hopes of pie in the sky or post-Mortem paradise, but the ethical quality and freedom of life lived on earth. This is further informed by attitudes to the things of earth themselves and different degrees of attachment to them. If earthly life is all there is then there is an incentive to hang onto it and all the material affords. If this body is all we have then there is an incentive to perfect and prolong it as much as possible. Contrary to the perception that it is always theology that defeats moves towards assisted dying or other forms of euthanasia theological views vary on the issue, as do non-theological views. The BMA[2] and RCN[3] have opposed such legislative changes just as much as any religious groups. Nor, amongst those who oppose euthanasia on the basis of theology, is the argument simply that only God decides when life should end. As noted there are also arguments about protecting the ill and vulnerable from pressures of feeling worthless or unproductive. The argument is not so much about usurping God's mandate over life as around the value of life regardless of productivity or function, the protection of each person regardless of what they can contribute and issues of dignity and quality of life that flow from such a view.

Another dimension of this difference is that if earthly life is temporary and relativized by the absolute of the eternal, divine and transcendent,

---

[2] https://www.bma.org.uk/advice/employment/ethics/ethics-a-to-z/physician-assisted-dying.

[3] https://www2.rcn.org.uk/__data/assets/pdf_file/0004/410638/004167.pdf.

then it can be lived more freely in the context of something beyond the self. This is not to say that faith-based ethics are superior or the only ethics concerned with altruism and wider community. However, the larger transcendent picture does free from the fear of death and attachment to what this world has to offer as if it is all there is. Perspectives and worldviews that foster a detachment from the material or relativize material wealth by reference to other values, has significant positive implications for environmental ethics. The injunction to live lightly on the earth and embrace poverty is not about privation, enforced and unchosen poverty needs to be tackled, but it is about recognizing that need not greed is sufficient. This is reinforced in a range of decisions not only about daily lifestyle and attitudes to consumerism but also for example in ethical investment, the most notable example being Shari'a-compliant Islamic investment that rejects the charging of interest as exploitative.

To the extent that theological reflection accepts harm, pain and suffering in the sense of recognizing harm as part of the conditions of creation, there is a further difference from utilitarian and some other secular philosophies. This is the case whether it is harm and pain intentionally inflicted or suffering more generally caused or simply inherent in existence. It is not a despair of human capacity but a realism that humanity, whatever their beliefs, is unable alone to perfect the world. This realism arises from recognition of the finite capacity and understanding of human agents. An acceptance of suffering does not diminish the incentive to mitigate it whether through addressing illness and pain or through detachment from the disappointments and expectations that often give rise to suffering. Yet that basic recognition that no matter how much material progress is made humanity still has a capacity for both experiencing and causing suffering provides a realism from which to address both the positive and negative dimensions of human capacity to build life and community together.

Theological realism about sin, including the temptations of power, lust, greed, self-delusion and limitations of finite experience should inform an ethics that is alive to human limitation and contingency. The recognition that all are in the same boat when it comes to falling short should give rise to a compassionate ethics, with forgiveness rather than retribution or vengeance. It is recognized that religious communities often fall short of their own theology into sectarian, sometimes nationalistic, sometimes judgemental traps. The failure to live up to the aspirations and hopes of theological ethics does not invalidate the voice any more than the incomplete realization of secular aspirations, for example to equality and justice.

In most instances theological ethics accepts and engages with scientific and other dimensions of secular epistemology to a similar degree to the majority of the population. Whilst there are minorities who reject medical science in favour of wholly faith-based healing or evolutionary theory in favour of creationism, they are minorities.[4] The presentation of religions as backward and irrational on the basis of minority views is in itself profoundly unscientific and unhelpful. Where there might genuinely be a difference between theological and materialist views generically is in the recognition that whilst science has some answers it does not have all of them. The belief that by mastery of science humanity can resolve the world's differences and solve its problems is not borne out by the evidence of divisions of wealth and resources or the levels of environmental damage actually present in today's global village. Theology brings to science, as has always been the case and as was set out by Al Ghazali, a recognition of the limits of human knowledge and science in the face of the whole creation. Science, like all human endeavour is relativized by God, the divine or however the transcendent is conceived.

For Gazali the experience of God in the sphere of prayer and contemplation was an extension of exploration of the world, as is the case for most of the natural law theologians in different traditions and others using different methodologies. Contrary to material empiricism's assumption that the divine and transcendent cannot be proved in empirical terms many people of faith do have particular experiences of

---

[4] A U.S. Gallup poll June 2014 found that 42% of the US Christians surveyed expressed some belief in aspects of Creationism, yet the extent of such beliefs in the US is falling. Equivalent research published by Forbes from Dr Amy Unsworth of the Faraday Institute, St Edmunds Cambridge found only 3–6% of UK Christians had a full belief in creationism not the 22% of reported by the Horizon research interrogated.

the divine and transcendent which have empirical validity and force. Whilst inevitably they remain subjective and personal they nonetheless have significant influence in peoples' responses to prayer and ethical and vocational decision-making. Whilst they are not objectively provable, neither are secular methodologies that include subjective criteria. For example, to the extent that pain and pleasure are often empirical but subjective experiences theology is not in fact so different as regards its entitlement to be brought to the ethical table. In that spiritual or theological and faith-based experience has a reality with significant ethical impact it needs to be acknowledged.

It is this perspective that also relativizes human autonomy. Theological and ethical assumptions of free will, judgement, consent particularly to marriage, conscience and karma all provide evidence that theological ethics in all traditions necessitates personal responsibility. However, the awareness that such faculties are exercised in a context larger than oneself, both in terms of community and relationships and of a bigger picture of the significance of ones life does provide a different perspective for individual decisions. The sense of being both a part of the miracle of creation and yet only one part of that miracle has implications for ethics throughout and particularly concerning the end of life. The Jewish and Muslim perspective that to save a life is to save a world illustrates the value of the individual life, which can never be a functional number. It is this factor that would tend to set theological perspectives apart from either a simple numbers game based on a utilitarian calculus or a bare argument for an autonomous right to take one's own life.

To Conclude

This is not to say that utilitarian calculus never has any place in theological ethics. There are the extreme examples where consequentialist analysis seems to be the only option; the case of just war, particularly under conditions of contemporary war and weaponry being the clearest example and allocation of limited resources being another. Yet theological ethics insists on conditions to make war just even if it has to be used as a last resort. Theological ethics also opposes care and protection of the vulnerable to any simple application of utilitarian calculus in distributing resources, along with the values of generosity and hope in assessing what resources are available.

As Malcolm Brown points out much ethical debate has developed by response and reaction to particular trends and arguments at any time,[5] for example utilitarianism and Kantian deontology in reaction to the Thirty Years War, contemporary virtue ethics in response to the failure of secularism in Nazism and Stalinism. The same is true, to a degree, of theological ethics in that non-theological developments and methods have been applied in response to changes outside theological circles. Examples include:

- William Paley's adaptation of utilitarianism to a Christian framework,
- 16th CE missionaries' appreciation of the human rights of indigenous peoples in response to their enslavement by mercantile explorers,
- Sikh reaction against the caste system in search of greater equality
- Mohamed's reaction against the tribal warring of his times
- The taking up of natural law philosophy as a partner in dialogue with theology's search to analyse and understand the world and
- The reaction to poverty and marginalization, using contemporary socio-political methods that has led to liberation theology.

The reality is that across its diversity theological ethics can and does draw on most ethical methodologies but in each case it also brings to the discourse its own resources dating from millennia ago. It does not, like the Enlightenment, seek to discard history but brings the tradition into dialogue with contemporary developments. The balance of history and contemporary in the application of ethical methodology varies according to other factors such as attitudes to wider culture and other sources of authority. Yet there is no faith community and no part of theological ethics that has not had to discern how its ethics, both meta-narrative and specific application, apply in a new setting and faced with new challenges. Thus arguments based on scriptural or traditional absolutism,

---

[5] Brown M. *Tensions in Christian Ethics*. SPCK, 2010 in particular at pp. 19–21 (Brown 2010).

inerrancy and changelessness simply do not reflect either the reality of historical development that has happened or the true meaning of tradition, which is handing it on.

Theological ethics therefore has the freedom to draw on the depths and complexities, nuances and paradoxes of its diverse traditions alongside other sources both of ethical method and epistemological understanding. This includes the different ways of conceiving ethics and recognizing that virtues are not incompatible with rights and other forms of ethics; they simply do different jobs. The inter-twining of theology over the centuries with methodologies and epistemologies outside the faith community, from the overlap of Hebrew commandments with the Hamurabi Code to contemporary adoption of liberation theology across a variety of settings, challenges any reading of theological ethics as pure, homogenous, self-contained or separate from wider society. However, insofar as Alasdair MacIntyre is correct in arguing that ethics requires a common narrative that contemporary international narrative is human rights. It is a narrative that requires consideration not only of broad maxims but also of substance and content, a common vision not only of what aspects of human dignity should be protected by rights but of the human beings to be protected. It is an ongoing narrative and discourse.

Theological ethics has much to contribute to that narrative, from claims to early development of rights based on human dignity to contemporary engagement with the challenges of cultural diversity, conscience and basic universal standards of justice and material provision. Theology and theological ethics also brings a vision of human rights and dignity that focuses on protection of the vulnerable not individual rights and property; it highlights the importance of conscience and engages with the diversity of understandings about how that dignity is understood. Theology also draws on the near-universal value of human dignity in context of wider creation and a relational approach to their implementation. The United Nations Convention on the Rights of the Child is an example of such a comprehensive approach to rights that has engaged all but two of the world's states, uniting parties who confirmed their differences yet were able to agree such a comprehensive document. It is not perfect and simply negotiating a form of words in a rights convention is only the start of the process. Yet the fact that it has been achieved and agreed in the vast majority of the worlds' nations is a positive start.

Looking to the Future

The fact that the world is a global village in which religion and theological narratives are a fact of life, means that all levels of that global community need to take theological ethics into account. Perpetuating a secular versus religious or faith versus non-faith based divide presents a false dichotomy to any such debates as no faith community is homogenous, any more than are non-religious communities. The fact that in many instances faith communities' more conservative elements quite often reflect unease in the wider population provides a useful barometer.[6] Despite the ease of its stigmatizing, religion is by no means uniquely conflictual, neither between religions nor between faith communities and wider society. In fact, in some arenas the coming together of interfaith groups from very different backgrounds, from local level to the World Parliament of Religions, provides some evidence that peoples of significant differences can work together. Yet theological perspectives need not only to be permitted at the table on condition that they buy in to dominant secular materialist theses but on their own terms so that they can bring the full riches of what they have that is distinctive to the table. There is also a need to engage with the difficult and entirely different as leaving them outside the fold will lead to separatism and in some cases adverse reaction. Engaging with Sinn Fein in Northern Ireland, the ANC in South Africa and David Ben Gurion in Israel are all examples of engagement with the extremes that in practice resolved conflict. Such a perspective is an example of the need for applied and pragmatic ethics that engages with the absolutist principle so as to understand and move on.

Gaps and differences will of course remain, that is the nature of democracy. Whilst some level of common language and narrative,

---

[6] Davie G. *The Sociology of Religion.* Sage, 2007, pp. 228–241 (Davie 2007).

such as rights, is needed there needs to be discussion about what they mean, not cheap assumptions that all agree at a superficial level without exploring more deeply. A key point is to be alive to the difference generated by language and perspective rather than substance. Moves to develop theologically literate language and practice, particularly for professionals with significant ethical decisions to raise with clients, are a move in the correct direction. It is a move that is needed in other contexts and may go some way to remove the 'othering' and hierarchy of religion summarized in Prakash Shah's comments about non-Christian faiths being treated as inferior religions.[7] Appropriate analysis of difference will also enable discussions on comparable terms identifying differences of premise, experience, worldview, epistemology or purpose as lying at the heart of the difference rather than negotiating along lines that do not meet. As highlighted in the introduction this exploration is far from exhaustive and the bias towards Christianity and the Abrahamic faiths is acknowledged. It is part of a bigger exploration and conversation, which seeks simply to set out some insights, historical perspectives and tools that may assist in future dialogue.

Theology can bring much that is positive to the table, as well as potential engagement with the minority of those who claim religion as justification for barbarism. The theological dilemmas of historical versus contemporary sources and negotiating development are in fact shared with all ethical systems and values; Bentham's world, even Rawls' world were different from contemporary society. Religion has been addressing these dilemmas and their changing range and scope, for centuries, unlike many other organizations that simply have not been around that long. Events like the Reformation, the split and foundation of new movements mean that theological ethics has been negotiating changing times, interpretations and contexts since its inception, including imperial rule, exile, division and reunification, as society has changed. There is also a continued valuing and search in society for integrity, authenticity,

---

[7] Shah Prakash. Judging Muslims, pp. 144–156. In *Islam and English Law: Rights, Responsibilities and the Place of Shari'a,* Ed. Robin Griffiths Jones. Cambridge University Press, 2013 at pp. 144–145 (Shah 2013).

human rights and doing right by personal relations, refugees, stopping war and protecting the environment. These issues pose huge challenges for all of society but the fact that people do still value these things despite the saturation and utilitarianism of market consumerism, suggests there is still scope and need for greater ethical discernment in tune with values that are not older but eternal.

Bibliography

Abdul Matin, Ibrahim. *Green Deen: What Islam Teaches About Protecting the Planet.* Leicester: Kube Publishing, 2012.

Adam Dr, Hans. *The Rape of Mother Earth.* Salzburg, 16 January 2002.

Adams, N. "Confessing the Faith: Reasoning in Tradition." In *The Blackwell Companion to Christian Ethics*, Eds. S Hauerwas and S Wells, 209–221. Oxford: Blackwell Publishing, 2004.

Ahmed, L. *Women and Gender in Islam.* Newhaven and London: Yale University Press, 1992.

Akhtar, S. *The Final Imperative: An Islamic Theology of Liberation.* London: Bellew Publishing, 1991.

Akhtaruddin, A, and A Clarke. Eds. *Islam and the Environmental Crisis.* London: Ta-Ha Publishers, 1997.

Akuppa. *Touching the Earth: A Buddhist Guide to Saving the Plant.* Cambridge: Windhorse Publications, 2002.

Alehossain, A. *Islamic Liberation: Theology for Women.* Munich: Grin Verlag GmbH, 2014.

Al Gazali. *The Faith and Practice of Al Ghazali.* Trans. W Montgomery Watt. Oxford: One World Publications, 1953 & 1994.

Al Gazali. Trans: Michael E Marmura. *The Incoherence of the Philosophers: A Parallel Engish-Arabic Text.* Chicago: University of Chicago Press, 2002.

© The Author(s) 2017

303

C. Shelley, *Ethical Exploration in a Multifaith Society*,
DOI 10.1007/978-3-319-46711-5

Al Hassan, Al Aidaros, S Faridahwati Mohd, and Kamil MD. Idris. "Islam and Ethical Theory." *International Journal of Islamic Thought* 4 (December 2013): 1–13.

Ali, SS. "From Muslim Migrants to Muslim Citizens." In *Islam and English Law*, Ed. R Griffiths Jones, 157–175. Cambridge: Cambridge University Press, 2013.

Alinsky, S. *Rules for Radicals.* London: Vintage Press, 2013.

Altheus Reid, Marcella. *Indecent Theology.* London: Routledge, 2000.

Andersen, S. Ed. Gotlind Ulshofer. *Die Rolle Theologischer Argumentation in Offentlichen Leben in Religion und Theologie in Offentlichen Diskurs.* Frankfurt Am Main: Haag und Herchen Verlaag, 2005.

An Na'im, AA. *Islamic Family Law in a Changing world.* London: Zed Books, 2002.

An Na'im, A. *Islam and Human Rights: Selected Essays of Abdullahi An-Na'im*, Ed. Mashood A. Baderin. London: Routledge, 2010.

Anscombe, E. "Modern Moral Philosophy, First Published." *Philosophy* 33(1958): 1–19; reprinted in *Ethics, Religion and Politics* (*The Collected Philosophical Papers of G. E. M. Anscombe*, Volume 3), Minneapolis, MN: University of Minnesota Press, 1981, 26–42.

Aquaviva, SJ. "On the Confession of Princes 1602." In *The Abuse of Casuistry: A History of Moral Reasoning*, Eds. S Toulmin and A Johnson, 147. Berkeley: University of California Press, 1988.

Aquinas, T. *Light of Faith.* Book of the Month Spiritual Classics. New York: Sophia Institute, 1993.

Aquinas, T. *Selected Writings.* London: Penguin Classics, 1999.

Aquinas, T. *Summa Theologica Prima Secunda Questions 1–5.* London: Beloved Publishing LLC, 2014.

Aristotle. *Nichomachean Ethics I (ii) & (v) The Object of Life.* London: Pengiun Classics, 1976.

Aristotle. Ed. Hugh Tredennick. *Nichomachean Ethics.* London: Penguin Classics, 2004.

Assman, J. *Of God and gods: Egypt, Israel and the Rise of Monotheism.* Madison: University of Wisconsin Press, 2008.

Averroes. Ed. Majid Fakhri, Trans. Ibrahim Naijar. *Faith and Reason in Islam: Averroes' Exposition of Religious Arguments.* London: One World Publishing, July 2001.

Awde, N. *Women in Islam.* London: Bloom & Bennett, 2005.

Badawi, L. *Women in Religion*. Eds. J Bowker and Holm. London: Continuum, 2000.

Bailey, T, and V Gentile. *Rawls and Religion*. New York: Columbia University Press, 2015.

Balagangadhara, SN. *The Heathen in His Blindness: Asia, the West and the Dynamic of Religion*. New Delhi: Manohar Books, 2005.

Banchoff, T, and R Wuthnow. *Religion and the Global Politics of Human Rights*. Oxford: Oxford University Press, 2011.

Barth, K. *Church Dogmatics Vol III.4 The Doctrine of Creation*. Eds. Torrance, F, and GW Bromily. London: T&T Clark, 2010a.

Barth, K. "Freedom in Fellowship: Man & Woman." In *Church Dogmatics Study Edition*, 109–231. London: T&T Clark, 2010b.

Barton, J, and J Bowden. *The Original Story: God, Israel and the World*. Grand Rapids Michigan and Cambridge, UK: Eerdmans, 2005.

Bentham, J. *1818 – Church of Englandism and its Catechism Examined*. Oxford: Oxford University Press, 2011.

Bergstrom, JC. *Principles of a Christian Environmental Ethic: With Applications to Agriculture, Natural Resources, and the Environment*. http://www.leaderu.com/science/bergstrom-enviroethics.html. Accessed 14 May 2016

Bigg, Charles. *The Christian Platonists of Alexandria*. Online only: Hardpress Publishing, 2012.

Biggar, N. *Behaving in Public: How to do Christian Ethics*. Michigan, Grand Rapids: Eerdmans Publishing, 2011.

Biggar, N. *In defence of war*. Oxford: Oxford University Press, 2013.

Bilimoria, P. "Indian Ethics." In *Companion to Ethics*, Ed. PA Singer. Oxford: Blackwells Publishing, 1991.

Blanchard, KD, and K O Brien. *An Introduction to Christian Environmentalism: Ecology, Virtue & Ethics*. Waco, Texas: Baylor University Press, 2014.

Block, W, and R Whitehead. "Compromising the Uncompromisable: A Private Property Approach to Resolving the Abortion Controversy." *Appalachian Journal of Law* 4, 1 (2005): 1–45.

Blond, P. *Post Secular Philosophy: Between Philosophy and Theology*. London: Routledge, 1997.

Boff, Leonardo. *The Cry of the Earth, the Cry of the Poor*. Maryknoll, New York: Orbis Books, 1997.

Bostick, William F. "Jesus and Socrates." *The Biblical World* 47, 4(April, 1916): 248–252, University of Chicago Press. http://www.jstor.org/stable/3143019.

Botterill, G. Hume on Liberty and Necessity. http://www.philosophy.dept. shef.ac.uk/papers/Botterill2002.pdf.

Bourdieu, Pierre. *The Logic of Practice*. Cambridge: Polity Press, 1990.

Bowring, B. "Misunderstanding MacIntyre on Human Rights." *Analyse & Kritik* 30(2008) (© Lucius & Lucius, Stuttgart): 205–214.

Bradley Dr, M, and M. Bendorf Utilitarianism, Deontology, Hinduism, and Buddhism on the Nature of Moral Right and Wrong. http://bendorfm. com/essays/PR202Essay1.htm. Accessed 28 May 2016.

Bradney, A. *Religion, Rights and Laws*. Leicester: Leicester University Press, 1993.

Bradney, A. "Faced by Faith." In *Faith in Law: Essays in Legal Theory*, 89–105. Ed. A. Bradney, Oxford: Hart Publishing, 2000.

Bretherton, L. *Christianity and Contemporary Politics: The Conditions and Possibilites of Faithful Witness*. Oxford: Wiley Blackwell, 2010.

Broderick, J. *Saint Francis Xavier (1506–1552)*. London: Burns, Oates & Washbourne Ltd, 1952.

Brody, H. *Studien zu den Dichtungen Jehuda ha-Levi's*. Berlin, 1895.

Brown, M. *Tensions in Christian Ethics*. London: SPCK, 2010.

Brown, Taylor Barbara. *The Preaching Life: Living Out Your Vocation*. Atlanta: Canterbury Press, 2013.

Bruce, S. "The Demise of Christianity in Britain." In *Predicting Religion: Christian, Secular and Alternative Futures*. Religion & theloogy in interdisciplinary perspective. Eds. G Davie, P Heelas, and L Woodhead. UK: Ashgate, Aldershot, 2003.

Butler, M, and AP Morris. *Creation and the Heart of Man: An Orthodox study of Environmentalism*. Acton Institute for Study of Religion and Liberty, 2013.

Byrnes, T. *Catholic Bishops in American Politics*. Princeton, New Jersey: Princeton University Press, 1991.

Cantwell Smith, W. *What Is Scripture?: A Comparative Approach*. Augsburg: Fortress Press, 1993.

Carter, Anthony J. *On Being Black and Reformed*. Phillipsburg, New Jersey: P&R Publishing, 2003.

Chadwick, H. *Augustine of Hippo: A life*. Oxford University Press, 2010; Augustine Trans. Mary T Clark. *Augustine of Hippo: Selected Writings*. London: SPCK, 1984.

Coakley, S. *Sacrifice Regained: Reconsidering the Rationality of Religious Belief*. Cambridge: Cambridge University Press, 2012.

Collard, A, and J Contrucci. *Man's Rape of the Wild: Man's Violence Against Animals and the Earth*. Bloomington, Indiana: Indiana University Press, 1998.

Cone, J. *A Black Theology of Liberation*. Maryknoll, New York: Orbis Books, 1970.

Couture, P. *Child Poverty, Love Justice and Social Responsibility*. Duluth: Chalice Press, 2007.

Coward, H. *Experiencing Scripture in World Religions*. Ed. Harold Coward. Maryknoll, New York: Orbis Books, Maryknoll – Interfaith series, Ed. Paul Knitter, 2000.

Dabashi, H. *Islamic Liberation Theology: Resisting the Empire*. UK: Routledge, 2008.

Dahlstrom, Daniel O. *Moses Mendelssohn: Philosophical Writings*. Cambridge: Cambridge University Press, 1997.

Darwin, Charles. *The Descent of Man and Selection in Relation to Sex*. New York: D. Appleton and Company, 1896.

Davie, G. *The Sociology of Religion*. London: Sage Publishing, 2007.

Davie, G. *A Sociology of Religion: A Critical Agenda*. London: Sage Publishing, 2013.

Davie, G. *Religion in Britain: A Persistent Paradox*. Oxford: Wiley-Blackwell, 2015.

Dawkins, R. *The God Delusion*. Boston: Houghton Mifflin, 2006 and London: Black Swan 2007.

Dennin, Michael. *Divine Science: Finding Reason at the Heart of Faith*. Cincinnati, Ohio: Franciscan Media, 2015.

De La Vitoria, Francisco. Ed. Pagden AG/Ed & trans: Lawrance J. *Vitoria: Political Writings*. Cambridge: Cambridge University Press, 1991.

Descartes, R. Ed. Williams Bernard. *Meditations on First Philosophy 1641*. Cambridge: Cambridge University Press, 1996.

Dodd, CH. *The Interpretation of the Fourth Gospel*. Cambridge: Cambridge University Press, 1968.

Donovan, O. *The Desire of the Nations: Rediscovering the Roots of Political Philosophy*. Cambridge: Cambridge University Press, 2006.

Donovan, Vincent J. *Christianity Rediscovered*. London: SCM, 2001.

Douglas, G, N Doe, S Gilliat-Ray, R Sandberg, and Asma Khan. *Social Cohesion and Civil Law: Marriage, Divorce and Religious Courts*. Cardiff: AHRC & Cardiff University, 2011.

Dunn, GD. *Tertullian (Early Church Fathers)*. London: Routledge, 2004.

Dusgupta, Surendranath. Ed. *A History of Indian Philosophy*. Cambridge: Motillal Barnasidas, 1922.

Easwaran, Eknath. *Essence of the Dhammapada: The Buddhist call to Nirvana*. California: Nilgiri Press, 2013.

Eberi, JT. *The Routledge Guidebook to Aquinas Summa Theologica*. London: Routledge, 2015.

Ellacuria, I, and J Sobrino. *Liberation Theology and Systematic Theology*. London: SCM Press, 2012.

Elliott, Larry, and Ed. Pilkington. New Oxfam report says half of global wealth held by the 1%. *The Guardian*, 2015.

Ellis Marc, H. *Towards a Jewish Theology of Liberation*. New York: Orbis Books, Maryknoll, 1987.

Ellul, J. *On Freedom, Love and Power*. Toronto: University of Toronto Press, 2010.

Esposito, J, and N De Long Bas. *Women in Muslim Family Law*. Syracuse, New York: Syracuse University Press, 2001.

Esposito, J, and D Mogaded. *Who Speaks for Islam*. New York: Gallup Press, 2007.

Fasching, DJ, D Dechant, and DM Lantigua. *Comparative Religious Ethics: A Narrative Approach to Global Ethics*. Oxford: Wiley Blackwell, 2011.

Fatani, Afnan. "Translation and the Qur'an." In *The Qur'an: An Encyclopaedia*, Ed. Oliver Leaman, 657–669. Great Britain: Routeledge, 2006.

Fiddian-Qasmiyeh, Dr E, and Ager Professor. A *Local Faith* communities and the promotion of resilience in humanitarian situations. Refugee Studies Centre, Oxford & Columbia University. https://www.rsc.ox.ac.uk/files/publications/working-paper-series/wp90-local-faith-communities-resilience-2013.pdf.

Finkel, Avraham Yaakov. *The Essential Maimonides: Translations of the RamBam*. Jerusalem: Yeshivat Moshe Press, 1993/4.

Finnis, J. *Natural Law, Natural Rights*. Oxford: Clarendon Law Series, 1980.

Finnis, J. *Moral Absolutes: Tradition, Revision and Truth*. Washington: Catholic University Press of America, 1991.

Fletcher, JF. *Situation Ethics: A New Morality*. London: Westminster: John Knox Press, 1999.

Fox, Matthew. *Creation Spirituality: Liberating Gifts for the Peoples of the Earth*. New York: Harper Publishing, 1991.

Fox, Matthew. *A Way to God: Thomas Merton's Creation Spirituality Journey*. California: New World Publishing, 2016.

Fraser, Giles. http://www.theguardian.com/commentisfree/2015/apr/29/lutfur-rahman-tower-hamlets-mayor-verdict-undue-spiritual-influence.

Freud Kandell, M, and N De Lange. *Modern Judaism an Oxford Guide*. Oxford: Oxford University, 2005.

Gill, R. *A Cambridge Companion to Christian Ethics*. Cambridge: Cambridge University Press, 2012.

Glahn, B, AM Emon, and MS Ellis. *Islamic Law and International Human Rights Law*. Oxford: Oxford University Press, 2015.

Gooder, Paula. *Heaven*. London: SPCK, 2011.

Griffel, F. *Al Gazali's Philosophical Theology*. Oxford: Oxford University Press, 2010.

Grisez, G. *Christian Moral Principles Vol 2 Living a Christian Life*. Cincinnati, Ohio: Franciscan Press, 1993.

Grotius, H. *On the Freedom of the Seas*, Indiana: Liberty Fund Inc, 1609.

Gunarsdottir, S. "Rapes of Earth and Grapes of Wrath." *Feminist Theology* 18, 2 (January 2010): 206–222.

Habermas, J. *Between Naturalism and Religion*. Cambridge: Polity Press, 2008.

Haleem, HA. *Islam and the Environment*. London: Ta-Ha Publishing, 1999.

Haleem, Abdel MAS. "Qu'ran and Hadith." In *The Cambridge Companion to Classical Islamic Theology*, 19–32. Cambridge: Cambridge University Press, 2008.

Hamer, MD. *The Rape of the Earth and the Human Ego*. Countercurrents, 14 May 2010

Hardy, Paul A. "Epistemology and Divine Discourse." In *The Cambridge Companion to Classical Islamic Theology*, Ed. T Winter, 288–307. Cambridge: Cambridge University Press, 2008.

Harris, James A. *Hume: An Intellectual Biography*. Cambridge: Cambridge University Press, 2015.

Hauerwas, SA. *Community of Character*. Indiana: University of Notre Dame Press, 1984 & 1991.

Hauerwas, S. *The Peaceable Kingdom: A Primer in Christian Ethics*. London: SCM Press, 2009.

Hauerwas, Stanley, and Samuel Wells. Eds. *The Blackwell Companion to Christian Ethics*. Oxford: Blackwell Publishing, 2006.

Hecht, NS, Jackson BS, and others. Eds. *An Introduction to the History and Sources of Jewish Law*. Oxford: Oxford University Press, 1996.

Heist, D, and Ram Cnaan. "A Faith-Based International Development Work: A Review School of Social Policy, University of Pennsylvania." *Religions* 7(2016): 19. doi: 10.3390/rel7030019. www.mdpi.com/journal/religions.

Henrix, Scott H. *Martin Luther Visionary Reformer*. Newhaven: Yale University Press, 2015.

Hobbes, T. Ed. MacPherson, CB. *Leviathon*. London: Penguin Classics, 1968.

Høgel, Christian. "An early anonymous Greek translation of the Qur'an. The fragments from Niketas Byzantios' Refutatio and the anonymous." *Abjuratio Collectanea Christiana Orientalia* 7 (2010): 65–119.

Holloway, R. *Godless Morality: Keeping Religion Out of Ethics*. Edinburgh: Edinburgh University Press, 1999.

Holloway, R. *Godless Morality*. London: Canongate Publishing, 2004.

Hooks, Bell. *Talking Back: Thinking Feminist, Thinking Black*. Boston: South End Press, 1988.

Hughes, J. *The End of Work: Theological Critiques of Capitalism*. Oxford: Wiley Blackwell, 2006.

Hull, John. *Touching the Rock: An Experience of Blindness*. London: SPCK, 1990.

Hull, John. *On Sight and Insight: A Journey into the World of Blindness*. London: One World Books, 1997/2001.

Hull, John. *In the Beginning there was Darkness: A Blind Person's Conversations with the Bible*. London: SCM Press, 2002.

Hutchings, K. *Global Ethics: An Introduction*. Cambridge: Polity Press, 2010.

Ilesanmi, S, WC Lee, and WJ Parker. *The Rule of Law and the Rule of God*. US: Palgrave MacMillan, 2014.

Ibn Tibbon, Judah. Trans. *Kitāb ul-'amānāt wal-i'tiqādāt* to Hebrew.

Jardine, L. *Erasmus Man of Letters: The Construction of Charisma in Print*. Princeton, New Jersey: Princeton University Press, 2015.

Kelsay, J. "The Just War Argument in Islam: Who's Up, Who's Down?" In *The Rule of Law and the Rule of God*, Eds. SO Ilesanmi, W-C Lee, and WJ Parker, 173–188. New York: Palgrave MacMillan, 2014.

Kenny, Anthony. *A New History of Western Philosophy*. Oxford: Oxford University Press, 2012.

Kessler, E, and M Arkush. *Keeping Faith in Development: The Significance of Interfaith Relations in the Work of Humanitarian Aid and International Development Organisations*. Woolf Institute of Abrahamic Faiths. http://www. woolf.cam.ac.uk/uploads/KeepingFaithinDevelopment.pdf. Cambridge: 2009

King, MS. *God v Darwin: The Logical Supremacy of Intelligent Design Creationism over Evolution*. Online Only: CreateSpace Independent Publishing, 2015.

Kirwan, M. *Political Theology: A New Introduction*. London: Darton Longman & Todd, 2008.

Kuehn M. *Kant: A Biography*. Cambridge: Cambridge University Press, 2001.

Ladikos, A. "The Trials of Socrates and Jesus Christ: A Comparison." *Phronimon* 8, 2 pp. 73–83 (2007).

Lawton, CA. "Judaism." In *Ethical Issues in Six Religious Traditions*, 2nd Edition, Eds. P Morgan and C Lawton, 168–215. Edinburgh: Edinburgh University Press, 2007.

Layman, D. The Qu'ran and historical criticism citing. Sayedd Hossein Nasr. http://www.firstthings.com/blogs/firstthoughts/2010/09/quran-historical-criticism.

Levine, S. *Mystics, Mavericks and Merry Makers*. New York: New York University Press, 2003.

Lewis, H. *Deaf Liberation Theology*. London: Routledge, 2007.

Lewis, CS. *The Problem of Pain*. London: Williams Collins, 2015.

Linzey, A. *Animal Theology*. London: SCM Press, 2000.

Lipner, J. *Hindus Their Religious Beliefs and Practices*, 2nd Edition. London: Routledge, 2010.

Logstrup, K. *The Ethical Demand*. Notre Dame, Indiana: Notre Dame University Press, 1997.

Long Stephen, D. *Divine Economy: Theology & the Market*. London & New York: Routledge, 2000.

Loughlin, G. *Queer Theology: Re-thinking the Western Body*. Oxford: Wiley Blackwell, 2007.

Lowney, C. *Heroic Leadership*. Chicago: Loyola Press, 2003.

Lubin, T, DR Davis, and JK Krishnan. *Hinduism and Law: An Introduction*. Cambridge: Cambridge University Press, 2010.

Malhotra, Namita. The World Wide Web of Desire – Pornography and Technology. http://cscs.res.in/events_folder/abevents.2007-03-17.5334271271/abevent.2007-12-20.5420095926 & Pink Chaddi Campaign. http://timesofindia.indiatimes.com/india/Pink-chaddi-campaign-a-hit-draws-over-34000-members/articleshow/4126529.cms.

Mann, Gurinder Singh. "Canon Formation in the Sikh Tradition." In *Sikh Religion, Culture and Ethnicity*, Eds. A. s Mandair and C Shackle, 10–25. London: Curzon Press, 2001 & Routledge, London, 2013.

Mann, Gurinder Singh. *The Making of Sikh Scripture*. United States: Oxford University Press, 2001.

Martin, D. "The Explosion of Protestantism in Latin America." In *Global Religious Movements in Regional Context*, Ed. J Wolffe, 247–266. Milton Keynes: The Open University, 2002.

Martin, DB. *Sex and the Single Savior*. London: Westminster John Knox Press, 2006.

Martyr, Justin. Ed. Donaldson, J, and A Roberts. *The Writings of Justin Martyr*. Berkeley, California: Apocryphile Press, 2007.

McClintock Fulkerson, M. *Women's Discourses and Feminist Theology*. Augsburg: Fortress Press, 1994.

McGinnis, Jon. "Scientific Methodologies in Medieval Islam." *Journal of the History of Philosophy* 41, 3 (July 2003): 307–327.

McGinnis, Jon. *Avicenna*. Oxford: Oxford University Press, 2010.

McIntyre, Alasdair. *After Virtue*. London: Duckworths, 1985.

McIntyre, Alasdair. *A Short History of Ethics*. London: Routledge, 1993.

Menski, W. *Hinduism in Ethical Issues in Six Religious Traditions*. Edinburgh: Edinburgh University Press, 2007.

Mernissi, Fatima. *Beyond the Veil: Male-Female Dynamics in a Muslim Society*, revised ed. London: Saqi Books, 1975, 1985, 1987, reprinted.

Meyer, SC. *Signature in the Cell: DNA and the Evidence for Intelligent Design*. New York: HarperOne, 2010.

Mill, JS, and J Bentham. *Utilitarianism and Other Essays*. London: Penguin Books, 1987, Originally Utilitarianism 1861.

Millbank, J, G Ward, and C Pickstock. *Radical Orthodoxy*. Routledge, 1998a; Ed. Millbank J. *The Radical Orthodoxy Reader*. London: Routledge, 2009.

Millbank, J, C Pickstock, and G Ward. *Radical Orthodoxy: A New Theology*. London: Routledge, 1998b.

Mir-Hossaini, Ziba. *Islam and Gender: The Religious Debate in Contemporary Iran*. Princeton, New Jersey: Princeton University Press, 1999.

Modood, T. *Multicultural Politics: Racism, Ethnicity and Muslims in Britain*. Edinburgh: Edinburgh University Press, 2005.

Modood, T. *Multiculturalism: A Civic Idea*. Cambridge: Polity Press, 2007/2013.

Modood, T. *Still Not Easy Being British: Struggles for a Multicultural Citizenship*. London: Trentham Books Ltd, 2010.

Modras, R. *Ignatian Humanism*. California: Loyola Press, 2004.

Mohammed, Khaleel. "Assessing English Translations of the Qur'an." *Middle East Quarterly* Vol 12, No.2 (Spring 2005): 58–71.

Montgomery Watt, W. *The Faith and Practice of Al Gazali*. UK: Allen and Unwin, 1953 & London: One World Publications, 1995.

Moore, G. *The Body in Context: Sex and Catholicism*. London: Continuum, 2011.

Morgan, P, and C Lawton. *Ethical Issues in Six Religious Traditions*, 2nd Edition. Edinburgh: Edinburgh University Press, 2007.

Nadler, S. *Spinoza: A Life*. Cambridge: Cambridge University Press, 2001.

Neff Stephen, C. *Hugo Grotius: On the Law of War and Peace: Student Edition.* Cambridge: Cambridge University Press, 2012.

Ner David, Haviva. *Life on the Fringes: A Feminist Journey Towards Traditional Rabbinic Ordination.* New Jersey: Ben Yehuda Press, 2000.

Niebuhr, HR. *Christ and Culture.* London: Harper Collins, 1951–2002 reprint.

Niebuhr, RH. *Christ and Culture.* London: Bravo Limited Press, 2002.

Nietzche, FW. *The Genealogy of Morals.* New York: Dover Publishing, 2003.

Nietzche, FW. Ed. Tanner, M. *On Good and Evil.* London: Penguin Classics, 2014.

Novak, M. *The Spirit of Democratic Capitalism.* New York: Madison Books, 1990.

Novak, D. *Tradition in the Public Square: A David Novak Reader.* Eds. Rashkover, R, and M Kavka. London: SCM Press, 2008.

Oborn, E. *Clement of Alexandria.* Cambridge: Cambridge University Press, 2009.

Olivelle, P. "Dharmasastra: A Textual History." In *Hinduism and Law: An Introduction*, Eds. T Lubin et al., 17–57. Cambridge: Cambridge University Press, 2010.

Origen. Ed. Henry Chadwick. *Contra Celsum.* Cambridge: Cambridge University Press, 2008.

Origen. *On First Principles.* Notre Dame, Indiana: Ave Maria Press, 2013.

O Sullivan, Maureen. *The Four Seasons of Greek Philosophy.* Athens: Efstatiadish Group S.A., 1982/1987.

Pais, J. *Suffer the Children: A Theology of Liberation by a Survivor of Child Abuse.* New Jersey: Paulist Press, 2001.

Paley, W. *The Principles of Moral and Political Philosophy.* Indiana: Liberty Fund Inc, 2003.

Pascal, Blaise. *Provincial Letters.* Particularly V-X. Eugene, Oregen: Wipf & Stock, 1997.

Peretz Elkins, Rabbi D. *Simple Actions for Jews to Help Green the Planet: Jews, Judaism and the Environment.* Online Only: Create Space Publishing, 2011.

Phillipson, Nicholas. *Adam Smith: An Enlightened Life.* London: Penguin, 2010.

Philo Scholer David, M. (Foreword), Yong CD (trans). *The Works of Philo: Complete and Unabridged.* Peabody, Massachusetts: Publishers Hendrickson, 1993.

Plaskow, J. *Standing at Sinai: Judaism from a Feminist Perspective*. London: Harper One, 1991.

Plato. *The Laws*. London: Penguin Classics, 1970.

Plato. *The Complete Works*. New York: Shandon Press, Kindle Edition, 2015.

Pope Francis. *Laudato Si or Praise be to You: On Care for Our Common Home*. US: Ignatian Press, 2015.

Porter, J, and N Wolterstorff. *Natural and Divine Law: Reclaiming the Tradition for Christian Ethics*. Grand Rapids, Michigan: Eerdmans Publishing, 1999.

Porter, J. "From Natural Law to Human Rights: Or, Why Rights Talk Matters." *Journal of Law and Religion* 14, 1 pp. 77–96 (1999–2000).

Potter, D. *Constantine The Emperor*. Oxford: Oxford University Press, 2015.

Powers, J. *Introduction to Tibetan Buddhism*. Boulder, Colorado: Snow Lion Publications, 2007.

Preston Ronald, H. *Explorations in Theology*, 9. London: SCM Press/Routledge, 1970–1981.

Pui Lan, K. *Introducing Asian Feminist Theology*. London: Bloomsbury, 2000.

Race, Alan. *Interfaith Encounter: The Twin Tracks of Theology and Dialogue*. London: SCM Press, 2012.

Ramadan, T. *Western Muslims and the Future of Islam*. Oxford: Oxford University Press, 2004.

Ramadan, T. *Radical Reform: Islamic Ethics and Liberation*. Oxford: Oxford University Press, 2009.

Rambachan, A. *A Hindu Theology of Liberation: Not Two is Not One*. Albany: State of New York Press, 2015.

Rashkover, R, and M Kavka. *Tradition in the Public Square: A Novak Reader*. Grand Rapids, Michigan: Eerdmans Publishing, 2008.

Rashkover, R, and M Kavka. Eds. Novak, D. *Tradition in the Public Square: A David Novak Reader*. London: SCM Press, 2008.

Rawls, J. "Public Reason Re-visited." *University of Chicago Law Review* 64 (Summer 1997): 765–807.

Reuther, Radford. *Liberation Theology: Human Hope Confronts Christian History and American Power*. Minnesota: Paulist Press, 1972.

Reuther, Radford. *New Woman/New Earth: Sexist Ideologies and Human Liberation*. New York: Harper Collins, 1989.

Reuther, Radford R. *Religion and Sexism: Images of Women in the Jewish and Christian Traditions*. New York: Simon & Schuster, 1974.

Reuther, Radford R. *Sexism and God-Talk*. Boston: Beacon Press, 1993.

Reuther, Radford R. *Gaia and God: An Ecofeminist Theology of Earth Healing*. London: Harper Collins, 1994.

Reuther Radford R. *The Development of Feminist Theology: Becoming Increasingly Global and Interfaith*. Svenska kyrkans forskardagar, Uppsala 12 September 2011. https://www.svenskakyrkan.se/default.aspx?id=863846. Uppsala, Sweden, 2011.

Reuther, Radford R, and P Bianchi. *From Machismo to Mutuality: Essays on Sexism and Woman-Man Liberation*. UK: Fowler Wright Books, 1976.

Richardson, L. *What Terrorists Want*. New York: Random House Trade, 2007.

Roald, AS. *Women in Islam: The Western Experience*. London: Routledge, 2001.

Robinson, Rt Rev Gene. *In the Eye of the Storm*. Atlanta: Canterbury Press, 2008.

Rocher, R. "Creation of Anglo-Hindu Law." In *Hinduism and Law An Introduction*, Eds. T Lubin, DR Davies, and KK Jayanth, 78–88. Cambridge: Cambridge University Press, 2010.

Rodriquez, J, and T Fortier. *Cultural Memory, Resistance, Faith and Identity*. Texas: University of Texas Press, 2009.

Romain, JA. *A Guide to Reformed Judaism*. London: Reform Synagogue of Great Britain, 1991.

Romain, JA. *Renewing the Vision: Rabbis Speak out on Modern Jewish Issues*. London: SCM Press, 2011.

Rosenblatt. Rosenblatt in 1948. *Book of beliefs and opinions*. Newhaven: Yale University Press, 1989.

Rothbard, M. *Personal Liberty for a New Liberty*. MacMillan, 1973.

Roy, Kamini. *The Fruit of the Tree of Knowledge Published in Talking of Power – Early Writings of Bengali Women from the Mid-Nineteenth Century to the Beginning of the Twentieth Century*. Eds. Malini Bhattacharya and Abhijit Sen. Kolkata: Popular Prakashan, c2003.

Rushton, Roger. *Human Rights and the Image of God*. London: SCM Press, 2004.

Russell, Bertrand. *History of Western Philosophy*. London: Routledge Classics, 2004.

Sabra, AI. "The Appropriation and Subsequent Naturalization of Greek Sciences in Medieval Islam:A Preliminary Statement." *History of Science* 25(1987): 223–243.

Sachs, J. *Radical Now, Radical Then*. London: Harper Collins/Continuum, 2004.

Saddar, Ziauddin. *Desperately seeking Paradise: Journeys of a Sceptical Muslim.* London: Granta, 2004.

Sanders, EP. *Paul, the Law and the Jewish People.* Augsburg: Fortress Press, 1983.

Sarah, Rabbi Elli Tikvah and Rabbi Dr Barbara Borts. *Women Rabbis in the Pulpit.* London: Kulmus Publishing, 2016.

Shah, Prakash. "Judging Muslims". In *Islam and English Law: Rights, Responsibilities and the Place of Shari'a,* Ed. Robin Griffiths Jones, 144–156. Cambridge: Cambridge University Press, 2013.

Sharpe, M, and D Nickelson. *Secularisations and Their Debates: Perspectives on the Return of Religion in the Contemporary West.* New York: Springer Press, 2013.

Sharpes Donald, K. *The Lord of the Scrolls: Literary Traditions in the Bible and Gospels.* New York: Peter Lang Publishing, 2005–2007.

Singer, P. "Famine, Affluence and Morality." *Philosophy and Public Affairs* 1, 3 (Spring 1972): 229–243.

Smith, WC. *The Meaning and End of Religion.* London: SPCK, 1978.

Smith, A. *Theory of Moral Sentiments.* London: Penguin Classics, 2010.

Smith, Adam. *Wealth of Nations.* Eds. Mark G Spencer and Griffith Tom. Ware, Hertfordshire: Wordsworth Editions: World Classics, 2012.

Sonderegger, K. "Barth and Feminism." In *The Cambridge Companion to Karl Barth,* Ed. J Webster, 258–273. Cambridge: Cambridge University Press, 2000.

Soskice, JM, and D Lipton. *Feminism & Theology.* Oxford: Oxford University Press, 2003.

Sowle, Cahill Lisa. *Teleology, Utilitarianism and Christian Ethics* 42, 601–629. Theological Studies London: Sage Publications, December 1981.

Stanford Encyclopaedia of Philosophy. http://plato.stanford.edu/entries/halevi/. Accessed 15 May 2016.

Stump, E. "The non-Aristotelian Character of Aquinas Ethics: Aquinas on the Passions." In *Faith, Rationality & the Passions,* Eds. S Coakley, 91–106. Oxford: Blackwell, 2012.

Swartz, DL. *The sociology of Habit: The perspective of Pierre Bordieu.* http://www.bu.edu/av/core/swartz/sociology-of-habit.pdf. Vol 22, Issue 1, 2002

Tanner, K. "Creation and Providence." In *The Cambridge Companion to Karl Barth,* 111–126. Cambridge: Cambridge University Press, 2000.

Taylor, Charles. *A Secular Age.* Harvard: Harvard University Press, 2007.

Te Velde, Rudi. *Aquinas on God: The 'Divine Science' of the Summa Theologiae.* Farnham: Ashgate, 2006.

Temple, W. *Christianity and the Social Order.* London: Shepheard-Walwyn Publishers, 1984.

Thatcher, A. *God, Sex and Gender.* Oxford: Wiley-Blackwell, 2011.

The Hitopadesha and Jataka folk tales

Tirosh-Samuelso, Hava. *Judaism and Ecology: Created World and Revealed Word.* Harvard: Harvard University Press, 2003.

Toulmin, S, and J Goodfield. *The Ancestry of Science: The Discovery of Time.* Chicago: University of Chicago Press, 1967.

Toulmin, S, and A Johnson. *The Abuse of Casuistry: A History of Moral Reasoning.* Berkeley: University of California Press, 1988.

Treanor, Jill (13 October 2014). Richest 1% of people own nearly half of global wealth, says report. *The Guardian.* At 06 December 2015.

Trigault, Nicolas SJ "China in the Sixteenth Century: The Journals of Mathew Ricci: 1583–1610." English translation Gallagher SJ, Louis J. New York: Random House, Inc., 1953.

Unsworth Amy Dr of the Faraday Institute, St Edmunds Cambridge Forbes, 2014.

Vacks, GJ. *The Rape of the Earth: A World Survey of Soil Erosion.* London: Faber & Faber, 1939.

Varden, H. "Kant and Lying to the Murderer at the Door... One More Time: Kant's Legal Philosophy and Lies to Murderers and Nazis." *Journal of Social Philosophy* 41, 4 (Winter 2010): 403–421. © 2010 Wiley Periodicals, Inc.

Ven Hsuan Hua. Biography. California: Buddhist Text Translation Society, 1981.

Vines, M. *God and the Gay Christian.* London: Random House, 2014.

Ward, K. *Religion and Community.* Oxford: Clarendon Press, 2000.

Ward, K. *The Big Questions in Science and Religion.* Philadelphia: Templeton Press, 2004.

Welchman, L, and S Hossain. *Honour Crimes, Paradigms & Violence Against Women.* London: Zed Books, 2005.

Weller, P, K Purdam, N Ghanea, and S Cheruvallili. *Religion or Belief, Discrimination and Equality: Britain in Global Contexts.* London: Bloomsbury Publishing, 2013.

Widdows, H. *Global Ethics: An Introduction.* London: Routledge, 2011.

Widdows, H, and H Marway, *A Global Public Goods Approach to the Health of Migrants.* Public Health Ethics, 2015.

Wilkins, WJ. *Hindu Mythology, Vedic and Puranic*, 1900. http://www.sacred-texts.com/hin/hmvp/index.htm.

Williams, R. *Islam and English Law*, 20–34. Ed. Griffiths, Jones R. Cambridge: Cambridge University Press, 2013.

Williamson, C. "Exploring the Failure of Foreign Aid: The Role of Incentives and Information." *The Review of Austrian Economics* 23, 1 (Springer Publishing, March 2010): 17–33.

Wilson, P (Professor). *The Thirty Years War: A Sourcebook*. Hampshire and New York: Palgrave MacMillan, 2010.

Wink, W. *Jesus and Nonviolence: A Third Way*. Augsburg: Fortress, 2003.

Winterson, Jeanette. *Boating for Beginners*. London: Vintage, 1990.

Winterson, Jeanette. *Weight*. London: Canongate, 2006.

Wolffe, J. "Evangelicals and Pentecostals: Indigenizing a global Gospel." In *Global Religious Movements in Regional Context*, Ed. J Wolffe, 13–108. Milton Keynes: The Open University, 2002a.

Wolffe, John. Ed. *Global Religious Movements in Regional Context*. Farnham: Ashgate, 2002b.

Wolterstorff, N. *Justice: Rights and Wrongs*. Princeton, New Jersey: Princeton University Press, 2010.

Wood, Alan. *The Groundnut Affair*. London: Bodley Head, 1950.

Woodhead, L. Religious leaders don't represent religious people, 20 August 2013. http://www.publicspirit.org.uk/religious-leaders-dont-represent-religious-people/.

Woolhouse. *A Locke: A Biography*. Cambridge: Cambridge University Press, 2007.

Yelle, RA. "Hindu law as performance." In *Hinduism and Law: An Introduction*, 183–192. Cambridge: Cambridge University Press, 2010.

Zonta, Mauro. "Possible Hebrew Quotations of Avicenna's Oriental Philosophy." In *The Arabic Hebrew and Latin Reception of Avicenna's Metaphysics*, Eds. Dag Nikolas Hasse and Amos Bertolacci, 177–196. Berlin: Walter d Gruyter & Co, 2010.

Legal References:

Legislation:

Corrupt & Illegal Practices Act 1883

Equalities Act 2010 Schedule 23

Human Rights Act 1998
Representation of the People Act 1983 s.115

Caselaw:

Arrowsmith v UK [1978] ECHR 7
DfE v Talmud Torah Matzikei School (1984) Times LR
Grainger plc v Nicholson [2010] IRLR 4 (EAT)
Re AB [2008] EWHC 1436
Re Begum ex p Denbigh High School [2005] UKSC 15
Re J [2001] 1 Fam (CA)
Re K sub nom LA v N & Others [2005] EWHC 2956
Re SA (Vulnerable Adult) [2005] EWHC 2942, [2006] 1 FLR 867
Re U sub nom J [2000] 1 FLR 57

Web Addresses:

http://ams-uk.org - Association of Muslim Schools
http://www.anglicancommunion.org/identity/marks-of-mission.aspx
https://www.bma.org.uk/advice/employment/ethics/ethics-a-to-z/physician-assisted-dying
http://sacred-texts.com/bud/sbe13/sbe1302.htm accessed 11.06.16
Catechism of the Roman Catholic Church
http://www.vatican.va/archive/ENG0015/__P86.HTM
http://www.catholicherald.co.uk/news/2015/04/10/sanctity-of-life-is-top-issue-facing-voters-say-scottish-bishops/
http://www.cbc.ca/news/politics/trudeau-defends-abortion-stance-amid-sharp-catholic-criticism-1.2649810;
http://www.CharityCommission.gov.uk
http://www.citizensuk.org
http://climate.nasa.gov/evidence/
https://www.cokesbury.com/FreeDownloads/BibleTransGuide.pdf
http://www.dalailama.com/messages/environment/buddhist-concept-of-nature
http://www.findajewishschool.co.uk/index.php
https://www.imf.org/external/pubs/ft/sdn/2015/sdn1513.pdf
http://www.thehindu.com/2000/04/03/stories/01030005.htm
https://humanism.org.uk

http://www.intelligentdesign.org/whatisid.php

http://jubileedebt.org.uk

http://www.lawandreligionuk.com/2015/05/04/spiritual-influence-and-the-law/

http://www.mishnehtorah.com/index.html

http://news.nationalgeographic.com/news/2004/12/1206_041206_global_warming_2.html

http://www.OFSTED.gov.uk

http://www.ohchr.org/EN/UDHR/Pages/Introduction.aspx

http://www.ons.gov.uk/peoplepopulationandcommunity/culturalidentity/religion/articles/religioninenglandandwales2011/2012-12-11

http://www.peta.org/about-peta/faq/how-does-eating-meat-harm-the-environment; http://science.time.com/2013/12/16/the-triple-whopper-environmental-impact-of-global-meat-production/

https://www.rsc.ox.ac.uk/files/publications/working-paper-series/wp90-local-faith-communities-resilience-2013.pdf

http://www.papalencyclicals.net - *Laborem Exercens, Laudato Sii, Rerum Novarum*

http://www.pewforum.org/2015/11/03/u-s-public-becoming-less-religious/

https://plato.stanford.edu/entries/hume-freewill/

http://pluralism.org/research-report/interfaith-and-faith-based-peace-organizations/

http://policy-practice.oxfam.org.uk/our-work/inequality - at 06.12.15

https://www2.rcn.org.uk/__data/assets/pdf_file/0004/410638/004167.pdf

http://www.religioustolerance.org/reciproc2.htm

https://www.rt.com/uk/347139-muslim-school-ofsted-racist/

http://www.sacred-texts.com/jud/khz/index.htm accessed 15.05.16

http://shaheed-khalsa.com/theology.html

http://sikhmissionarysociety.org/sms/smsarticles/advisorypanel/gurmukhsinghsewauk/sikhismandhumanrights.html

http://www.sikhs.org/nosymbol.htm

http://www.thinkhumanism.com/the-golden-rule.html

http://www.torahphilosophy.com/2011/09/atheist-ethics.html

http://www.unhcr.org/uk/news/latest/2016/6/5763b65a4/global-forced-displacement-hits-record-high.html

www.unicef.com

https://www.wider.unu.edu/article/what-inequality

http://data.worldbank.org/indicator/SI.DST.FRST.10

References from Scripture:

The Bible – from New Revised Standard Version & New International Version

וְשָׁמַעְתָּ יִשְׂרָאֵל יְהֹוָה ,אֱלֹ הֵינוּ יְהֹוָה.אֶחָד
Genesis 1 & 2; 7; 9:1 & 7; 19; 35:11
Exodus 20:14; Exodus 22:26;
Leviticus 18: 22-3; 19: 34; 20:13
Deuteronomy 10:19; 22:22; 24:12-13
1 Kings 10
Jonah
Psalms 148-151
Proverbs 13:24, 19: 18, 22:15, 23: 13-4
Song of Songs
Isaiah 61
Jeremiah 23.3
Amos 5
Matthew 5: 17 NRSV
Matthew 10:34-39; Matthew 15: 21-28;; Matthew 19:6&9
Mark 2: 23-27 & 3: 1-6; Mark 7:10-12; Mark 7: 25-30
Luke 11: 46 & 52; Luke 12:5; Luke 15: 11-32
John 2; 4 & 7; John 15-17; 1 John 2: 16
Acts 16
Romans 1: 26-7; 7: 15-20; 7-9; Romans 16: 1
1 Corinthians 11:14-15; 6: 9-10
Ephesians 2: 15; 5: 25-31
Galatians 3: 28; 8
Hebrews 11.1
1 Timothy 1: 1-10; 2: 12
Book of Judith NRSV Apocrypha

The Qu'ran:

Trans. N.J. Dawood Penguin Classics 1993
Surah 21, 41 & 79
Surah 24:2;
Surah 7: 80-84

Surah 2:228 and 33:35; 2:282 and 4:11
Surah 7:143-4 & S.11 and 71
Surah 4:1
Surah 70:29-31
Surah 2:197, 2:222, 24:2
Surah 16:97, 40:40
Surah 4: 34, 30:20, 38:52, 37:44, 52:20, 56:10-25
Surah 26:165 Lut
Surah 4:124
Surah 2: 31 & 30-31
Surah 53:45, 92:3 and 75:39

Hindu Texts:

Trans. Eknath Easwaran Classics of Indian Spirituality 2007 Nilgiri Press
The Baghavad Gita
Gita Ch.7:11

Buddhist texts:

http://www.buddhisma2z.com/content.php?id=71#sthash.caNevWPr.dpuf;
Agannah Sutta
Vinaya pittaka sadàrasantuññho, A.III,348
Saüyutta Nikàya
Indriya saüvara, màtucitta, bhaginàcitta, dhàtucitta

Sikh Texts:

http://www.sikhs.org/english/eg_index.htm
Guru Granth Sahib 74
Guru Granth Sahib Ji, 773-4 & 963
Guru Granth Sahib Ji, 152
Guru Granth Sahib Ji, 473
Guru Granth Sahib Ji 425 & 349 & 1426

Index

© The Author(s) 2017
C. Shelley, *Ethical Exploration in a Multifaith Society*,
DOI 10.1007/978-3-319-46711-5

Printed by Printforce, the Netherlands